Baseball and Social Class

ALSO EDITED BY RONALD E. KATES AND
WARREN TORMEY AND FROM MCFARLAND

Baseball/Literature/Culture: Eassays, 2008–2009 (2010)

Baseball/Literature/Culture: Essays, 2006–2007 (2008)

Baseball and Social Class

Essays on the Democratic Game That Isn't

Edited by RONALD E. KATES
and WARREN TORMEY

McFarland & Company, Inc., Publishers
Jefferson, North Carolina, and London

LIBRARY OF CONGRESS CATALOGUING-IN-PUBLICATION DATA

Baseball and social class : essays on the democratic game that isn't / edited by Ronald E. Kates and Warren Tormey.
    p.   cm.
Includes bibliographical references and index.

ISBN 978-0-7864-7239-0
softcover : acid free paper ∞

1. Baseball—Social aspects—United States. 2. Baseball—Political aspects—United States. 3. Sports—United States—Sociological aspects. 4. Social classes—United States. 5. United States—Social conditions. I. Kates, Ronald E. II. Tormey, Warren.
GV863.A1B37647 2012
796.357—dc23   2012037143

BRITISH LIBRARY CATALOGUING DATA ARE AVAILABLE

© 2012 Ronald E. Kates and Warren Tormey. All rights reserved

No part of this book may be reproduced or transmitted in any form or by any means, electronic or mechanical, including photocopying or recording, or by any information storage and retrieval system, without permission in writing from the publisher.

On the cover: Baseball game at a Farm Security Administration migratory labor camp in 1942 in Robstown, Texas (Photograph by Arthur Rothstein, FSA/OWI Collection, Library of Congress)

Manufactured in the United States of America

McFarland & Company, Inc., Publishers
  Box 611, Jefferson, North Carolina 28640
  www.mcfarlandpub.com

Table of Contents

Acknowledgments — vii

Preface (Ronald Kates and Warren Tormey) — 1

Gothic Baseball: The Death of Mary Rogers and the "Birth" of Baseball History (Steve Andrews) — 7

Freedom and Baseball: The Uplift of Sport (Janaka B. Lewis) — 28

Born a Busher; or, How Journalists-Turned–Fiction Writers Made Baseball Safe for the Middle-Class Readers of the *Saturday Evening Post* (Scott D. Peterson) — 44

"Disgraceful employment": The Gentleman Amateur in Eric Rolfe Greenberg's *The Celebrant* (Mark Bresnan) — 60

Rings Born of Impulse: Gift-Exchange Economies in Greenberg's *The Celebrant* (Ronald E. Kates) — 74

Playing the Field: Rube Marquard's Performance of Class Identity in Early Twentieth Century Baseball and Vaudeville (Andrew Friedman) — 85

"The Old College Try": Eddie Collins and the 1919 Black Sox (Warren Tormey) — 98

The "Lost Art" of Baseball: James Weldon Johnson, the Negro Leagues and the "Black Bohemia" of the Harlem Renaissance (Daniel Anderson) — 112

The Gentle Player: Baseball and the "Gentle People" in Irwin Shaw's Short Fiction (Nathaniel Valle) — 126

Setting a Place for Mickey Mantle: Baseball, Class and Local Identity in Philip Roth's *Goodbye, Columbus* (Matthew Bruen) — 139

Table of Contents

Phillip Roth's Comic Corrective (JOSHUA DANIEL-WARIYA)   148

Class (Un)Consciousness: The Unusual Case of Jackie Robinson (ANDREW HAZUCHA)   162

Commonwealth: Hardt, Negri and the Contemporary Class Struggle for the National Pastime (CARL F. MILLER)   173

About the Contributors   191

Index   195

Acknowledgments

This collection was ultimately made possible because of the gracious support given by various individuals and funds at Middle Tennessee State University. Select individuals within MTSU's College of Liberal Arts deserve mention as valued supporters of the Baseball in Literature and Culture Conference, which generated many of the essays in this collection. The first is "The Dean," Dr. John McDaniel, whose interest in and recognition of baseball as a viable academic interest was invaluable to us as we began hosting the yearly conference in 2006. McDaniel's support helped an established event retain its viability after the conference moved from Indiana State University to MTSU, and without him our efforts to keep the conference afloat would have been much more difficult. We also thank Mark Byrnes, Dean McDaniel's successor, who continued the gracious assistance that has allowed our conference to continue to produce collaborative academic works like this present volume. Lastly, we thank the chair of MTSU's English department, Tom Strawman, who has apportioned department resources and supported our organizational and scholarly efforts, and has likewise recognized that baseball has viability as a field for academic study.

In addition, we are grateful for the support of various funding sources at MTSU, including the Virginia Peck Trust Fund, the Distinguished Lecturers Fund, Black History Month Committee, and the College of Liberal Arts. It is appropriate to acknowledge as well the helpful contributions of Chris Torgusen of the Major League Baseball Speakers Bureau, whose suggestions about conference luncheon speakers help us to build programs which continue to draw interest from scholars across the country and from local baseball fans alike. Likewise, we are most grateful to McFarland, whose support of our earlier proceedings volumes led to our collaboration in this current project. We look forward to working together on future projects in this growing "field" of study.

Finally, we'd also like to thank our peer reviewers and early editors, who bore the task of subjecting early drafts to rigorous critical scrutiny. These folks include Crosby Hunt, Peter Carino, David Cicotello, Kevin Grace, Laura Dubek, Shawn O'Hare, Sekou Franklin, Will Brantley, Don Roy, and David

Lavery. This volume is much strengthened by their efforts, especially by those whose interest in baseball is subordinate to their insistence on effective scholarship. Material in Carl Miller's "*Commonwealth:* Hardt, Negri, and the Contemporary Class Struggle for the National Pastime" is reprinted by permission of the publisher of *Commonwealth* by Michael Hardt and Antonio Negri (The Belknap Press of Harvard University Press), copyright Michael Hardt and Antonio Negri.

Likewise, Ronald Kates's "Rings Born of Impulse: Gift-Exchange Economies in Eric Rolfe Greenberg's *The Celebrant*" appeared in *NINE: A Journal of Baseball History and Culture* 17, no. 2, and has been reprinted by permission of the University of Nebraska Press.

We give a final shout-out to Peter Carino of Indiana State University, who noted our enthusiasm for baseball-themed scholarship in our yearly visits to the Baseball in Literature and Culture Conference, which was hosted by Indiana State University in the years between 2000 and 2005, and saw fit to hand us the reins in 2006. We hope that we've been able to carry the field forward.

Preface

The French philosopher Jacques Barzun famously commented on baseball's unique position as a point of entry into larger aspects of American society, indirectly providing justification for academic studies of the game that would come later. Presented in his 1954 collection of essays, *God's Country and Mine*, Barzun wrote that "whoever wants to know the heart and mind of America had better learn baseball, the rules, and reality of the game." This timely and prophetic declaration has proved a useful sound byte for generations of scholars who valorize the place of America's game within its larger social fabric.

Appearing within an essay that spoke to the complexity of the game, however, the quote has taken on a life of its own. Those who read the whole essay from which Barzun's quote appears also come to appreciate his respect for baseball's opaque multi-facetedness, and his awareness of the buried contradictions beneath its veneer of singularity. Sounding subtle cautionary notes in what is otherwise a celebration of America's game, Barzun writes that "[b]aseball takes its mystic nine and scatters them wide. A kind of individualism thereby returns, but it is limited — eternal vigilance is the price of victory." In subtly discordant notes, Barzun speaks to the game's complexity beyond its simplicity, its subtle dynamics of chance, intelligence, and fate that captivate its followers. For example, he describes the experience of the beginner, the newcomer, the outsider, who struggles to "read" the box score, the journalist's account, the grammar of the game: "To read [these things] with profit you have to know a language that comes easy only after philosophy has taught you to judge practice. Here is scholarship that takes effort on the part of the outsider, but it is so bred into the native that it never becomes a dreary round of technicalities." One can usefully invoke Barzun's essay to explain baseball's appeals to democratic idealists, but his words also speak of the game's exclusivity and impenetrability to non-native outsiders. In other words, Barzun voices appreciation for the complexity of the game that exists beneath the veneer of simplicity, and this aspect of his essay provides a useful framework for the project undertaken in this volume.

Many of our contributors seek to understand aspects of baseball in the sense highlighted by Barzun's acknowledgment of baseball's subtler language. This collection examines the general perceptions of egalitarianism that are fundamental to the game and traceable to its earliest American origins, and the myriad contradictions that lie beneath this idealized premise. The inspiration for this project emerged from conversations and presentations that took place at the Baseball in Literature and Culture Conference, which we have been fortunate to host at Middle Tennessee State University here in Murfreesboro since 2006. The conference, initiated in 1995 by Peter Carino of Indiana State University, has produced five proceedings volumes and has encouraged collaboration leading to other scholarly publications. Baseball historians, creative writers, and scholars of sports literature and culture have enjoyed the opportunities for the exchange of ideas and the presentation of creative efforts. Building on these conversations, the editors of this volume approached the topic with only a vague sense of its dimensions and complexity. As the collection grew, a fuller picture emerged, pointing to the conclusion that America's game, infused from its earliest origins with a democratic mythos and founded on high-minded principles of meritocracy, is nonetheless fraught with class contradictions. Each contributor to this collection has attempted to engage one fundamental question about America and its game: To what extent do the democratic ideals imposed on both contradict the inherent divisions and stratifications within?

To that end, each writer has explored class standing and its influence on some aspect of the game as experienced by those who play it, those who watch it, those who write about it, and those who market it. Class is an amorphous concept, and in tying it to baseball one subsequently must also consider matters of race, education, locality, integration, assimilation, and cultural standing. In that spirit, each contributor articulates the value of class capital within a specific context within the game's history and makeup. This capital is crucial to understanding how baseball creates, preserves, reinforces, and, occasionally, assails class divisions among those who watch, play, and own the game. The collection is organized in a largely chronological narrative, but we do leave room to highlight particular contextual associations within select works.

The title of Steve Andrews's essay, "Gothic Baseball: The Death of Mary Rogers and the 'Birth' of Baseball History," makes self-evident its place as an appropriate starting point for this collaborative inquiry into baseball's class dimensions. Andrews establishes how class contexts figure into the organized game's origins as an outgrowth of the value systems of Victorian–era New York City. He connects the formation of the New York Knickerbocker Baseball club and its early games on Hoboken's Elysian Fields with the sensationalized story of murder victim Mary Rogers, and considers the background of Alexander Cartwright, one of the more celebrated pioneers of early baseball.

Andrews weaves an interconnected narrative that situates baseball's formal beginnings within several shifting and problematic class contexts. Building on Andrews's reading, Janaka B. Lewis likewise considers the many opportunities that sport — and particularly, baseball — offered to upwardly mobile blacks from the game's early days as a sport of the Reconstruction era. In "Freedom and Baseball: The Uplift of Sport," Lewis looks at select game accounts from the late 19th century, reading these within the context of larger narratives of class mobility and arguing that they reveal how "baseball offered a new politics of physical engagement which African Americans could participate in and eventually gain recognition from."

A number of our contributors explored the class dimensions of baseball in the two decades immediately following the turn of the 20th century. In "Born a Busher; or, How Journalists-Turned–Fiction Writers Made Baseball Safe for the Middle-Class Readers of the *Saturday Evening Post*," Scott D. Peterson notes that "baseball journalists promoted the character-building and democratic elements of the game," deliberately transforming the perceptions of ballplayers as "ruffians" and "roustabouts." Baseball fiction offered fertile ground, Peterson argues, for narratives of upward mobility from the social margins, and select fictions of popular sportswriters Charles Van Loan, Ring Lardner, and Bozeman Bulger offer bildungsroman narratives that depict a character's growing realization of middle class codes and values.

Next, in "'Disgraceful employment': The Gentleman Amateur in Eric Rolfe Greenberg's *The Celebrant*," Mark Bresnan considers class in Greenberg's representation of pitcher Christy Mathewson, another college-educated star whose privileged background figures prominently in the narrative of upward mobility of the main character, Jackie Kapp. Mathewson's character, argues Bresnan, depicts a larger deep-seated and ultimately contradictory impulse to impose nostalgic notions of amateurism upon baseball players of all time periods. In an essay previously published in *NINE: A Journal of Baseball History and Culture* (17.2), Ronald E. Kates offers a useful counterpoint to Bresnan's study. Kates approaches the story's assimilationist narrative from another angle, focusing on the class dynamics implied in the "gift sphere" that defines the relationship between Kapp, the immigrant, and Mathewson, the all–American icon. This distant, impulsive relationship, defined by the rings which Jackie crafts to commemorate the pitcher's growing list of accomplishments, actually comprises his commitment to the success of his family's growing commemorative jewelry business. Asked to design comparable rings to celebrate (and ultimately, to create for market) the accomplishments of the pitcher's Giant teammates Jeff Tesreau and Rube Marquard, Jackie can find no comparable inspiration. His ambivalence places him at odds with his profit-minded brothers, partners in the increasingly profitable family business that is devoted to pulling the immigrant family into the middle-class mainstream. Throughout his essay, Kates highlights the problematic class dimensions of the "gift exchange economy" that the jeweler and pitcher maintain in the face of growing endorsement and profit opportunities.

Mathewson's teammate Marquard stands within a complicated class nexus of his own, as shown in "Playing the Field: Rube Marquard's Performance of Class Identity in Early Twentieth Century Baseball and Vaudeville." In this study, Andrew Friedman examines a select example of the then-common practice of off-season stage performance, which allowed select ballplayers to supplement their incomes. In the case of Marquard and others, argues Friedman, ballplayers traded on the symbolic capital of contradictory and often self-generated narratives which privilege class mobility and the emergence into the middle class. Working within a slightly later time frame, Warren Tormey examines the class dynamics pervasive within the toxic team culture and clubhouse of the 1919 Black Sox. Arguing that college-educated star second baseman Eddie Collins' place on a roster with underpaid, working-class teammates has escaped the consideration it merits, Tormey sheds light on the second baseman's policy of "strategic inaction" in the face of the gambling scandal that rocked the game.

Moving forward into the 1920s, Daniel Anderson considers the game as perceived by intellectuals within the Harlem Renaissance. In "The 'Lost Art' of Baseball: James Weldon Johnson, the Negro Leagues and the 'Black Bohemia' of the Harlem Renaissance," Anderson begins by considering black intellectuals' odd silence toward baseball and other sports, which were paradoxically gaining a growing foothold within the larger development of an African American middle class consciousness. James Weldon Johnson, argues Anderson, was a notable exception, a writer willing to consider the economic significance of baseball businesses that were owned, operated, and played by blacks.

Moving into the pre- and post-war years, a quartet of contributors examine how baseball fiction speaks to the negotiation of class boundaries within the larger pattern of demographic shifts and the greater levels of prosperity realized within the cold war era. In "The Gentle Player: Baseball and the 'Gentle People' in Irwin Shaw's Short Fiction," Nathaniel Valle considers Shaw's portrayal of baseball as an urban game that affirmed communities defined by ethnicity, while also offering avenues of assimilation to an increasingly professionalizing middle class. Identifying how baseball shaped Shaw's "*gentle people*," those upwardly mobile characters who simultaneously sought community in working-class environs (especially sporting arenas) and embraced middle-class value systems, Valle considers how Shaw's characters articulate the struggles of his own assimilationist narrative. These concerns also resonate, as the next two contributors reveal, in the Philip Roth works *Goodbye, Columbus* and *The Great American Novel*. In "Setting a Place for Mickey Mantle: Baseball, Class and Local Identity in Philip Roth's *Goodbye, Columbus*," Matthew Bruen considers how notions of local identity, as shaped by baseball loyalties, are inscribed on Roth's portrayal of an upwardly mobile family's move from urban Newark to the more highbrow North Jersey suburbs. Joshua Daniel-Wariya's "Philip Roth's Comic Corrective" investigates the association between Roth's baseball-themed "wildly excessive" *Great American Novel* and Albert Spalding's *American National Game*, the 1911 work that sought to affirm baseball's unique stature as the most overt metaphor of American meritocracy. Reading the former as an interrogation of the democratic ideals of the latter, Daniel-Wariya highlights Roth's attempt to reinvent "Spalding's paean to the American dream in terms that point to its contradictions and points of dislocation."

In "Class (Un)Consciousness: The Unusual Case of Jackie Robinson," Andrew Hazucha considers the pioneering player's unlikely political leanings and loyalties, which belied the role he took as an "increasingly public spokesperson about racial politics in America." Collectively, these readings highlight baseball's continuing place in the growing middle class consciousness that mirrored national demographic shifts from city to suburb.

Finally, Carl F. Miller offers a take on the implicit class dimensions within baseball's current economic model in "*Commonwealth*: Hardt, Negri and the Contemporary Class Struggle for the National Pastime." Applying the theories of two Cambridge economic theorists, whose latest work focuses on the concepts of "globalization and labor," Miller peers beneath the glossy exterior of big league baseball and its modernized, fan-friendly ballparks and massive marketing apparatus. He finds an increasingly stratified, polarized game that is at risk of a "cultural exodus" that will relegate major league baseball to a "second-tier professional sport" if it continues to dismiss the egalitarian appeals that speak to the common good. Thankfully, Miller describes a scenario in which the game might reinvent itself with a closer eye on the class dimensions of its economic model.

Collectively, the contributors explore the complicated class dynamics that have always existed within that great American sporting institution that has historically defined itself according to an egalitarian ethos of classlessness. Our aim is to uncover baseball's subtler, class-based dimensions and provide a clear view of those barriers, dynamics, and contradictions that have simmered beneath the idealism of American Democracy from its earliest origins.

Gothic Baseball:
The Death of Mary Rogers and the "Birth" of Baseball History[1]

STEVE ANDREWS

Given the primacy of baseball talk in American culture, it should surprise no one to know that there is an Internet site dedicated to "Hoboken, New Jersey — Where Baseball was Born!" After offering the usual information one would expect, such as "On 19 June 1846, the first officially recorded, organized baseball match was played under Alexander Cartwright's rules on Hoboken's Elysian Fields," the site goes on to offer a not totally unexpected debunking of the claim of origin on the part of Cooperstown and Abner Doubleday. If such a move is utterly conventional, the website at least has the good sense to cite the last paragraph from the Hall's own "A Short History of the Hall of Fame," thereby hoisting the Cooperstown claim by its own petard. "Whatever may or may not be proved in the future concerning Baseball's true origin is in many respects irrelevant at this time," the Hall intones. "If baseball was not actually first played in Cooperstown by Doubleday in 1839, it undoubtedly originated about that time in a similar rural atmosphere." Baseball historians will take some pleasure — "undoubtedly" — in the vagaries of the Cooperstown conditional, as well the phrase "whatever may or may not be proved in the future." But the following from the Hoboken site-manager is surely an attention-grabber: "I originally included the words 'Birthplace of Baseball' in this site's designs," he informs us, "[b]ut then, thanks to the searchable data-bases of the US Government's Patent & Trademark Office, I discovered that the Cooperstown folk have those words trademarked for a number of uses." "So," he goes on to say, "I opted for 'Where Baseball was Born,' instead" (Hoppe).

Both the trademark and the solution underscore the tenacious hold that the extended metaphor of birth has on discussions about the origins of baseball. And if, as our state-sanctioned vernacular suggests, baseball can be born and can have a birthplace, then it surely must have a father, someone more tangibly embodied in the twists and turns of lived experience than is the office of patents and trademarks. As it turns out, baseball doesn't have *a* father; rather, as preeminent baseball historian John Thorn would have it in his latest book, *Baseball in the Garden of Eden: The Secret History of the Early Game*, baseball has *four* fathers (with pun intended, one presumes, on "forefathers"). All played for the Knickerbocker Base Ball Club of New York and none are named Alexander Cartwright. The four whom Thorn credits with "legitimate claims to baseball's paternity" are William Rufus Wheaton, Daniel Lucius "Doc" Adams, William H. Tucker, and Louis Fenn Wadsworth (26). Add to these the usual suspects for baseball paternity — the aforementioned Doubleday, Cartwright, plus Henry Chadwick[2] — and we are just two persons short of being able to take the field with a team made up entirely of men who at one time or another were purported to have fathered the game.

The hubbub over paternity tends to obscure the fact that there are related questions never asked. How, for instance, can baseball have so many claimants to paternity yet never once have nominated a single, historically viable candidate for maternity? By way of addressing that maternal absence, this essay explores two potential candidates, one of whom is the Mary Rogers of the title, and the other of whom is still alive and kicking but whose identity, for now, will be kept secret.

Inventing/Paternity

In a footnote to his 1845 edition of "The Mystery of Marie Roget," Edgar Allan Poe notes that the Mary Rogers case of 1841 had "occasioned an intense and long-enduring excitement" among New Yorkers (723). The desire to capitalize on that initial excitement led Poe in 1842 to use the second of his three Dupin tales as a narrative frame with which to solve the case. The first of these tales, entitled "The Murders in the Rue Morgue," would have been enough to establish Poe as "the father of detective fiction" (Thoms 133). Poe sold the second, "The Mystery of Marie Roget," to Snowden's *Ladies' Companion* to be printed in three installments, in November and December of 1842 and January of 1843. Rogers was initially thought to have been brutally raped and murdered at the hands of a gang, but Poe, setting his story in Paris, France, had his detective, Dupin, debunk the rape/murder-by-gang theory in favor of a theory of death-by-strangulation at the hands of one man, most likely a naval officer of a "dark and swarthy" complexion (769). By November of 1842, after the supposed death-bed confession of Hoboken innkeeper Mrs. Frederika Loss, it was generally conceded by most that Rogers had died the victim of a botched abortion, or what in those days was euphemistically called "premature delivery" (Walsh 55). According to John Walsh, "sometime in late November" of 1842, too late to do anything with the December installment, Poe returned to New York from Philadelphia and "persuaded Snowden to postpone the third segment of *Marie Roget* to the February issue so that changes could be made to it" (63). Enough changes, however slight, were made for the February 1843 installment to at least prevent Poe's literary reputation from being buried alive by the "premature delivery" of his "lonely assassin" theory (Poe 771).

For the 1845 edition of *Tales*, Poe went on to make 15 changes within the story in addition to footnotes (Walsh 69). Designed to resituate the tale more securely within the context of the abortion hypothesis, these changes, as Walsh explains, have, over time, become devastatingly effective. As Thomas Ollive Mabbott reminds us in his introduction to the tale, "The Mystery of Marie Roget" is the "first detective story in which an attempt was made to solve a real crime" (Poe 715). Poe's initial solution, as we have seen, was wrong. However, by virtue of what Walsh refers to as a "classic performance ... of literary hugger-mugger," the now apparently prescient commitment to "premature delivery" audaciously trumpeted in the first footnote of the 1845 edition hoodwinked generations of critics into thinking that Poe had actually solved the case, thus ushering Poe and his detective into a special place in literary history (73). As implied in the subtitle of chapter six of Amy Gilman Srebnick's important 1995 cultural analysis of the Mary Rogers case, that special place turns out to be at the "birth of detective fiction." Srebnick offers a twist on the birth metaphor that has the added value of positioning readers closer to the embodied contribution of the mother than to the hopes and aspirations of any expectant father.

Since Srebnick's analysis, it has become commonplace to attribute to the Rogers case the mobilization of social energy—call it outrage—that led the state legislature to pass "An Act for the Establishment and Regulation of the Police of the City of New York," which went into effect in 1845. In their recent history of the New York Police Department, in a chapter entitled "A Cry from the Bottom of the Hudson," James Lardner and Thomas Reppetto describe that Act as "the child of the press" (23), by which they mean the penny press that stoked the outrage in which the mishandling of the Rogers case played a "decisive" role (18). In addition, and due in large part to circumstances surrounding the Rogers case, the legislature in 1845–46 passed an act criminalizing the procurement or performance of abortion, an act that was aimed at the notorious and highly successful abortionist, Madame Restelle. These two Acts are manifestations of "the criminalization of private life" for which the Mary Rogers case served as "catalytic event" (Srebnick 87).

To better understand the cultural significance of the Rogers case, we turn to an altogether serendipitous ally, Bill James, known in baseball circles as "the father of sabermetrics." In a recent foray into the annals of *Popular Crime*, as his new book is entitled, James concludes his commentary on the Mary Rogers case with the following thoughts:

> [I]f you read a history of metropolitan police departments, I am certain that it will reference the significance of the Mary Rogers case in leading to the reorganization of the New York police department in 1845. If you read the early history of abortion law, I am confident that it will reference the Mary Rogers story. If you study the history of the detective story, I feel sure that you will find that the Mary Rogers stories were critical to that genre's breaking out of its narrow early trench, and becoming a part of the culture. If you know anything about the history of journalism, you certainly know that the newspaper business rode on the backs of crime stories for a hundred years, the Mary Rogers case being one of the sturdiest carriers. But if you read a history of America in the 1840s, it is likely that not a word will be said about Mary Rogers [22–23].

James's is a curious way of affirming the understated social significance of the Mary Rogers case. The listing of specific histories—of the police department, of abortion law, of the detective story, and of the newspaper business— seems to insist on the very idea of historical probity, even as the conditionals (those five "ifs") undercut that authority while seemingly valorizing the writer's intuition *of* that history. Why the conditionals? Surely James has studied the very histories that he is "certain," "sure," and "confident" will back up his claim that the Mary Rogers case was singly important in the "reshaping" of 1840s Manhattan culture. Should we, then, read those conditionals as a rhetorical ploy geared toward casting the writer in the guise of the detective who, like a good lawyer, knows beforehand the answer to every question asked? And if no "history of America in the 1840s" is "likely" to say anything about Mary Rogers, are we to ascribe to James a certain degree of forensic authority for having brought to our view the social consequences of the Rogers case, as if—presto!—he were somehow privy to secrets the rest of us are not? Readers may claim I pay undue attention to a rather minor portion of James's overall project, but I see James's concluding comments on the Rogers case, in which historical significance is all too coyly underscored without paying any dues to the historians who bring that history back to us, as emblematic of the often vexed relationship between the facts of baseball (its historiography) and the myths of baseball (its hagiography).

The tensions between baseball historiography and baseball hagiography are addressed more self-consciously early on in Thorn's book. There, he tells his readers that he once dismissed, out of hand, baseball's "whole history" as "a lie from beginning to end, from its creation myth to its rosy models of commerce, community, and fair play" (ix). But once he began to drill down into the reasons for that collective "nostalgia," Thorn realized that the "driving question" of his book (xi) is a question of historiography, of the tension between the work of "*historians* as that term once was understood," who were concerned "to create a national mythology," and a newer, "analytical impulse that marks modern historiography" in which, and by which, "large narratives and small pieties are swept away" (xii, emphasis in original). Because "modern historiography" must always compete with the older, mythologizing histories that seek to account for baseball as our national epic, modern students of the game are as likely to be haunted by the self-serving pleasures of nostalgia as to be turned on by "the bright if not warming light of truth" (xii). Thus the revelation of "secrets," as the subtitle of Thorn's book, *The Secret History of the Early Game*, suggests, becomes an important part of the debunking process that attends the construction of what he implies is the "real" history of baseball.

"Secrets" also happen to be a constitutive part of what we mean when we say "gothic." Where the gothic haunts, as it surely must, it does so, according to literary critic Eric Savoy, not through the agency of the dead, or undead, but by way of the "*gaps left within us by the secrets of others*," often manifested as "the shadow of history itself" ("Rise," 174, emphasis in original). Speaking more broadly of history, critics David Mogen, Scott P. Sanders and Joanne B. Karpniski explain that "Gothicism results when the epic moment passes and a particular rift in history develops and widens into a dark chasm that separates now from what has been." For these critics, the moment of "rift" occurs when an alternative history threatens to destabilize the integrative, "logocentric" function of a "privileged" or "authorized" history that, until recently, had allowed us to transform our experience of "the world and its landscape" into a "comfortable" and "coherent" narrative (qtd. Savoy 1998, 7). Logocentric history, as Savoy goes on to gloss it, "is an essentially nostalgic mode, *if nostalgia is understood as a will to sustained cultural coherence, a desire for the seamless authenticity of national narrative*" (7, emphasis added).

What the literary critics above refer to as "logocentric history" is what Thorn, in reference to the products of old-school baseball historians, calls "national mythology."

The gaps created by Thorn's two types of historiography are formational in producing the gothic effect, but such gaps can also be imagined, as critic Anne Williams does, as a "fault-line" that signals "a revolution within the established system" (66). In this system, "the patriarchal family provides the organizing 'myth' of the literature we now call Gothic" (29), and it stands to reason that gothic plots would themselves be "organized," in part, "around anxieties and uncertainties generated" by concern for "the principles of 'legitimate' succession and inheritance" (68). Thus the gothic, for Williams, is reliant on a set of "conventions that emerged toward the end of the eighteenth century" that are "crucially concerned with exploring the 'rules' of patriarchy, such as the relative powers and qualities of the masculine and the feminine and the interrelated and mutually supportive social structures like the family, the monarchy, and the church" (35). Once we substitute "the government" for "the monarchy," we can begin to recognize that in the American idiom baseball historians' seeming obsession with troping their history as a form of paternity is really a way of underscoring the "rules" of American patriarchy and of legitimizing that history in relation to those rules. Could any tale, then, be more conventionally gothic than one in which there are so many claimants to the throne of paternity? In such a story, the symbolic value of paternity is undeniable; but with so many claims, and the alternative histories that each portends, the application of its value is rendered mysterious and uncanny, if not altogether empty.

Whereas words like "birth" and "paternity" dominate the debate between Cooperstown and Hoboken, a different word surfaces in the discursive swirl surrounding the Mary Rogers case. That word is "invention." In *The Beautiful Cigar Girl: Mary Rogers, Edgar Allan Poe, and the Invention of Murder* (2006), true-crime writer and mystery novelist Daniel Stashower picks up where historian Srebnick left off, again making strong links between the botched investigation and the "ambitious slate of social and political reforms"—including the Police Reform Act and the Abortion Law—occasioned by it (4–5; 342–3). Thus the "invention" of murder, as Stashower figures it, relates to the formation of the detective story and to the modernization of New York City's law enforcement procedures, both of which result from the intersection of fact, fiction, and sensationalist journalism surrounding the Rogers case. More conventionally, as a quick scroll down Google will show, it is by way of the "invention of the detective story" that we have canonically come to understand Poe's role in shaping the literary significance of his Dupin stories. Even so, the invention of murder and detection has an additional Manhattan complement: in his 2009 biography of Cartwright, Jay Martin states unequivocally that "Alexander Joy Cartwright Jr. invented baseball in 1845" (11).

The word "invention" has meant many things over its lexical lifespan. We normally think of it in the Edisonian sense of "something devised or produced by original contrivance; a method or means of doing something, an instrument, an art, etc., originated by the ingenuity of some person, and previously unknown; an original contrivance." That last phrase, "an original contrivance," brings us round, in the *Oxford English Dictionary*, to another meaning, especially relevant in the context of origins: "the action of devising, contriving, or making up; contrivance, fabrication," as in the phrase "Cooperstown is the Birthplace of Baseball." This last, as Thorn reminds us by way of citing occasional base-ball player Catherine Morland's skeptical musings on history in Jane Austen's *Northanger Abbey*, is pure "invention" (ix). Ironically enough, the appropriateness of the term "invention" is further validated by "the Cooperstown folk" taking out a trademark through the agency of the U.S. Patent and Trademark Office. What I have been building up to is the idea that where baseball and Mary Rogers are concerned, "invention" (implying design, coherence, order and managerial competence) and "birth" (intersected as it is by discourses of sex, gender, class and race) are complementary aspects of related social phenomena.

Occupying the same geographic locales of lower Manhattan along publishers' row and across the Hudson to Elysian Fields during the early to mid–1840s, Mary Rogers and Alexander Cartwright lived blocks apart in Manhattan and both were shaped by similar cultural codes. By October of 1844 and early into 1845 when he once again began revising "The Mystery of Marie Roget," Poe himself was working at the *Evening Mirror*, located "at the corner of Nassau and Ann streets, only a few doors down from Mary Rogers' old home" (Walsh 67), and literally "across the street" from the bookselling business that Cartwright and his brother started in 1845 (Nucciarone 8). Let me be clear from the outset: I am not espousing a cause and effect relationship (as implied in the tropes of paternity and invention) between the Mary Rogers case, the "birth" of detective fiction, and the playing of regulated baseball at Elysian Fields in 1846. I am instead proposing a part to whole relationship — as of a matrix — in which "the invention of baseball" is included in the shared context in which the Rogers case, as Bill James so coyly reminds us, was a circumstance of no little cultural significance. As Poe himself wrote in regard to the murder trial of Polly Bodine, "Not the least error, in such investigations, is the limiting of inquiry to the immediate, with total disregard of the collateral, or circumstantial events" (*Doings* 66). Similarly, in an effort to move baseball historians away from "'top-down' models of the game," models in which "an authority figure dictates the answers," Peter Morris advocates instead a "'bottom-up' perspective, in which a wide range of ideas are considered and the best suited one triumphs" (5). While I would urge us to give up on the idea of the ultimate survival of a "single" fittest idea, I nevertheless join Morris in encouraging greater focus on the collateral or circumstantial context whence baseball arises.

The era in which Alexander Cartwright and Mary Rogers came of age in New York City was, by all accounts, a period of tremendous social and cultural upheaval brought about by an influx of immigrants as well as thousands of young men and women from the rural hinterlands on a scale not seen before. According to historian Elliott Gorn, "in 1800, the city's population stood at roughly sixty thousand people" (393); by 1840 the population was approximately 300,000 (NYPD 9), with a stunning 750 percent increase from 1825 to 1850 (Wilentz 109). As thousands flocked into the city, changes in work relations and living arrangements destabilized accepted codes of middle class propriety. The labor market in the lower wards of Manhattan, for instance, was dominated by young, single men who "earned their livings with their muscles, then sought rough and exuberant pleasures after hours" (Gorn 408).

No longer living in the homes or workspaces of their employers as in the old master-apprentice relationship, young men now lived in boarding houses where they were usually free to come and go as they pleased. These "unregulated youth," to use historian Patricia Cline Cohen's term, could now "construct their own youth culture, one greatly at variance with moralistic employers' and parents' expectations. They could construct and adopt multiple identities and put them on and off like masks" (46). Cline's conclusions stem from her analysis of the Helen Jewett murder of 1836. The body of Jewett, a well-known prostitute and a great favorite of young clerks, was found hacked to death and burned. Richard P. Robinson, a young clerk from a "respectable family," stood accused of the crime but was eventually found not guilty. The Jewett case drew national attention that brought with it, according to historian Timothy Gilfolye, an unsettling sense among middle class observers that the moral codes they took for granted—"self-control, chastity, domesticity, sobriety, and frugality"— were, at best, unstable (98). "Robinson's sexual behavior," Gilfoyle suggests, "mocked" middle-class ideals of propriety and "put the tension of what constituted 'respectable' sexuality on public view" (98). Additionally, Robinson's "popularity among large numbers of urban youths" indicated "the emergence of a 'sporting male' culture. Organized around various forms of gaming—horse racing, gambling, cockfighting, pugilism, and other 'blood' sports—sporting male culture defended and promoted male sexual aggressiveness and promiscuity" (99).

If prostitution, which brought upper class males into competitive proximity with working-class gang members, was the great leveler of class at the core of this subculture, "blood sport" further blurred the already troubled delineations of category and label. The word "pugilist," as Gorn explains in his analysis of working class male culture of this era, referred not only to the professional boxer on whom men from different classes might bet, on the assumption that the ring was a place of honor where the fighting was fair, but it also referred to the working-class street brawler whose reputation hinged on "his ferocity, on his reliability in a gang fight, on his defiance of police and other outsiders, and on his total devotion to his chums" (403). Devotion to after-hours violence was as much a function of the "tedium" and sometimes life-threatening danger of daytime jobs as it was a compensatory reaction against limited economic prospects (408). As "real wages fell in the city's major trades" in the 1830s and 1840s, by 1850 the trade worker's average wages were at three-fifths of the minimum required to support a family of four (Wilentz 117–18). Given such bleak prospects, volunteer firefighting "offered a chance for real heroics, rough masculine camaraderie, and colorful display, qualities lacking in the prosaic bourgeois world of work, home, and church" (Gorn 408).

As with prostitution and the sporting life, fire-fighting brought men from different classes together, sometimes in violent competition to defend turf and honor (Nucciarone 8). As Herbert Asbury describes in his *Gangs of New York,* "the rivalry between the fire companies whose membership included men of substance was friendly if strenuous," and the Bowery Boy, "who loved his fire engine almost as much as he did his girl ... considered both himself and his company disgraced if his apparatus was beaten to a conflagration" (31). Indeed, engine company associations were important points of social and recreational contact for different classes of men and women. Thorn suggests that in the 1820s activities associated with engine companies and target companies were considered "respectable" as compared to the "dubious" recreation of baseball, which was then already being played in the City (65). One could easily infer from this that volunteer engine companies gave the cover of "respect" to adult males devoted to baseball as a leisure activity. While this may have been true on the surface, an even more important force might have been at play. By the 1840s and '50s, factory workers in Newark, for example, "tended to join three leisure groups: volunteer fire companies, militia and guard units, and baseball teams" (Gelber, "Working" 14–15). According to Susan E. Hirsch, "all three of these institutions" involved "highly organized teams that emphasized precision and cooperation," and "all three wore similar uniforms, required practice and drill, and provided moderate outdoor ... exercise and fellowship" (qtd. in Gelber, "Working" 15). While these parallels and similarities may seem striking, they become less so if, with historian Steven M. Gelber, we understand that the shared structures of organization and the common values of precision and cooperation were replicating and reinforcing an increasingly more ordered and regulated *workplace* experience that, by the end of the 19th century, would culminate in Frederick Winslow Taylor's near total "mapping of the body onto the machine" in a process of rationalization in which individuals were "reembodi[ed] ... as the 'head' and 'hands' of a new corporate whole" (Seltzer 95). Such regulation produced a workplace ethos of teamwork and discipline that was shared by increasing numbers of American males, an ethos with which organized, rule-bound baseball was clearly "congruent" (Gelber, "Working" 8).

By 1845, as more and more "fire companies began to think of extending their competition in fighting fire to competition on the ball field," the Cartwright brothers and their friends formed the Knickerbocker Base Ball Club, so named, Martin claims, "after their fire company," Knickerbocker Engine Company Number 12 (8). As fire-fighter and ball player, Cartwright and his fellow "clerks," "merchants," "brokers," "professional men," and the odd (if topically intriguing) "Seegar Dealer" (Seymour 16), would have had ample opportunity to come into rough contact with clubs like the Magnolia Ball Club of New York, which might have included "shoulder hitters and fire laddies, Bowery Boys and ward heelers, Nativists and anti–Masons, brothel owners and saloonkeepers, sporting men and subterraneans ... who played the game not to rise above their social caste but to affirm it" (Thorn 86). Such individuals may have taken pride in their workplace efforts, but as Gorn explains, "it was in the strut and swagger of leisure-time activities—centered around saloons, theaters, boxing matches, pleasure gardens [such as Elysian Fields], sporting houses, boardinghouses, and brothels—that these young men found their deepest sense of individual identity" (407). Think, now, about Asbury's Bowery Boy, whose competitive passion for beating all-comers to a fire could now be transferred to the baseball field. "[F]orged in the heat of an urban sporting culture" (Thorn 86), the rules and regulations of baseball ascribed to the "whiggish" Knickerbockers affirmed identity by way of providing a re-creation of the values increasingly congruent with various kinds of work experience while simultaneously providing a recreational contrast with the perceived lack of regulation beyond the field of play. Or, as Gelber phrases it, "baseball was the antidote produced by the same plant that produced the poison" ("Hands" 19).

For Cartwright biographer Martin, "regulation" turns out to be a key concern. "Baseball was henceforth to be a regulated and refined game," he writes, "[b]aseball, no less than American social life, was to be guided by the rule of law and Victorian etiquette" (11). Rather than steep Cartwright and the codification of the rules of baseball into the seething roil of New York street life of the 1840s, much of which was expressly *not* guided by either the rule of law or the proprieties of Victorian etiquette, Martin will make what has become a conventional move in baseball historiography, a move toward abstract idealization that verges more on myth than on history: "The quest in America for a national identity had extended from its roots in revolutionary politics and social egalitarianism to a national capitol and a national flag and a national bird and national arts. Now it went all the way to baseball as the national game" (11). Echoing philosopher Michael Novak, Martin underscores his idealization of baseball as a metonym for the best of American institutions by equating the expanded role that the umpire would now play with the checks and balance system of our three branches of government: "If the batter was like the president and the fielders like the Congress, the umpire was the Supreme Court" (Martin 13).³ All of this is very appealing for those of us who want baseball to have done, and to do, the kind of cultural work that Martin ascribes to it. But can we really imagine that in establishing those early rules this motley crew of lawyers, doctors, clerks, salesmen — most of whom were familiar with and comfortable with the hurly-burly world of volunteer firefighting — was taking on the burden of crafting out a new *national* institution? Why wouldn't we instead imagine that the drive toward regulation of morals, fines for "profane or improper" language and the codification of behavior through the regulation of the diamond, player positions, distance between bases, number of innings, and outs (Martin 10–12), why wouldn't we imagine *that* sort of regulation as a reaction to the local context which, as the Mary Rogers case all too explicitly highlighted, was itself much unregulated?

The sporting life thrived on unabashed sexual aggression and profanity-laced passion for blood sport, a passion that mocked the pieties on which the Victorian concept of the good home was based. Nowhere was the impropriety of that passion more surprisingly on display than at the ever popular Elysian Fields, which a writer in the New York *Herald* extolled for "the beauty of its groves" and the "picturesqueness of its cliffs and creeks" (Stashower 89). Beautiful as it was, by the 1840s Elysian Fields had become a gathering place where members of all classes came into contact with each other — sometimes roughly, sometimes intimately — and where, as with New York lawyer George Templeton Strong, one might walk in "momentary expectation of stumbling on some couple engaged in ... 'the commission of gross vulgarity'" (qtd. Mann 91). Elysian Fields, then, was an unregulated social space which the Knickerbockers, when they played their baseball games there, did fair to turn into a rule-governed place in which "hands" — with all the implications for embodied, regulated labor that such a term implies— would be safest on base with the ultimate goal of getting home. (Ironically enough, the rules we usually associate with the Knickerbocker club also helped enable statistical re-description of games in local newspapers— Chadwick would "invent" his version of the box score in 1859 — thus making it more attractive for sportsmen to gamble on each game.⁴) In order to appreciate such "regulation" in the way Martin does, shouldn't we understand the *difference* that the men of Engine Company 12 were striving for as being *in relation to* the rough profligacy of the adherents of the sporting life? Keep in mind, too, that theirs was not the only new set of regulations involving activities associated with engine companies. Since the city lacked a professional firefighting department, it should come as no surprise to hear that one of the duties of the newly formed police department's precinct captains was, "at any alarm of fire," to "proceed to the [location] with one-half of the number of the policemen off duty, [and] to be diligent in preserving order and protecting property" (Valentine Art. I, §11, p. 57). Partly as a result of the Mary Rogers case, the hitherto unregulated space of the volunteer engine companies would now be appropriated by the regulations of the Police Reform Act of 1845.

Authorizing Baseball "Motherhood"

Wednesday, July 28, 1841, promised to be another scorcher in the 90s, the tenth in a row for Manhattanites. For Henry Mallin, "a young vocalist and music teacher," and his friends, including James Boulard, relief was just a ferry ride away, across the Hudson to Elysian Fields in Hoboken, New Jersey (Stashower 90). In seeking such relief at Elysian Fields, Mallin and friends were no different from thousands of other New Yorkers. Indeed, the day before, the *Tribune* had promoted the resort's unique combination of sanative benefit and convenient proximity by reminding its readers that they could "enjoy the pleasures and health bearing breezes of the Country without purchasing them at the dear rate of sweating over dusty roads" (Srebnick 18; Stashower 89). As the young men neared the famous hand-hewn Sybil's Cave, where strollers could refresh themselves (for a small fee) with water from the natural spring there or with something stronger in taprooms close by, Mallin and Boulard saw "a body floating between two tides, two or three hundred yards from shore" (Srebnick 18). They quickly commandeered a scull at a boathouse nearby and began rowing toward the body. Mallin and Boulard could hardly have been prepared for what they found next. A reporter from the *Herald* was among the crowd who gathered as Mallin and Boulard towed the body back to shore, and his is one of the first descriptions of the badly decomposed body: "Her forehead and face appeared to have been battered and butchered to a mummy. Her features were scarcely visible, so much violence had been done to her ... and altogether she presented the most awful spectacle that the eye could see" (Stashower 91). Leisurely consumption of the beautiful and the picturesque may very well have been on the docket for that day, but the discovery of a young woman's badly decomposing body brought home the complementary aesthetics of the sublime and the grotesque, aspects that the penny press, headed by the notorious James Gordon Bennett, founding editor of the New York *Herald*, would exploit to great effect.

Shortly after the body was brought ashore, a young clerk named Alfred Crommelin happened on the scene. Crommelin had been busy looking for a young woman named Mary Rogers, who had been missing from her home in Manhattan since Sunday morning, when she left her mother's boarding house on Nassau Street ostensibly to visit an aunt. A onetime boarder at the house and a failed suitor of the young woman in question, Crommelin had been on the search since Sunday night. He recognized Mary's body almost immediately, and soon after submission of the first coroner's report the penny press took up the gauntlet on behalf of what was now deemed the "tragedy of Mary Rogers," raped and murdered by a gang of brutal thugs. Once her identity was established, word quickly spread that this was *the* Mary Rogers, "the Beautiful Seegar Girl" who had until recently worked for John Anderson at his tobacco emporium located at 319 Broadway. There, Anderson served the needs of a wide clientele that included publishers, government workers, and glittering literati such as Washington Irving and James Fenimore Cooper, and perhaps even Poe. But since cigar stores were places where men from all walks of life could, and did, spend time "exchanging information" and "carrying out business," his emporium, sometimes to his regret, also had a "special reputation as the center of lively young sporting culture" (Srebnick 53). It was here, in this cross-class milieu, that young Mary Rogers attracted the kind of attention from the kind of young men that had spent money on and written letters of love and longing to Helen Jewett. However, unlike Helen, who, when she turned out to be more genteel than her profession might suggest, merely surprised those who investigated her murder, Mary would be constructed rather quickly as, in the words of the coroner, Dr. Cook, "a person of chastity and correct habits" (Srebnick 19).

Such assumption of virtue actually may have hindered investigators from thinking beyond the possibility of rape and murder — to abortion, for instance. After all, Mary had disappeared once before, back in 1838, a disappearance attracting no little interest in the local papers. That time, she had left behind a note that said she would kill herself (Walsh 11). No one knows for sure just exactly what happened in relation to the usual suspects in such cases — abduction, seduction, publicity stunt or hoax (14–15). But based on things that her then employer, Anderson, was to say years later, that earlier disappearance might very well have been for an abortion, and, according to Walsh, Anderson might quite plausibly have been involved (80). After all, Mary and her mother had lived for a short while with Anderson when they first came to the city in 1837. Shortly after that episode, supposedly with money supplied by her brother, she and her mother were able to open a boarding house, and Mary quit working for Anderson in order to help her mother (16).

The boarding house helped shore up the family's sagging fortunes a bit, but as Srebnick details, Mary's "working roles as tobacco girl and boarding-house keeper placed her within a world of working- and lower-class women, on the borderline of respectability" (51). The borderline was made even more problematic for being located at the threshold — what Anne Williams might call the "fault line" — where that which should be private becomes all too public. Perhaps this confounding of public and private is why Poe turns the thicket, wherein lie the clues for the solution of the case of *Marie Roget*, into what Laura Saltz calls a "natural parlor" (256). As Poe himself emphasizes, "within its naturally walled enclosure were three extraordinary stones, *forming a seat with a back and footstool*" (Poe 761; qtd. in Saltz 256). Saltz, who focuses, in part, on the increasingly public nature of abortion discourse during the time when the Rogers case was at its peak, takes the occasion of Poe's domestic figuration to make a point about why he would move the solution from the initial theory of a gang of men to that of a single man: "[Dupin] resolves the outrage against Marie by understanding the ways in which the crime disturbs patterns of rightful ownership" (261). As outrageous as this murder by a single man might be, it at least has the social value, for Dupin, of reaffirming "who owns what" (261) and thus of preserving the patriarchal status quo within the domestic precincts of the private home. Private home? Unfortunately, in antebellum Manhattan "the distinctions between public brothels, parlor houses, houses of assignation, furnished-room houses, and panel houses were often unclear." Gilfoyle goes on to say that "[a] house filled exclusively with prostitutes was outwardly indistinguishable from a female-run boardinghouse with a few tenants" (166). Given the all too public and transitory nature of the space of the boarding house, the Rogers's house, like the thicket around which Marie Roget's clothes were strewn, could never quite qualify as a home in the Victorian sense, an idea that is underscored by the fact that several men who had boarded there, Alex Crummelin and Daniel Payne, among them, were either infatuated with or considered themselves Mary's suitor. Thus the boardinghouse and tobacco shop milieus, with their male-dominated clientele that was less a function of class than of ability to pay, heightened the perception of Mary's "open availability and sexuality" and "made her a representation of the eroticized culture of the metropolis" (Srebnick 51). For the men who idealized her "face value," as Saltz aptly phrases it (and I would include Poe among them), Mary is "both a sign and an object of exchange" (249), perpetually oscillating between the possibility of being owned and the inability to own her.

Whereas the City, as Srebnick describes, is gendered feminine and is figured most often as a dangerous siren who beckons the unwary, "home" is its domesticated counterpart. No one knew that better than did novelist and social reformer Lydia Maria Child, who wrote about her September 1841, visit to Elysian Fields when it was still thought that Mary had been gang-raped and murdered. Child focuses her attention on the stillness of the scene, and as she approaches what she terms the "Gothic interior" of Sybil's Cave in moonlight, her writing takes its own gothic turn: "All else was still — still — so fearfully still, that one might almost count the beatings of the heart. That my heart *did* beat, I acknowledge; for here was the supposed scene of the Mary Rogers' [sic] tragedy; and though the recollection of *her* gave me no uneasiness, I could not forget that quiet lovely path we were treading was near to the city, with its thousand hells, and frightfully easy of access" (21). Those "thousand hells" notwithstanding, as Child's ferry approaches the New York shore, she points out for her readers the "lamps of the city gleaming in the distance," and with a dutiful remembrance of "the houseless street-wanderer," Child "gratefully" acknowledges "that one of those lights illuminated a home, where true and honest hearts were ever ready to bid me welcome" (21–2).[5] With that nod to the "street-wanderer," Child underscores the notion that a truly middle-class home, in the Victorian context in which the Cult of True Womanhood prevailed, was "the de-eroticized counterpart of the dangerous city" (Srebnick 48).

The idea of a home as a sanctuary from the unregulated flux and fluidity of the City was echoed in a funeral sermon for murdered Nativist icon, Butcher Bill Poole, delivered by the aptly named Reverend J.B. Wakely: "What improvement can we make of this sad catastrophe? I trust it will have an influence in checking sporting gentlemen — pugilists — and preventing rowdyism; that we shall get rid of this fearful, withering curse; that his death will give to this a death blow, and that men will cease to destroy each other. It shows us the danger of carrying weapons of death. It shows us the evil of keeping open saloons, if they must be kept open at all, till a late hour in the night.... Home! Home! is the place of happiness—the place of safety" (qtd. in Gorn 405–6).

Baseball fans do not need to be told about the symbolic importance of being safe at home. But I hope I have shown the significance of locating that home in its Manhattan context of the 1840s in which the Mary Rogers case was both historically durable and culturally transformative. Once we recognize what Charles Springwood calls the "invented tradition" of the "immaculate conception" of baseball in Cooperstown in 1839 (30), we can better attend to the development of the game in Manhattan, at Elysian Fields, and elsewhere. And to the extent that such histories too readily seek the comforts of hagiography and the attractions of closure in order to turn baseball into a fraternal organization centered on the notion of a transcendental origin, we are in the realm of gothic baseball. For it is precisely Cooperstown's "premature delivery" *in relation to* the development of the game *elsewhere* that creates the gaps whence baseball history — the *secret* history — develops. As in the case of our master practitioner of the gothic idiom, Poe, whose fictive tale must confront its own historical matrix in the form of a death-bed tale of Loss, even biographies with the best of intentions, as is Martin's of Cartwright, will find itself face to face with its corrosive doppelganger.

The notion of Cartwright as one among a significant group of inventors during the heyday of American invention (Martin 11) is complicated, and many points debunked outright, in another recent biography of Cartwright by Monica Nucciarone, entitled *Alexander Cartwright: The Life behind the Baseball Legend* (Nebraska, 2009), with a foreword written by John Thorn. Nucciarone titles her concluding chapter, *Alexander Cartwright, Father of Modern Baseball.** Both the italics and the asterisk are in the original, and Nucciarone's point, as she clearly declares, is that Cartwright's historical identification as "the father of modern baseball" "deserves an asterisk" (225). (The asterisk, according to Wikipedia, is "derived from the need of the printers of family trees in feudal times for a symbol to indicate date of birth."[6]) Perhaps aware of the impending publication of Nucciarone's biography, Martin provides something in the way of his own asterisk in the form of an "appendix" in which he makes explicit reference to baseball historians such as Thorn. In it, he asks, "Did [Cartwright] 'invent' baseball? 'Father' baseball? 'Codify' or 'promote' various streams from ballgames?" Good questions all; and Martin's response? "He did a little of each. But his central claim for being singled out in baseball history is that he appeared at a certain crucial time in the 'making' of the game and through his keen organizing ability he clarified the game and continued to be involved with its development" (133). *A little of each?* Since it is now possible to do "a little" bit of fathering, we must be but a Nassau Street-corner away from being "just a little bit pregnant." At any rate, the qualified and hedged language in Martin's appendix is a far cry from the indicative assurance of "Alexander Joy Cartwright Jr. invented baseball in 1845" (11).

Arguing on behalf of larger recognition for Doc Adams in establishing the rules that regulate our national pastime, Thorn quotes the venerable Henry Chadwick on the topic of baseball's paternity: "Like Topsy, baseball never had no 'fadder'; it jest growed [sic]" ("Doc Adams, n.p.). When we trace that line back to its source in Harriet Beecher Stowe's *Uncle Tom's Cabin* (1852), another work of fiction that sought to pull back the veil of "real" history, we find that what Topsy actually said in response to Miss Ophelia's queries is that "I spect I grow'd. Don't think nobody ever made me" (356). Miss Ophelia was nothing if not persistent, for earlier, Topsy had phrased it this way: "Never was born ... never had no father nor mother, nor nothin.' I was raised by a speculator, with lots of others" (356). Topsy, speaks, of course, for the condition of the slave, and Chadwick's invocation of her implicitly underscores the color line in baseball and in American social life in general. By invoking Topsy, Chadwick, perhaps unwittingly, reminds us that the writing of history, if we are attuned to its relationships to power and to the subject positions of its historians, is unavoidably a species of speculation. Baseball history has, indeed, been raised by a whole host of such speculators, and even if we could find out the "biological" identity of its father, the child, as in the case of Topsy herself, would follow the condition of its mother.

What do we get when we follow through on that condition? As the New York *Journal of Commerce* warned its eager readers in regard to Mary Rogers' post-mortem condition, it may not be pretty and it may be "difficult ... for the most imaginative mind to conceive a spectacle more horrible or humiliating to humanity": "There lay, what was but a few days back, the image of its Creator, the loveliest of his works, and the tenement of an immortal soul, now a blackened and decomposed mass of putrefaction, painfully disgusting to sight and smell. Her skin, which had been unusually fair, was now black as that of a negro" (Stashower 105). *The child follows the condition of its decomposing mother, "now black as ... a negro."* I really am not as interested in the grotesque, racialized or not, as was Poe and the penny press. But I do know that we have always been a little too good at abstracting out — subliming — the paradise portion of the classical meaning of Elysian Fields and of turning a blind eye to its material conditions. Such indifference or blindness to an informing matrix shaped by men and women from all classes and races is what leaves "baseball" susceptible to the corrosive effects of its own history.

Allow me, now, to make one more turn of the screw of baseball historiography. In *Chasing Baseball: Our Obsessions with Its History, Numbers, People and Places* (2010), Dorothy Seymour Mills reflects on the role that her late husband, Harold Seymour, played in legitimizing baseball historiography within the academy. She reminds us that fellow baseball historian Steven Riess had famously dubbed Seymour the "father of modern baseball history." Mills goes on to affirm an analogy made by William M. Simons equating Seymour's work on behalf of baseball history with that of Frederick Jackson Turner, the legendary historian who "redirected examination of the nation's past to new sources and new themes" (51) in essays such as "The Significance of the Frontier in American History," delivered to the American Historical Association at the Columbian Exposition in Chicago in 1893. Well, so much for the usual pieties. The second half of *Chasing Baseball*, as the title for Part Two indicates, is devoted to baseball as "A Womanly Pursuit." There, Mills details a long neglected history in which women both played the game and participated in its development behind the scenes. The analogy, now, is with racial discrimination. "Women, like blacks," Mills writes, "are used to discrimination in baseball" (185).

Mills saves the best for last, however, in her description of her own contributions to the three-volume work that for so many years we ascribed purely to the efforts of her late husband. In an article she published in 2000, as she explains, "I finally revealed to the world of scholarship ... that I was Harold

Seymour's co-author" (218). In spite of the fact that these claims were backed by reams of research notes in her handwriting, when the Society for American Baseball Research (SABR) named the recipients of its inaugural Henry Chadwick Award in March of 2010, Harold Seymour was honored, along with other luminaries of baseball history such as Lawrence S. Ritter and Bill James, but Dorothy Mills, who had done so much of the research and, by the third volume, most of the writing for "Seymour's" history, was not honored (Schwarz n.p.). After some 48 hours of "heated discussions" involving Mills, the selection committee that included John Thorn, and the vociferous support of "329 female members of SABR," Mills was told that she would be "honored equally with Seymour." This decision to finally set the public record straight meant that some of the stakeholders, like committee-member Thorn (who that spring was likely putting the finishing touches on his *Baseball in the Garden of Eden: The Secret History of the Early Game*) had to work through their personal sense that this was a private domestic issue — a family squabble — between a deceased man and his still living former wife. As Thorn said, "It was easy for me to say, 'Well, Harold's not here to defend himself in this spousal fight; I'm not getting into it." But Thorn eventually came around, and in explaining the decision to include Mills, had this to say: "I do believe I have a heightened sense because of this unusual experience this week.... A heightened sense of responsibility — to correct historical error" (Schwarz, n.p.). Stuck between choosing sides in a domestic disturbance or coming down on the right side of history, Thorn was able to resist the "small pieties" demanded by the protocols of a flawed patriarchal authority — in this case the "father" of his discourse — in favor of the "analytical impulse" of the newer history that Thorn would so forcefully advocate in his then forthcoming book (c.f. Thorn xii). Making his own strong link to the ghosts of Topsy's speculators, Steve Gietschier, "former chief of research at *The Sporting News*," insisted that Seymour did more than appropriate Dorothy's work: "He stole her personhood" (Safya, n.p.).

If Mills was off to a hot spring of 2010, summer would prove to be gangbusters, as more good news arrived by way of Oxford University Press, the publishers of the three-volume history. "I am happy to announce," said OUP executive editor Tim Bent, "that at long last Dorothy Seymour Mills will be given formal credit on the books she wrote with her late husband" (Reid n.p.). What exactly does formal credit mean? It means that in all future editions of their history, her name will "now accompany her late husband's on the books' covers and title pages" (Reid n.p.). The world would finally get a chance to know who owned what.

Perhaps the appropriate coda to the symbolic meaning of Mills' restoration can be found in an earlier book she wrote entitled *A Woman's Work: Writ-*

ing *Baseball History with Harold Seymour* (McFarland, 2004). There, in describing the publication of the first volume of their history, Mills informs us that "[i]n those days publishers took nine months—*the length of a pregnancy*—to produce a book, so *Baseball: The Early Years* appeared in the spring of 1960" (68, emphasis added). "At long last," then, we arrive at our "secret mother" of baseball history. And because she is a secret no more, and because, even if in spite of a cultural order that is still fundamentally patriarchal, she has been given all due credit, we arrive as well at the beginning of the end of what I have been calling *"gothic baseball."*

Notes

1. This is a revised version of a paper entitled "Gothic Baseball: Mary Rogers, Alexander Cartwright, and Manhattan in the 1840s," presented at the 15th Annual Baseball in Literature and Culture Conference, Middle Tennessee State University, March 26, 2010. My thanks to the anonymous reader for helpful comments, to Phil Jones, reader services librarian at Grinnell College for help in locating historical documents, and many thanks to Ron Kates and Warren Tormey for their generosity and patience as they awaited completion and delivery of this chapter.

2. Monica Nucciarone writes that in the nineteenth century Chadwick was known as "the Father of Baseball" (225). Jules Tygiel refers to Chadwick as "Father Baseball," and his contributions to the game, especially in relation to the development of statistics, has inspired the bestowal of credit along the lines of invention. Tygiel, for example, credits Chadwick with having "invented the game's historical essence." See *Past Time: Baseball as History* (New York: Oxford University Press, 2000), 16.

3. For Novak, "baseball is designed like the federal system of checks and balances," as the "umpires provide a kind of judiciary; the offensive players ... learn like our executive that 'the buck stops here'; the defense attempts to play in concert, a congress checking the power of the hitters." See *The Joy of Sports: End Zones, Bases, Baskets, Balls, and the Consecration of the American Spirit* (New York: Hamilton Press, 1988), 63.

4. For the importance of gambling, statistics, and newspaper publicity in bringing sporting culture to baseball, see Thorn, p. 87.

5. Both Srebnick (4–5) and Walsh (31–2) cite this passage.

6. This historical sense of the "asterisk" is validated on the website retinart.net, which tells us that one traditional use of the asterisk has been "to indicate a person's birth," used in tandem with appropriate date. See "Typographic Marks Unknown," retinart.net/typography/marksunknown.

Works Cited

Asbury, Herbert. *The Gangs of New York: An Informal History of the New York Underworld.* New York: Old Town Books, 1927, 1928; New York: Dorset Press, 1992. Print.

Child, Lydia Maria. "Letter IV." *Letters from New York: A Portrait of New York on the Cusp of Its Transformation into a Modern City.* Ed. Bruce Mills. Athens: University of Georgia Press, 1998. Print.

Cohen, Patricia Cline. "Unregulated Youth: Masculinity and Murder in the 1830s City." *Radical History Review* 52 (Winter 1992): 33–52. Print.

Gelber, Steven M. "'Their Hands Are All Out Playing': Business and Amateur Baseball, 1845–1917. *Journal of Sport History* 11.2 (Spring 1984): 5–27. Print.

_____. "Working at Playing: The Culture of the Workplace and the Rise of Baseball." *Journal of Social History* 16.4 (Summer 1983): 3–22. Print.

Gilfoyle, Timothy J. *City of Eros: New York City, Prostitution, and the Commercialization of Sex, 1790–1920.* New York: W.W. Norton, 1992. Print.
Gorn, Elliot J. "'Good-Bye Boys, I Die a True American': Homicide, Nativism, and Working-Class Culture in Antebellum New York City." *Journal of American History* 74.2 (1987): 388–410. Print.
Hoppe, Randolph. "Hoboken, New Jersey — Where Baseball was Born!" *Hoboken Baseball.com.* Mar. 28, 2010. Web. Sep. 9, 2011.
James, Bill. *Popular Crime: Reflections on the Celebration of Violence.* New York: Scribner, 2011. Print.
Lardner, James, and Thomas Reppetto. *NYPD: A City and Its Police.* New York: Henry Holt, 2000. Print.
Mann, William A. "The Elysian Fields of Hoboken, New Jersey." *Base Ball* 1.1 (Spring 2007). Print.
Martin, Jay. *Live All You Can: Alexander Joy Cartwright and the Invention of Modern Baseball.* New York: Columbia University Press, 2009. Print.
Mills, Dorothy Jane. *A Woman's Work: Writing Baseball History with Harold Seymour.* Jefferson, NC: McFarland, 2004. Print.
Mills, Dorothy Seymour. *Chasing Baseball: Our Obsession with Its History, Numbers, People and Places.* Jefferson, NC: McFarland, 2010. Print.
Morris, Peter. "Whatever Happened to Baseball History: Keynote Speech to the Sixteenth Annual NINE Spring Training Conference, 14 Mar 2009." *NINE* 18.2 (2009).
Novak, Michael. *The Joy of Sports: End Zones, Bases, Baskets, Balls, and the Consecration of the American Spirit.* New York: Hamilton Press, 1988. Print.
Nucciarone, Monica. *Alexander Cartwright: The Life behind the Baseball Legend.* Lincoln: Nebraska University Press, 2010. Print.
Poe, Edgar Allan. *Doings of Gotham by Edgar Allan Poe as described in a series of letters to the editors of the Columbia Spy together with various comments and criticisms by Poe; also a poem entitled "New Year's Address of the Carriers of the Columbia Spy." Now collected by Jacob E. Spannath; with preface, introduction and comments by Thomas Ollive Mabbott.* Pottsville: J.E. Spannath, 1929. Print.
_____. "The Mystery of Marie Roget." *Tales and Sketches*, volume 2: 1843–1849, ed. Thomas Ollive Mabbott. Urbana: University of Illinois Press, 2000. Print.
Reid, Calvin. "OUP Gives Long Overdue Credit to Female Baseball Historian." *Publishersweekly.com.* Aug. 20, 2010. Web. Nov. 1, 2011.
Safya, Ana. "Baseball wife comes from dugout." *bighaber.com.* Web. Mar. 3, 2012.
Saltz, Laura. "'(Horrible to Relate!)': Recovering the Body of Marie Rogêt." *The American Face of Edgar Allan Poe.* Eds. Shawn Rosenheim and Stephen Rachman. Baltimore: Johns Hopkins University Press, 1995. Print.
Savoy, Eric. "The Face of the Tenant: A Theory of American Gothic." *American Gothic: New Interventions in a National Narrative.* Eds. Robert K. Martin and Eric Savoy. Iowa City: University of Iowa Press, 1998. Print.
_____. "The Rise of American Gothic." *The Cambridge Companion to Gothic Fiction.* Ed. Jerrold E. Hogle. New York: Cambridge University Press, 2002. Print.
Schwarz, Alan. "Straightening the Record." *NYTimes.com.* Mar. 6, 2010. Web. Nov. 1, 2011.
Seltzer, Mark. *Bodies and Machines.* New York: Routledge, 1992. Print.
Seymour, Harold. *Baseball: The Early Years.* New York: Oxford University Press, 1960. Print.
Springwood, Charles Freuhling. *Cooperstown to Dyersville: A Geography of Baseball Nostalgia.* Boulder: Westview Press, 1996. Print.
Srebnick, Amy. *The Mysterious Death of Mary Rogers: Sex and Culture in Nineteenth-Century New York.* New York: Oxford University Press, 1995. Print.

Stashower, Daniel. *The Beautiful Cigar Girl: Mary Rogers, Edgar Allan Poe, and the Invention of Murder.* New York: Berkley Publishing Group, 2006, 2007. Print.
Stowe, Harriet Beecher. *Uncle Tom's Cabin, or Life among the Lowly.* New York: Penguin Classics, 1992. Print.
Thoms, Peter. "Poe's Dupin and the Power of Detection." *The Cambridge Companion to Edgar Allan Poe.* Ed. Kevin J. Hayes. New York: Cambridge University Press, 2002. Print.
Thorn, John. *Baseball in the Garden of Eden: The Secret History of the Early Game.* New York: Simon & Schuster, 2011. Print.
_____. "Doc Adams." *The Baseball Biography Project.* Web. Nov. 1, 2011.
Tygiel, Jules. *Past Time: Baseball as History.* New York: Oxford University Press, 2000. Print.
Valentine, D.T. "Police Department. An act for the Establishment and Regulation of the Police of the City of New York. Passed May 13, 1846." *Manual of the Corporation of the City of New York for the Year 1847.* New York: Casper C. Childs, 1847. Print.
Walsh, John. *Poe the Detective: The Curious Circumstances behind* The Mystery of Marie Roget. New Brunswick: Rutgers University Press, 1968. Print.
Wilentz, Sean. *Chants Democratic: New York City and the Rise of the American Working Class, 1788–1850.* New York: Oxford University Press, 1984. Print.
Williams, Anne. *Art of Darkness: A Poetics of Gothic.* Chicago: University of Chicago Press, 1995. Print.

Freedom and Baseball: The Uplift of Sport

JANAKA B. LEWIS

In spite of difficult racial environments for its participants, baseball has served as an equalizing ground in African American cultural history. Late 1800s narratives about African American participants in baseball examine their individual and collective subjectivity, their attempts to assert control over hands and minds under and within the law, and the general absence of African Americans from the American body politic. Even so, aspiring professional and, later, college participants, negotiated social issues through their dominance in the game. Thus, baseball offered a new politics of physical engagement which African Americans could participate in and eventually gain recognition from.

Rather than offering a detailed and comprehensive history of African American involvement in baseball, this essay analyzes the shift between the social and physical emphasis of the sport in its mainstream environments. This shift was also mirrored in African American communities in the nineteenth century. Using Frederick Douglass and Booker T. Washington as two examples of how African American authors interpreted sport in their everyday lives, I argue that baseball presented a framework across communities for determining social conduct, manipulating stereotypes, and articulating social norms.

The contributions to and participation in baseball of African Americans often follow the lines or exist within the margins of mainstream narratives of "American" baseball. In his introduction to *Out of the Shadows: African American Baseball from the Cuban Giants to Jackie Robinson*, Bill Kilwin writes: "Partially hidden and ignored by the general population, black baseball emerged as a parallel version of the National Pastime subsisting on the margins of society" (vii). Even so, as Robert Peterson documents in *Only the Ball Was White*, the story of African American involvement in athletics offers its own narrative of freedom and mobility from the late nineteenth century until the beginning of the Negro Baseball League in 1920 (and during the years of the "gentlemen's agreement" from the 1880s through the 1940s that perpetuated African American exclusion from the major leagues). Likewise, Sol White's *History of Colored Base Ball with other documents on the early Black Game, 1886–1936,* and additional news accounts of black baseball games in local newspapers in the early 1900s, suggest that although baseball has origins as a white American middle class game, African American institutions and communities also used the game to increase educational opportunities and to promote racial respectability amongst themselves. Gaining recognition from outside communities was often a secondary goal to re-shaping the ways in which African Americans chose to interact with and be seen by each other. Importantly, the history of black baseball emerges from and intertwines with a dominant narrative of social transition through sport.

Baseball's Histories

Baseball is classified as one of oldest major American team sports—referred to as the "nation's pastime," among other terms of endearment. In *Touching Base: Professional Baseball and American Culture in the Progressive Era,* Steven Riess writes: "The game of baseball supplanted cricket as the most popular American team sport in the 1850s and toward the end of the decade was already gaining consideration as *the* national pastime" (4). Indeed, according to Peterson,

> by 1867 there were more than a hundred baseball clubs in the North, and the game's first league, the National Association of Base Ball players, was nine years old. It was a loose confederation with the primary purpose of making rules for member clubs. On December 11 and 12, the NABBP held its annual convention in Philadelphia, with 237 delegates attending, some from as far away as Wisconsin [16].

Peterson goes on to say, however, that those who met for the purpose of advancing the game also could not be "oblivious to the nation's moral dilemma—what to do about its four-and-a-half million new citizens, all of them black" (16). This conundrum, creating rules for a "game" when society itself had contradictory rules, eventually helped to shape the history of baseball itself.

Despite the number of accounts contributing to the history of the sport, New Yorker Alexander Joy Cartwright, then a young bank clerk, was credited with "founding" modern American baseball with his creation of the Knickerbocker Base Ball Club in 1845 (Goldstein 12). As Goldstein describes, "his fellows liked the idea, and, constituting themselves as the Knickerbocker Base

Ball club, they drew up a constitution, wrote down their playing rules, and rented a field and dressing rooms in the Elysian Fields of Hoboken, New Jersey" (12). According to Goldstein, initially the sport was "a club-based fraternal pastime grounded in the respectable local culture of urban artisans, clerks, and small proprietors" (4). Baseball's "first" year of 1845 is also, however, significant in African American literary history as the year that the *Narrative of the Life of Frederick Douglass* was first published. As Douglass reflected on his life of and an escape from bondage, the game played by middle and upper-middle class business men was taking root in New York, where he would move in 1847, to start his antislavery newspaper, *The North Star*, in Rochester.

Though coincidental, the sport's establishment and publication of the *Narrative* mark the beginning stages of baseball's growing social emphasis, making a parallel examination of both narratives significant. Goldstein discusses the game as a social ritual, arguing that "The game was embedded in a set of fraternal rituals and club activities in the 1850s and 1860s" (13). He continues: "Only later did the baseball contest emerge as the focal point for players, spectators, and the press" (13). Though brief, this account highlights the focus on the social construction of baseball as an activity of middle-class origins.

Douglass's text is also a social and cultural marker, and he had a less than favorable view of sport as it related to enslavement of and prospects for freedom. Even before established leagues and athletic programs included African Americans, games and play were essential to documenting mobility (or lack thereof) in slave narratives. Douglass writes: "The days between Christmas and New Year's Day are allowed as holidays; and, accordingly, we were not required to perform any labor, more than to feed and take care of the stock. This time we regarded as our own, by the grace of our masters; and we therefore used or abused it nearly as we pleased" (*Narrative* 62). Douglass argues that even the time of enslaved persons during "holidays" did not belong to them:

> The staid, sober, thinking and industrious ones of our number would employ themselves in making corn-brooms, mats, horse-collars, and baskets; and another class of us would spend the time in hunting opossums, hares, and coons. But by far the larger part engaged in such sports and merriments as playing ball, wrestling, running foot-races, fiddling, dancing, and drinking whisky; and this latter mode of spending the time was by far the most agreeable to the feelings of our masters. A slave who would work during the holidays was considered by our masters as scarcely deserving them ... [*Narrative* 62].

Although Douglass does not specify the type of "ball" that was played, he categorized the game, along with other sports, in the same way as dancing and drinking — as wastes of time compared to the more industrious tasks that slaves could complete for their own benefit. Furthermore, masters sanctioned this "free" time, as one who worked instead proved not to need unscheduled time. Play, then, as Douglass saw it, became part of the institutional oppression of slavery rather than games of leisure.

Saidiya Hartman analyzes the vexed notion of "play" as it relates to activities in which enslaved persons participated: "Not only was pleasure posed in contrast to labor, but the negation or ambivalence of pleasure was to be explained by the yoking of the captive body to the will, whims, and exploits of the owner and by the constancy of the slave's unmet yearnings, whether for food or for freedom" (49). Douglass also analyzes holidays within a framework that points to the restrictive nature of the slave's pleasure, describing them as "the most effective means in the hands of the slaveholder in keeping down the spirit of insurrection ... as conductors, or safety-valves, to carry off the rebellious spirit of enslaved humanity" (62). Without the "safety-valves" available to their masters, he argues, slaves would give in to desperation. They are "part and parcel of the gross fraud, wrong, and inhumanity of slavery.... Their object seems to be, to disgust their slaves with freedom, by plunging them into the lowest depths of dissipation" (62). In this text, slavemasters are both initiators of and partakers in this degradation — they engage the slaves in the "game" of freedom, a game where the victor has already been determined.

Douglass outlines the real game as such: "When the slave asks for virtuous freedom, the cunning slaveholder, knowing his ignorance, cheats him with a dose of vicious dissipation, artfully labeled with the name of liberty" (63). In the end, the "liberty" is false, the games do not lead to a transformation of reality for the enslaved, and the slaves realize that the masters will always win. As Douglass illustrates, the enslaved realize "victory" only within the sense of a larger defeat, when the deceit has seemingly ended: "when the holidays ended, we staggered up from the filth of our wallowing, took a long breath, and marched to the field — feeling, upon the whole, rather glad to go, from what our master had deceived us into a belief was freedom, back to the arms of slavery" (63).

Hartman analyzes this negotiation of enslaved bodies to subjugation through physical labor and amusement:

> Generally, the response of the enslaved to the management and orchestration of "Negro enjoyment" was more complex than a simple rejection of "innocent amusements"; rather, the sense of operating within and against these closures made the experience of pleasure decidedly ambivalent ... pleasure was less a general form of dominance than a way of naming, by contradistinction, the consumption and possession of the body and black needs and possibilities [49].

In this assessment, pleasure is used as an instrument of control to possess black bodies. However, it also seems to allow that leisure can be a way for blacks to repossess their bodies from those who dominated them by the same means. Douglass revisits the idea of game as a potentially revolutionary activity in his 1855 narrative, *My Bondage and My Freedom*, reiterating that the activities of slaves "generally most agreeable to their masters" included "ball playing, wrestling, boxing, running foot races, dancing, and drinking whisky," adding "fiddling, dancing, and 'jubilee beating'" as activities through which enslaved persons simultaneously express defiance toward and submit to the enforcement of their masters (184):

> The performer improvises as he beats, and sings his merry songs, so ordering the words as to have them fall pat with the movement of his hands. Among a mass of nonsense and wild frolic, once in a while a sharp hit is given to the meanness of slaveholders. Take the following, for example: "We raise de wheat,/ Dey gib us de corn;/ We bake de bread,/ Dey gib us de cruss;/ We sif de meal,/ Dey gib us de husss;/ We peal de meat,/ Dey gib us de skin,/ And dat's de way/ Dey takes us in" [184].

In this instance, physical games complement rhetorical ones, suggesting a means to reclaim one's authority within a manipulated timeframe. In this revisitation of the topic of sport, "play" can also serve as resistance.

Returning to the mainstream history of baseball, in which the sport emerged from larger social frameworks, Warren Goldstein argues: "The earliest baseball organizations were genuine social clubs, in which baseball playing was an important but far from the only activity. As one club constitution put it, the objects of the Club shall be to 'improve, foster and perpetuate the American game of Base Ball,' and advance morally, socially, and physically, the interests of its members'" (17). This focus on "moral, social, and physical" advancement in addition to fraternal activities such as meals, "toasts, speeches, and songs" establishes a parameter that is evident across racial lines (17–18). Indeed, the constructed social aspect of games is likewise as important to black baseball history as is physical talent of the players. Consequently, as African Americans became more prominent in ownership of the game, their social aspirations became a part of that transition.

Legal emancipation was instituted in many places with the Emancipation Proclamation of 1863; but this growing consciousness relating to sport remained independent from any legislation. In 1867, the National Association of Base Ball Players took the stand that African Americans could not participate alongside the white players of the sport. Robert Peterson argues: "The Negro was a political subject in 1867, but politics was a secondary consideration for the NABBP. Simple prejudice brought baseball's first color line. The members of the Association were all Northerners, but most shared with Southerners the belief that the Negro was inferior and not fit company for white gentlemen" (17). Alongside the black codes that prevented Negro mobility, especially in the south, baseball became an area in which color lines were instituted as well. Indeed, "the NABBP addressed itself to the Negro question and came down on the side of repression, barring Negroes and the clubs to which they belonged from membership. The Association's nominating committee penned the first color line in baseball, unanimously calling for exclusion 'of any club which may be composed of one or more colored persons'" (16–17).

The National Association of Professional Base Ball Players, the successor of the NABBP, continued to exclude persons of color as the game and its players became more professionalized; indeed, with its formation in 1871, "the NAPBBP never had a written rule against Negro players. It did not need one, for there existed a 'gentleman's agreement' barring Negroes from this first professional league and from its successor, the National League" (Peterson 17). Despite this exclusion, African Americans negotiated the game and its terms within their own communities and on their own terms, even before the institution of Negro Leagues in 1920. As Peterson points out, "if Negroes could not play baseball with Association clubs, there was nothing to forbid them from playing among themselves. And they did. Nothing is known about the earliest Negro clubs, but by 1867 teams were sufficiently well-organized, at least in the North, to have challenge matches for supremacy" (17). Throughout the history of Reconstruction in the South, officially documented from 1865 to 1877, and into the Post-Reconstruction period, African American teams competed among themselves, gaining both audiences and mobility through participation in the game.

These early players came from varied backgrounds, and their pursuit of respect transcended their class struggles, as across the sport the game drew players from a broader pool of participants. In "The Birth of the Cuban Giants: The Origins of Black Professional Baseball," Jerry Malloy argues that a physical and competitive focus emerged within mainstream baseball as the game grew more distant from its upper middle class origins:

> White baseball had long abandoned its origins as a gentlemen's social romp, little more than a good excuse for a smashing buffet. A muscular professionalism had propelled the game to new heights of national prestige—and commercial reward. Now, in the mid–1880s, African American baseball took a similar plunge into professionalism. Black baseball established itself as a viable economic entity when the Cuban Giants were born [Malloy 1].

Sol White relates how the Giants grew out of a group of waiters at the Argyle Hotel in the Long Island resort community of Babylon: "The Cuban

Giants, born in 1885, enriched a wide range of communities across the sprawling province of nineteenth-century baseball. They set a standard for black baseball excellence that would be unequalled, though not unchallenged, for ten years" (qtd. in Malloy 1). Both writers offer reasons for the team's success. White wrote that several players had played in Havana, hence accounting for the team's name, and Malloy, incorporating coverage of the team's trip to Boston by the *New York Age*, a "prominent African American newspaper," wrote that the team was a consolidation of "Keystone Athletics, the Manhattans of Washington, D.C., and the Orions of Philadelphia" (3). Together, these accounts suggest both that there was more than fleeting interest in the competitive aspects of the sport, and that the players had common vocations outside the game.

Once the team was established, they planned to play year round, despite not having a permanent home base. While in Florida, Malloy writes, the team was associated with Henry Flagler of the Royal Poinciana hotel. Traveling during their first summer season, the Giants won their first forty games, only to lose to the Major League St. Louis Browns on May 28, 1886. Eventually establishing a home base in Trenton, New Jersey, the team depended on their athleticism, and also on white communities from their very beginning. Malloy writes:

> For entire seasons, the Cuban Giants would be the only viable black professional team in the East, due to the increasingly toxic atmosphere of the 1890s and beyond.... In large part, the Cuban Giants were successful because of this commerce between wealthy whites and ball-playing blacks, this mixture of America's most and least favored classes [6].

Further, in developing connection, Neil Lanctot argues that because they were "unable to survive solely through the support of the black community, black teams earned the bulk of their income playing white independent 'semi-pro' clubs outside Organized Baseball...." (4). Other historical and literary accounts, however, reveal this competition as the means of securing opportunities for a broader population, and even for future generations, through social policy within African American communities. Though by no means exhaustive, various social histories of black baseball suggest similar behind the scenes investments to make baseball a viable vehicle for African American success.

Steven Riess offers that "the professionalization and commercialization of baseball began in the 1860s when the first players were paid to play and the fields were enclosed so that promoters could charge admission fees to spectators" (4). However, despite the beginning of the National Association of Professional Base Ball Players in 1871, followed by the National League of

Professional Base Ball Clubs (NL) in 1876, the International Association in 1877, the Northwestern League in 1879, and the American Association in 1882, only the National League and thirteen minor leagues were still in place at the end of the nineteenth century (Malloy 5). More widespread than other emerging sports, the game reached its "peak of popularity as the country's leading sport" in the early twentieth century, so that "by the early 1900s, when boxing and horse racing were operating, if at all, under severe legal and social restrictions, and football was an amateur sport mainly limited to the college crowd, professional baseball teams played in nearly every city" (Malloy 5). The sport's visibility was evident in amateur arenas as well, and African American organizations, such as the Giants, realized the class mobility that the game could offer.

Offering a different perspective of the sport in the early 1860s, Warren Goldstein cites the "sharp differences" that "had already emerged among players, clubs, spectators, and the press over how much emphasis ought to be placed on the game itself—on practice, skillful play, and playing to win—as opposed to the 'social' side of the game—post-game dinners, club balls, and playing for 'fun and exercise'" (4). However, he also offers the early connection between baseball and labor during the same time period: "As early as 1860 the language reporters used to describe a successful team was the language of self-disciplined, productive craft labor ... Club captains exercised wide authority over the conduct of their players on and off the field, while club rules—which had been collectively determined and enforced guidelines for club behavior—became instruments of labor discipline" (5). Gaining "discipline" through labor offered early black players the means to gain esteem through behavior and performance on and off the field.

Booker T. Washington, the noted author and founder of Tuskegee Institute (now University), offers an example of social progress realized through sport, considering the connection between baseball and education. As articulated in *Up from Slavery* (1901), Washington describes a memoir of labor that both contributed to his own uplift from slavery, and later became part of his "programme" of creating student self-reliance and self-sufficiency, first at Hampton Institute (now University), and then at Tuskegee. Washington describes a philosophy in which students make most of the items they needed or used, even down to bricks from straw, but does not offer much concerning the school's overall curriculum. Even though he excluded these details from his memoir, which garnered great attention for his work at Tuskegee, components of that "education" included a focus on athletics.

Significantly, Tuskegee's website notes that the school's first Athletic director James Washington — Washington's brother — was hired in 1890. Yet, Booker T. Washington's original narrative suggests that sport did not play a part in his own life, which he devoted instead to African American vocational advancement. He writes:

> I was asked not long ago to tell something about the sports and pastimes that I engaged in during my youth. Until that question was asked it had never occurred to me that there was no period of my life that was devoted to play. From the time that I can remember anything, almost every day of my life has been occupied in some kind of labour; though I think I would now be a more useful man if I had had time for sports [3].

His self-described image of being "too busy" for sports speaks both to the challenges of his background, as Washington was born into slavery and even as a free youth had to work, and to the outward image that he wants to project in his later years, as being too industrious for play. As Washington continues, he analyzes sport within the context of his industriousness:

> Games I care little for. I have never seen a game of football. In cards I do not know one card from another. A game of old-fashioned marbles with my two boys, once in awhile, is all I care for in this direction. I suppose I would care for games now if I had any time in my youth to give to them, but that was not possible [266].

Standing alone, these are two unremarkable statements; however, together they reveal his contradictory position toward others who see channels to success through participation in sports. In the first statement, he considers how sports might have made him useful if he were not too busy bringing himself up through work. In the latter statement, Washington seems more elite in his interests, except for occasional games with his sons. In both cases, he reflects upon games not available to him as a youth, but also suggests that something inherently useful might emerge for those with time to play these same games.

Washington positions himself at times against his own sport affirming efforts, yet Tuskegee's legacy proves that room exists for non-industrial activity—including "sport" in the school's educational "programme." Perhaps, to this extent, although he suppresses an instinct to validate the value of games in his narrative, Washington correctly identified baseball, and later other sports, as channels for competition, mobility, and visibility, key elements in the project of racial uplift that Washington's curriculum tried to promote.

First played at Tuskegee in 1893, baseball preceded football, which began the following year. Within Washington's educational philosophy, sport came to represent the game of life—a "field" (or "common ground") with training and rules through which individuals as well as teams could succeed. With the early success of the school's baseball and football teams, men's and women's basketball followed in 1905. As recorded on the school's website, in the years that followed, Tuskegee joined nine other schools to form the Southeastern Intercollegiate Athletic Conference (1913). Men's and Women's track teams formed in 1916, the same year the men won the SIAC championships in both football and track and field. While many other collegiate athletic conferences did not integrate until after the Civil Rights movements of the 1950s and 1960s, independent schools created their own programs much earlier to insure student success. Although Washington may have made only passing references to sport in his narrative, he planted the seeds of athletic success within his larger educational practice.

Yet Washington's legacy as an advocate for black sports in general, and baseball in particular, extended beyond Tuskegee. As Neil Lanctot points out:

> Facing discrimination and segregation, local blacks organized their own teams, most notably the amateur Pythian Club in the late 1860s. The Pythians, however, were subsequently barred from membership in two amateur organizations: the National Association of Base Ball Players and the Pennsylvania state association, foreshadowing the eventual de facto exclusion of African Americans from white professional baseball later in the century. In response, African Americans in Philadelphia and elsewhere embraced the self-help strategy advocated by Booker T. Washington in the late nineteenth century ... blacks began to build separate institutions of their own, forming their own amateur and later professional teams by the mid–1880s [4].

Leadership testimonies from Washington's contemporaries and peers typically do not mention his advocacy of sports. However, he clearly saw sport as a contributing factor in the larger project of racial uplift, beginning with baseball, and gradually including other sports and games. When viewed together, these late nineteenth and early twentieth century narratives demonstrate the stories of opportunity and possibilities realized through athletic participation. Eventually, sports teams and programs offered access to a stage that existed beyond the local realm. Further, this first generation of African American athletes, liberated from slavery or born into freedom, assumed control of their own physical prowess. Even today, on the secondary school level, sport combines with other curricula to offer a ground on which African Americans can compete for recognition and mobility. I offer the example of Booker T. Washington's perspective of sport as a necessary stage in this process of reflection.

Additionally, through the example of black baseball, one finds the negotiation of African American self-perception. In *Uplifting the Race* (1996), Kevin Gaines examines how "African American spokespersons [have] answered the widespread charge that people of African descent were noncitizens, less than fully human..." (xiii). His own response is that "a sustained reflection on their contradictory position as both an aspiring social class and a racially subordinated caste denied all political rights and protections, struggling to define themselves within a society founded on white dominance, offers a profound understanding of the historical nexus of race, class, national and sectional politics, and black leadership in our society" (xiii). Describing the "self-help ideology of racial uplift" as "the response of educated African Americans, who ... numbered roughly 2 percent of the black population in the 1890s," Gaines maintains, "Through racial uplift ideology, elite blacks sought the cooperation of white political and business elites in the pursuit of race progress" (xiv).

Baseball serves as a model for the ideology of racial uplift in both Washington's Tuskegee model, and also in the history of Solomon "Sol" White himself, who was a student and athlete at Wilberforce University, who played for both integrated and black teams prior to the ban, who managed several all-black teams, and eventually authored *Sol White's History of Colored Base Ball*, which first appeared in 1907.

As Robert Peterson notes, "a ballgame in those days (for both blacks and whites) was as much a social occasion as an athletic contest. Announcing plans for a visit by the Excelsiors of Philadelphia to play the Uniques and the Monitors in October 1867, the *Brooklyn Daily Union* commented: 'These organizations are composed of very respectable colored people, well-to-do in the world ... and include many first-class players'" (17). This quote establishes baseball as a high class affair (though not exclusively so) in African American communities where the paper enjoyed wide circulation. Additionally, the black media promoted the game's players as embodiments of a particular class ethos, explaining that "'the visitors will receive all due attention from their colored brethren of Brooklyn; and we trust, for the good of the fraternity, that none of the "white trash" who disgrace white clubs, by following and bawling for them, will be allowed to mar the pleasure of these social colored gatherings'" (17).

By emphasizing the conduct, rules, and social standing prevalent among the game's players and watchers, the article reflects how the participants and spectators wished to be represented more so than it documents a particular social group. Positing that "pleasure was ensnared in a web of domination, accumulation, abjection, resignation, and possibility" (49), within the African American experience, Hartman also suggests a "search for oppositional culture," which seemingly emerged from within the African American community and was realized by incorporating mainstream activities. Indeed, Jackie Robinson symbolized a long process of the sport's integration, which developed out of a long held desire for recognition and respectability that came through competing on a national field.

Even as Sol White documents the discouraging stories of brothers Moses

Fleetwood and Welday Walker, who, along with other African Americans, were dropped from major and minor-league rosters in the 1880s per the Gentlemen's Agreement, he also writes the history of the Cuban Giants, the Page Fence Giants (1895), the Cuban X Giants, and the Chicago Columbia Giants that developed from these teams. According to the Negro League Baseball Players Association website, in 1902, still many years before the advent of the Negro Leagues, White, with Caucasian sportswriter H. Walter Schlichter, founded the Philadelphia Giants, and both played and managed a team that would claim national titles three times under their co-ownership. White would go on to manage the Brooklyn Royal Giants (1910) and the New York Lincoln Giants (1911–1912) and came back from retirement even in the following decade to manage the Columbus Buckeyes (1920), the Cleveland Browns (1924), and the Newark Stars (1926). Through his career, he also became an important African American journalist who wrote for and granted interviews to African American press including "the *Cleveland Advocate*, the *New York Amsterdam News*, the *New York Age*, and the *Pittsburgh Courier*" (Bond).

In Washington's conception, athletic competitions helped to establish a standard of prowess and excellence among historically black colleges, eventually leading to cordial cross-racial contact. Athletic exhibitions offered a means to achieve this standard. *The Augusta Chronicle* advertises a game between Haines Institute (a school started by former slave Lucy Craft Laney that also boasted a classical curriculum) and Lincoln University of Pennsylvania. Though several decades removed from Washington's initial articulation of his "programme," this article demonstrates its continuing influence. A summary entitled "Haines and Lincoln in Baseball Classic," is listed in the *Chronicle's* "Notes on the colored people" (4–5-25) as follows:

> The followers of baseball and Augusta at large will have a chance of seeing two crack teams play at Southview Park on April 9, 3 o'clock. This game will be the climax of the season so far as seeing fast baseball teams of ability to play the American game, which the people have wanted to see for some time. We who have been hankering for a game of class will do well to see these teams from different sections cross bats [5].

The occasion generates regional interest, and conjoins the game with other cultural activities: "aside from the game proper, the K. of P. Band will be on the sidelines and at night Dr. Josey, president of Lucy Laney (L)eague, has put on a dance of merit for the visitors" (5). Documented in a mainstream newspaper, the account expresses the connection between baseball and the aspiration of social respectability, indicated by the later "dance of merit" put on by a black social organization. Sanctioned by African American institutions, baseball demonstrated the ability of black teams to "play the American game," one which "the people have wanted to see for some time" before a large crowd. Organized, controlled, and closely followed, these activities brought young African American adults into closer association with baseball's middle-class origins.

In the same issue, the *Chronicle* also covers a baseball game between Morehouse College (founded as Augusta Institute in 1867) and Walker Baptist Institute of Augusta: "Tuesday, April 7, Morehouse will face Walker Baptist at Southview Park. This is the first time the champions among colored colleges in baseball has been to this city, which itself ought to be a big drawing card. Morehouse has played four games and won all four" (5). The account suggests that this contest will be a huge draw for the city, and also that this "classic" game is intended to draw a profit at $.50 a ticket.

In addition to promoting baseball games, these articles also appear alongside advertisements suggesting additional ways "for the younger men to show their worth in the community ..."— an orphanage fundraiser, a Men's Bible Class, the observance of National Health Week at the Blue Triangle Y.W.C.A., and even a spring festival to raise funds for McClain Business College, during which "a well trained chorus of 75 voices will render a number of selections including several negro spirituals by some of the foremost composers of the race" (5). The article adds, "The proceeds from this festival will go towards improving the facilities of the McClain Business College, an institution that promises to do much for the community" (5). With the cost of admission at $.25, the festival likely draws from the same seekers of racial uplift. Reflecting their socially-progressive impetus, these accounts also document community agendas, as each event is calculated to represent the local African American population well and to advance its interests. Drawn from local institutions, the participants often both played sports and supported endeavors for the community's betterment

In *Creating the National Pastime: Baseball Transforms Itself*, G. Edward White analyzes baseball as first a working class, and then middle class sport: "Its early history included close connections with gambling, drinking, and general rowdiness. Its early owners were not, for the most part, representatives of the wellborn classes, but entrepreneurs seeking upward mobility and public recognition" (4). Reflecting a parallel desire for social advancement, baseball became the preferred sport of middle class families. In discussing the inconsistent segregationist policies where "Latins, Asians, and Native Americans" were accepted while African Americans were not, White argues that baseball "publicized itself as a 'democratic' game, one personifying the 'melting pot' theory of ethnic assimilation in America" (5). Over time, those of diverse ethnicities and class backgrounds were expected to shed their distinctiveness and blend into American society. Blacks, however, were not treated as capable of 'melting'"—into the mainstream (5).

Adrian Burgos, Jr. explores these contradictions further in *Playing America's Game: Baseball, Latinos, and the Color Line*. Calling Latinos the "central actors in the negotiation of the color line," Burgos argues that "most [Latinos] occupied a position between the poles of white (inclusion) and black (exclusion)" (4). Justifying its exclusion of blacks by its tolerance for other ethnic groups, baseball simultaneously discriminated while also making interracial progress. Paradoxically, the black professional game evolved from this exclusion: "Playing baseball for money offered at least a temporary respite from the apparently inexorable future of low-paying, low-status jobs available to male blacks for the first fifty years of the twentieth century" (White 129). Out of this legacy of discrimination, and evolving in conjunction with philosophies of racial uplift, black baseball became a marker of growing athletic and social influence.

White cites the growing attendance at the East-West game between Negro League teams from 8,000 in 1933 to 21,000 in 1936 as a reflection of the growing influence of black baseball: "Part of the reason for increased attendance had been the [*Pittsburgh Courier*'s] self-conscious description of the All-Star Game as a spectacle frequented by 'society'" (142). White continues:

> In another edition the [Chicago] *Defender* described the All-Star Game as "a highlight in the affairs of the elite." "The East-West baseball game," it added, "has been popularized to a fine social point. Social registerites take a greater interest in the game now than ever before. Rest assured that society will be represented at Comiskey." The *Defender* printed a list headed, "Socialites to Attend East-West Ball Game" [143].

Despite the decline of the Negro League enterprise during the depression (Lanctot 3), the game continued to figure in African American social behavior through baseball into the period of major league integration.

Lanctot cites Branch Rickey's 1946 address to the Carlton Branch of the Brooklyn YMCA, "a predominantly black organization whose members included a high number of professionals ... doctors, lawyers, realtors, teachers, a minister, and a judge" (155). Rickey emphasized the "necessity of black baseball fans behaving with propriety and moderation toward the prospect of blacks playing in the major leagues," arguing that "the biggest threat to [Robinson's] success ... is the Negro people themselves" (155). Rickey's concern was that blacks [would] "'go and form parades and welcoming committees,' that 'you'll strut,' and 'wear badges,' that 'you'll get drunk,' 'fight,' and 'be arrested'"(qtd. in Lanctot 155). Rickey's audience resisted these stereotypes and responded instead through committee action:

The committee, using "Don't Spoil Jackie's Chances" as a slogan, began to operate throughout the New York area in the spring of 1947, encouraging blacks not to drink liquor before attending baseball games and not to indulge in ceremonies honoring Robinson at ballparks [156].

The committee's efforts apparently yielded the desired response, as

> when the Dodgers made their first road trip, black fans flocked to see him in all cities. Mike Royko, columnist for the *Chicago Daily News*, reported blacks "[coming] by the thousands, pouring off the north-bound ELS and out of their cars at Wrigley Field." "They didn't wear baseball-game clothes," Royko noted. "They had on church clothes and funeral clothes—suits, white shirts, ties, gleaming shoes, and straw hats" [157].

The message within this narrative is clear. The legacy of Washington's "programme" of uplift survived into the integration of the Major Leagues, reflecting the desire of black society to assist in Robinson's representation to the world. Collectively, these narratives continue to acknowledge that African Americans positioned sports, and particularly baseball, as a means to combat prejudices against them.

Works Cited

Bond, Greg. "King Solomon 'Sol' White." *Negro League Baseball Players Association.* N.p., n.d. Web. 20 January 2011.
Burgos, Adrian, Jr. *Playing America's Game: Baseball, Latinos, and the Color Line.* Berkeley: University of California Press, 1999. Print.
Douglass, Frederick. *My Bondage and My Freedom.* 1855. New York: Penguin, 2003. Print.
_____. *Narrative of the Life of Frederick Douglass.* 1845. New York: Borders, 2006. Print.
Gaines, Kevin. *Uplifting the Race: Black Leadership, Politics, and Culture in the Twentieth Century.* Chapel Hill: University of North Carolina Press, 1996. Print.
Goldstein, Warren. *Playing for Keeps: A History of Early Baseball.* Ithaca: Cornell University Press, 1989. Print.
Hartman, Saidiya. *Scenes of Subjection: Terror, Slavery, and Self-Making in Nineteenth Century America.* New York: Oxford University Press, 1997. Print.
Kilwin, Bill, ed. *Out of the Shadows: African American Baseball from the Cuban Giants to Jackie Robinson.* Lincoln: University of Nebraska Press, 2005. Print.
Lanctot, Neil. *Negro League Baseball.* Philadelphia: University of Pennsylvania Press, 2004. Print.
Malloy, Jerry. "The Birth of the Cuban Giants: The Origins of Black Professional Baseball." *Out of the Shadows: African American Baseball from the Cuban Giants to Jackie Robinson.* Ed. Bill Kilwin. Lincoln: University of Nebraska Press, 2005. Print.
"Notes on the Colored People." *Augusta Chronicle.* 5 April 1925: 5. Print.
Peterson, Robert. *Only the Ball Was White: A History of Legendary Black Players and All-Black Professional Teams.* New York: Oxford University Press, 1992. Print.
Riess, Steven A. *Touching Base: Professional Baseball and American Culture in the Progressive Era* (Revised Edition). Urbana: University of Illinois Press, 1999. Print.

Washington, Booker T. *Up from Slavery*. 1901. *3 African-American Classics: Up from Slavery, The Souls of Black Folk and Narrative of the Life of Frederick Douglass.* New York: Dover, 2007. Print.
White, Edward G. *Creating the National Pastime: Baseball Transforms Itself, 1903–1953.* Princeton: Princeton University Press, 1996. Print.
White, Solomon. *Sol White's History of Colored Baseball with Other Documents on the Early Black Game, 1886–1936.* 1907. Lincoln: Bison Books, 2006. Print.

Born a Busher; or, How Journalists-Turned–Fiction Writers Made Baseball Safe for the Middle-Class Readers of the Saturday Evening Post

SCOTT D. PETERSON

In the early twentieth century, baseball journalists helped to write the game into American popular culture, combining versions of *Bildung* narrative with early public relations methods. Both techniques were required to improve the late nineteenth century image of baseball players as ruffians, roustabouts, and low social others, thus allowing owners of major league teams to win middle class audiences in the dead-ball era. As baseball journalists promoted the character-building and democratic elements of the game, they actively ignored the more unsavory aspects of the players' activities. And thus, a symbiotic relationship grew up between the press and team owners. The resulting images of players' experiences both captured an American culture that was redefining the male maturation process, and revealed the competition between the character-driven Victorian values of the nineteenth century and the developing consumer-driven personalities of the twentieth century.

With the growth of *The Saturday Evening Post* and other middle-class magazines, fiction writers— many of whom were initially journalists— began to incorporate journalistic techniques into their popular short stories. In this way, they created a blend of fact and fiction that continued to promote the game, redact the image of the players, and create a place for baseball in American popular culture. This paper will examine how Charles Van Loan, Ring Lardner, and Bozeman Bulger translated journalistic practices into their popular fiction to shape the game's image for middle class readers. Specifically, Bakhtin's concept of the chronotopic *Bildung* narrative helps to illuminate how the stories of these journalists fulfilled the needs of *Saturday Evening Post* editor George Horace Lorimer, both personally and in his project to make the *Post* a beacon and a bastion of the average middle-class American reader.

Background: Three Key Transitions of the Early 20th Century

While baseball was developing into America's pastime during the late nineteenth and early twentieth centuries, other aspects of American culture were also undergoing significant transitions. As a product of corporate capitalism, the Professional-Managerial Class (PMC) emerged around 1880 and by 1910 could be described as a "social class" with an "identity achieved through consumption" (Ohmann 135). This group of "middle-managers" served as a buffer between the industrial entrepreneurs and the wage-earning proletariat and helped manage the transition from local ownership to the corporate structure that required off-site management and bookkeeping.

As the PMC was taking shape, the "magazine revolution" facilitated a changing of readership as publishers actively sought to reach the middle class in addition to their primarily upper-class audience (Ohmann 24). To differentiate themselves from *Harper's*, *Century*, *The Atlantic* and other highbrow periodicals, *McClure's*, *Cosmopolitan*, *Munsey's* and other magazines dropped their prices, sold ads to pay production costs and make a profit, and set out to bring "culture" to middle class readers (Ohmann 24, Tassin 341). These middle-class magazines would soon help shape the ideology of their readers, allowing them to "fix their bearings amid social change"(Ohmann 220). Soon enough, the "confluence of historical currents" made the PMC ready for "national culture and commodities to create the best self" (Ohmann 223). Reflecting this transition, *The Saturday Evening Post* and other middle-class magazines measured their circulation in the millions by the middle of the second decade of the twentieth century, marking these periodicals as significant shapers of mass culture tastes (Tebbel and Zuckerman 78).

The last key transition was a move from the nineteenth century Victorian concept of an interior-based character to a more consumption-driven sense of identity, one built around personality and self-expression:

> All of these changes, and many others, undermined the basis for Victorian masculinity; the republican notion of proprietary ownership was obviated by the new corporate business structures, and many men began to question whether the virtues of self-restraint, dedication, honesty, and integrity really meant much anymore [Pendergast 13].

Into this matrix of class development, magazine mass culture, and shifting value structures, the Busher was born into the pages of the *Saturday Evening Post*, one of the most widely read and thus most widely influential middle-class magazines of the era (Appleton 425).

Early 20th Century Influences of *The* Saturday Evening Post

As a product of mass-market magazine fiction, the Busher also figured in *Saturday Evening Post* editor George Horace Lorimer's project to create the "average American" and provide stories that appealed to the "wholesome tastes" of his middle-class readership (Cohn 28). Appearing in a number of stories by different authors, the Busher became a staple figure:

> The recurring characters in *Post* fiction, like those on the *Post* covers, were woven out of stereotypes deeply embedded in American popular consciousness. As such, they reaffirmed popular attitudes and strengthened the values and prejudices of the broad middle-class, middle-brow community that made up the audience of the *Post* [Cohn 85].

As Cohn illustrates here, Lorimer's nineteenth century upbringing contributed to his belief in the self-made man, the concept of hard work and ethical behavior championed by Horatio Alger. The *Post*'s middle-class audience was thus further defined by its efforts to elevate itself without the influence of upper-class assistance. Lorimer's editorial policy sought to "find a place within modern corporate capitalism for the nineteenth century self-made man of character" (Pendergast 47). Furthermore, when Lorimer and other editors of middle-class magazines printed the best fiction available without tailoring it to standard patterns, their actions, according to Ohmann, implied three points about that fiction:

> First, that those pages of the magazine charted a space of individual creativity and imagination, free from rules and prescriptions; there might be found autonomous literature. Second, that the audience was a discriminating one, and able to form its own judgments, sensitive to nuance and variety, and ready to experience new styles. And third, that writers, editors, and audience were participating in a discourse of high culture associated with education, money, leisure, and social respectability [295–6].

One way to tap into the audience's drive for social respectability — as well as for education, money, and leisure — was to follow the British model of using the *Bildung* narrative to help guide young men and women toward maturity (Alden 2, Castle 18). According to Karen Tolchin, the protagonists in American *Bildung* narratives — or *Bildungsheld* — often promote themselves, exhibit manic behavior, indulge in self-pity, engage in embarrassing self-revelation, and reveal themselves to be generally self-absorbed (Tolchin 6–15). The Busher — or any young player who leaves home and "begins to climb," according to Van Loan ("The Busher" 193) — becomes a stand-in for the young men and women in the *Post*'s audience who have left their hometowns and tried to make their way in the big city by ascending the corporate ladder. In reflecting this demographic current, works by Van Loan, Lardner, Bulger, and other journalists-turned-fiction-writers take on a new importance, illustrating how their fiction mirrored the experience of PMC readers of the Post, and shaped their middle-class ideology (Ohmann 2). Lorimer's proclivity for publishing such instructive fiction is perhaps further illustrated by the fact that none of the stories published in other magazines by these authors contained successful *Bildung* narratives in the Horatio Alger mode.

Using Journalistic Techniques to Make the Busher Middle Class

Sports writing in the early twentieth century reflected the tensions created by the transitions underway in American culture, including a blending of the interests of journalism and advertising to create the modern commercial concept of "publicity" (Lears 203). With baseball established as a mass spectator sport by 1900, the "reciprocal affinity" between newspaper coverage and ticket sales encouraged the owners of major league teams to develop a positive working relationship with the press (Anderson 14). In the pages of the *Saturday Evening Post*, Charles Van Loan, Ring Lardner, and Bozeman Bulger used three techniques in their fiction to help write baseball into American culture and make it more acceptable to the magazine's middle-class readers. First, each writer encouraged identification between characters and readers by using what Hemingway would later call the "real thing." Secondly, Broun's concept of personality encouraged further identification, putting a human face on the ball players. Finally, those writers used vernacular to make the identification process more authentic by holding up a mirror to Lorimer's average middle-class American.

Tying their narratives into "real life" was the first technique used by these writers to win the respect of their audiences and to demonstrate the connections between sport narratives and middle class aspirations. By making references to actual baseball players — both famous and obscure — and events from "real life," such as memorable World Series contests, Lardner and other journalists turned fiction writers illustrated what Heywood Broun's biographer O'Connor calls "a journalist's appreciation of topicality as a stimulus to book sales" (122–3). This blending of fact and fiction was a natural outgrowth of journalistic training, as identified by Hemingway:

> You told what happened, and with one trick or another, you communicated the emotion aided by the element of timeliness which gives a certain emotion to any account of something that has happened on that day. But the real thing, the sequence of motion and fact which made the emotion and which would be valid in a year or ten years or, with luck and if you stated it purely enough, always was beyond me and I was working hard to get it [qtd. in Kazin 331].

Using these tricks, the journalist enhanced the emotional impact of "timeliness" on an audience.[1] The account would become all the more significant when the journalist began to transform "fact into symbol," whether consciously or unconsciously, because the verisimilitude created by such fiction had the potential to reflect middle class aspirations more powerfully. The result was a kind of journalism that reflected what Alfred Kazin called "that perfect conversion of natural rhythm into an evocation of the necessary emotion, that would fuse with the various phrases of contemporary existence—love, war, sport—and give them a collective grace" (333). Thus, just as Hemingway would seek a comparable authenticity decades later, Lardner et al used similar storytelling methods in their baseball fiction, thus illustrating how the metonymic qualities of sport shape individual and collective identities. These accounts run parallel with actual realities, instead of linking a reader with a story thematically or through symbolism. (Blain 250–2).

The second technique used by these authors to encourage the identification of their middle-class readers involved a shift from a Victorian character type to the more modern concept of "personality." This shift enabled the writers to distance their work from the ideal, unrealistic, Merriwell–type ball player found in children's pulp magazines. In this way they revealed the foibles of their protagonists more authentically, as attested by this quote from Heywood Broun about his days as the sporting editor of the New York *Tribune*. "I'd concentrate on personalities in sport," Broun said:

> Just the usual stuff about a great baseball player having started his career with a sand-lot team is not news. But if my reporter finds out that a baseball player struck out with the bases full because he was out on a beer party the night before the game, that's the story I want [qtd. in Knight 34].

Writing about baseball players as "personalities" was also part of Ring Lardner's *Chicago Tribune* column, "In the Wake of the News," which brought forward the literary concepts of Robert Park's new journalism (Trachtenberg 124). Like others, Lardner used vernacular speech, anecdote, and "rainy day" interviews to develop the figure of the Busher, which would become a staple in baseball journalism and fiction through the 1930s (Orodenker 41–2). In focusing on "personalities" instead of attributes of Victorian character, Broun and Lardner thus reveal the larger transition underway in American culture, as observed by Pendergast and other critics. Also, these writers encouraged readers to identify with the players more fully by "putting a human face" on them, even as they continued to protect the images of Cobb, Chase, and other real ball players.

The third technique used by journalists in the early twentieth century to connect their ballplaying characters with their middle-class audiences involved developing a realistic vernacular. The ability to render speech accurately was identified by Edmund Wilson as a sign of skillful writing:

> So Lardner has marked the distinction between the baseball player's slang and the prize-fighter's slang.... And he understands the difference between the spoken language of these semi-literate types and the language they will use when they write. Finally, what is most important, he writes the vernacular like an artist and not merely a clever journalist [97].

In this way Lardner, Van Loan, Bulger, and the other sports-journalists-turned- fiction-writers, portrayed characters with a distinctive vernacular, best demonstrated by the Busher, who spoke with a rural accent that marked him as a "rube" or a "hick" that had recently arrived in the city. As soon as the Busher is offered a major league contract, however, he achieves middle-class status — with regard to his income, if not his manners and mindset. Thus, even as Lorimer's average Americans laughed at the Busher, the satirical mirror used by Lardner et al. encouraged them to recognize their own circumstances in his portrayal as a recent arrival to the city and seeker of upward mobility.

The use of realism, personality, and the vernacular collectively imbued the Busher with characteristics of his time, giving him greater cultural significance and impact. The Busher stands out as more than a mere symbol of his times. He embodies the tenor of these times as the subject of a *Bildung* narrative, in which he follows the path laid out by the self-made man of Horatio Alger's novels: get a job, get ahead, and get married (Sharnhorst 186). In this way, the Busher becomes a significant cultural artifact of American history, according to the pattern of Bakhtin's chronotope:

> The transition is accomplished in him and through him. He is forced to become a new unprecedented type of human being. What is happening here is precisely the emergence of a new man.... It is as though the very foundations of the world are changing, and man must change along with them [Bakhtin 23].

In this context, the *Bildung* narratives of the Busher can be seen as extensions of those of the Western vernacular hero, a character type from late nineteenth century fiction that evolved from a regional hero into a national one through the efforts of Teddy Roosevelt and his Rough Riders. This kind of character was given access to the upper classes through marriage or wealth or both, as in the case of the main character of *The Virginian* (Saxton 341).[2] Thus, in order to help fill the vacuum that was created when the frontier was proclaimed "closed" by Frederick Jackson Turner in 1893, Van Loan, Lardner, and Bulger used *Bildung* narratives and employed these three distinctive journalistic techniques, giving the Busher the cultural significance that enabled Lorimer's average middle-class American readers of the *Saturday Evening Post* to identify with him.

Analysis 1: Van Loan's "The Bone Doctor"

Nine of Van Loan's eleven baseball stories that appeared in the *Post* featured *Bildung* narrative, which illustrates his dedication to George Horace Lorimer's project of promoting the self-made man. Like many of Van Loan's *Post* stories, "The Bone Doctor" applies all three journalistic techniques in a class-elevating narrative structure in which the Busher learns a lesson of some kind; thus the story serves as a representative example of how Van Loan created stories that connected with Lorimer and his middle-class audience.[3]

Making a reference to an actual player recognizable even to even the casual baseball fans of the period, Van Loan invokes Christy Mathewson within the first words of the story to establish verisimilitude and provide a journalistic context that is continuous with real life. At the same time, Van Loan uses this reference to contrast Mathewson with Jones, the story's *Bildungsheld,* who is characterized as "the swelled-up bush pitcher who hasn't done anything yet and ain't sure he can, but is proud of it just the same" ("Bone Doctor" 8).[4] When Jones "sticks" with the big club, he gets the opportunity to perform in his hometown in an exhibition game arranged by Murph — whom Van Loan places in the same realistic context, describing him as once being "the best catcher in the National League" (8). Van Loan invokes Mathewson again in the narrator's description of the pre-game speech by the "local orator" of Jones's hometown:

> A stranger listening to that address would have got the idea that Jones was Mathewson, Ty Cobb, Theodore Roosevelt and Napoleon Bonaparte all rolled into one. In between references to Jones — yes, he called him Verbena's favorite son — he gave us the history of baseball from the Garden of Eden down to date; and every little while he would slap Jones on the back and the cheering would bust loose again [32].

Not only is "Verbena's favorite son" tied to recognizable sports and historical figures, but he is also linked to a cultural movement that would resonate with the *Post*'s audience. Van Loan's *Post* audience would have recognized Roosevelt not only as a former president, but also as a proponent of the Physical Culture movement, which sought to revitalize American society by encouraging middle-class men to play baseball, football and other sports as a means of returning to a more authentic and active existence (Riess 16–17).

Recalling Broun's observation about revealing a player's indiscretions, Van Loan characterizes Jones's personality and shows him as a product of his time. For example, Jones is aware of the media and he talks about how his former minor league opponents "pull all that inside stuff that you read about in the magazines" (8). Making a date to play pool with "the newspaper boys" to give them "some good stuff" (8), Jones comes across as the typical self-promoting and publicity-seeking American *Bildungsheld* who is a product of modern consumer culture. In this way Van Loan contrasts him to the quiet, industrious, do-your-duty qualities of a Victorian character (Tolchin 6). Van Loan completes this description of the self-promoting Jones by noting how he is "dressed in a gambler's plaid that you could play checkers on" and that he "was all diked up with a lot of cheap jewelry" such that he "looked like a cross between a small-time vaudeville actor and a hick hotel clerk" (8). Dressed in loud, ready-made clothes, promoting himself like a minstrel band, and pulling on his gloves "like a villain in a melodrama" (10), Van Loan's Busher figure is thus a product of modern consumer and popular cultures. He is also marked as a dynamic — or chronotopic in the Baktinian sense — *Bildungsheld* — with human qualities that would appeal to the *Post*'s readers.

In total, Van Loan creates a realistic story and uses the *Bildungsheld*'s personality as the center of the "local boy made good" plotline. Both elements work together to reveal the Busher as an avatar for Lorimer's *Post* audience of "average Americans." Beginning the story as something of an antagonist, Jones becomes a momentarily sympathetic figure when his roommate reports that the ballplayer has been sitting up nights to write his homecoming speech. The narrator further reveals that Jones can't sit still as the train approaches his hometown (10). This homecoming means much to Jones, and thus Van Loan encourages his contemporary middle-class readers to look past the humor of the Busher figure and identify with him as a fellow human who was trying to "make good" in the big city.[5] Murph uses the exhibition game as an occasion to cure the "swelling" in Jones's head, and also to give the team a better chance of winning the pennant — and the piece of the World Series money that went with it. Thus Van Loan appeals to business-minded members of the *Post*'s Professional-Managerial Class audience.[6] Through the agency of his "bitter medicine" (33), Murph "cures" Jones in a way that follows the progress of interior development on the part of the *Bildungsheld*: "There is a wonderful improvement in Jonesy. He has a relapse now and then; but if he gets going too strong somebody is sure to ask him the time of day. That stops him" (33).

The narrator's affection for "Jonesy" might have been echoed by readers who also felt sorry for him. But the Busher can be taught and also emulated, as shown by the young pitcher's response to the hard lesson on the field, and later, his response to receiving a watch at the post-game banquet. Always skeptical about the Busher's personality, Van Loan nevertheless shows that he can be taught to take his place in the middle-class fold populated by readers of the *Post*. Furthermore, by using Murph's nineteenth century values of hard work, self-reliance, and duties of citizenship through collective effort, Van Loan's story also serves as an example of how Lorimer added middle-class baseball fans to his audience without losing his original readers, who valued Alger's self-made man (Prendergast 55).

Analysis 2: Lardner's You Know Me Al

Exactly half of Ring Lardner's 48 *Post* stories, published between 1914 and 1920, were baseball stories; the overwhelming majority of those (21 of 24) featured a *Bildung* narrative of some kind. Thus, not only could Lardner claim to be more of a "baseball writer" than Van Loan, but he also wrote more directly to a specialized audience, exclusively publishing his work in the mass market magazines aimed at the middle class, foregoing the lower-paying pulps. Just as Van Loan made use of all three journalistic techniques to connect with readers, Lardner uses these to an even greater degree and perhaps achieves a deeper connection. His daily column in the *Chicago Tribune*, "In the Wake of the News," afforded him the occasion to refine these techniques and use them on a regular basis.[7]

Taken together, the six Busher stories that make up *You Know Me Al* comprise Jack Keefe's first-person *Bildung* narrative. Breaking into major league baseball, Keefe fails to "stick," eventually "makes good," marries, and "gets ahead" enough "at the office" to be asked to tour the world with a select group of players. Keefe could also be considered an early series hero in the Frank Merriwell mode, as Lardner continued to develop his character in subsequent stories that took him to basic training (*Treat 'Em Rough*, 1918), to France at the end of World War I (*The Real Dope*, 1919), and back to the major leagues with the White Sox in a series of stories published in the *Post* in 1919 — the same year that the actual White Sox threw the World Series. While a cautionary element runs underneath this *Bildung* narrative, and is signaled by Lardner's use of humor and satire, he clearly goes to greater lengths than Van Loan to make Jack's stories contemporaneous with the events and players of

Jack's times. Several actual White Sox players, managers, and front office personnel appear in the stories as characters, from Harry Lord to Kid Gleason and Charles Comiskey. Many of the plot elements are consistent with the contemporary baseball seasons, from the spring training trip to California in 1913 to the advent of the Federal League in 1914 (Hilton 23–5). These elements of Lardner's Busher stories, which middle-class readers of the *Post* also encountered in other first-person player narratives like Christy Mathewson's *Pitching in a Pinch* (originally published in 1912), avoided the heavily formulaic fiction of pulp magazines and allowed readers to identify with the Keefe stories more readily.[8]

As in Van Loan's portrayal of Jones from "The Bone Doctor," Lardner's Jack Keefe is also caught in the transition from nineteenth century Victorian virtues and twentieth century conceptions of personality and self-expression. For example, Jack begins by watching his money carefully, but ends up going through his savings over the course of the winter. Jack recognizes his own spendthrift habits when he talks about how the hired girl — a definite middle-class luxury — doesn't have to work very hard because "we generally run round downtown till late and don't get up till about noon. That sounds funny don't it Al, when I used to get up at 5 every morning down home" (Lardner 110). The Victorian virtues of thrift, hard work, and industry, as demonstrated by Jack's careful accounting of his wedding expenses (100) have been thrown over for habits of conspicuous consumption that prompt him to spend $110 on new furniture when his apartment is already furnished (105). Thus, in addition to being self-absorbed, brash, boastful, and something of a clothes horse, Jack buys into the lifestyle encouraged by the ads at the back of the *Post* and other mass market magazines aimed at the middle class. And yet Lardner's narrative makes him an example of what can happen to the nineteenth century self-made man if he loses sight of his origins. Using satire within his own specific brand of journalistic skepticism, Lardner shows how Jack is a product of early twentieth century cultural aspirations and must resist the inherent dangers of the times (Peterson 42).

Lardner moves past the occasional "ain'ts" and "'ems" of Van Loan's narrator, building the stories around the vernacular of Jack's letters, which he writes exactly as he speaks. The letters are filled with Jack's carefully constructed grammar and syntax, and with dialogue that contains the double modals of rural speech: "That sent him right up in the air and he bawled me awful.... He says Boy you shouldn't ought to talk like that to Cal" (Lardner 65). This strategy works on a number of levels for Lardner. First, this strategy adds the "real thing" element to the stories, as the letters purport to be written by an actual ball player. Secondly, this vernacular allows Lardner to create some distance between his character and his audience, even as he encourages his readers to see in Jack what they might have become had they not kept to their — and George Horace Lorimer's — nineteenth century values. Thirdly, like the early American vernacular characters identified by Saxton, Lardner's portrayal of Keefe allows him to champion the class mobility of working-class baseball players seeking to rise into the middle class (113). In so doing, he also defends against those higher class biases that would inhibit such a rise (113).

As a result of Lardner's deeper and more concerted use of the three journalistic techniques identified above, the stories of *You Know Me Al* are authentic to a greater degree than Van Loan's stories. Likewise, in using Jack Keefe's evolving personality as the center of his *Bildung* narrative, Lardner creates a Busher figure that serves as an avatar for Lorimer's *Post* audience of "average Americans," even as the satire of the stories maintain the distance of the baseball player as a social inferior. Although Jack's self-absorption and self-expression must have annoyed Lardner's contemporary readers, only the most critical would not have empathized with Jack in his final story when he faces a choice between doing what is right by his wife and child and gaining the honor and life-broadening experience of playing baseball around the world. Jack's careful accounting of his finances proves to Al that he is a capable self-made business man (except when it comes to paying back all the money he owes to Al), and he also maps out his entire thought process to demonstrate the depth of his humanity beneath the blustering exterior of the Busher. In this way, Lardner improves upon the figure created by Van Loan, breathing life into Jack and letting him tell his own story to the middle-class readers of the *Post*. Overall, Lardner's stories advance George Horace Lorimer's project of reinforcing middle class ideology through the *Post*'s content. This content, which adheres to the nineteenth century values of the self-made man, shows Lardner's resistance to patterns of conspicuous consumption, encouraged by the very same ads that Lorimer sold to keep his magazine solvent (Prendergast 61). Therefore, Lardner's style demonstrates the significant aspects of the fiction selected by Lorimer; this style also applies to detractors who dismiss it as the monolithic product of the hegemony of the growing corporate capitalism of the early twentieth century, in the process allowing him to act as a tour guide for Lorimer's middle-class readers who would like to know more about baseball (Ohmann 322).

Analysis 3: Bulger's "A Pinch Hit in Vaudeville" and "A Major-League Mother-in-Law"

Similar to Van Loan and Lardner, Bozeman Bulger was a journalist turned fiction writer. Between 1908 and 1925, Bulger published ten stories, eighteen articles, and twelve columns in the *Post*, with four of the stories being about baseball. Two of those stories, "A Pinch Hit in Vaudeville" and "A Major League Mother-in-Law," feature the same Busher figure who models an actual major league player. However, the former story makes more use of personality and vernacular, while the latter contains a *Bildung* narrative that replicates the Victorian conception of manhood. The differences between these two stories illustrate two contrasting strategies for reaching the middle-class readers of the *Post*.[9]

In both "A Pinch Hit in Vaudeville" (published in 1915) and "A Major League Mother-in-Law" (which appeared a year later), Bulger's *Post* readers who were either fans of baseball, vaudeville, or both, would have recognized Rube Vick as a thinly veiled portrait of Rube Marquard. A left-handed pitcher for the New York Giants, Marquard set a major league record that still stands by winning 19 consecutive starts in 1912. This feat made him an instant celebrity — as evidenced by the number of contemporary mass market short stories that reference the streak — and gave him the opportunity to earn extra money on the vaudeville stage (Edelman 47–8). In the first story, Bulger deviates from actual events when he makes Vick's vaudeville partner unmarried, thus avoiding the scandal that occurred when Marquard and Blossom Seeley became romantically attached after appearing together on stage. Even if he did not suggest this change, George Horace Lorimer would have no doubt approved of how it kept tabloid gossip out of the pages of the *Post*. Bulger sidesteps the Blossom Seeley issue once again in the second story by portraying Vick as already married. Bulger's use of the "real thing" in these two stories illustrates both the benefits and the difficulties of basing his character on an actual player, even though he could redact Marquard's image with a simple change or two.

Beyond portraying Rube Vick as yet another "crazy left-hander" in the first story, Bulger depicts him in the fuller context of nineteenth century character and twentieth century labor issues. In this way, his Busher figure differs from those of Van Loan and Lardner. Due to Bulger's use of the vernacular in Rube's speech in the first story, the character comes across a more fully rounded Busher figure "I ain't no quitter. But say," he added, "if you let a ball player in here before I get this stuff off my face I'll shoot the doortender. There ain't a one of them that wouldn't call me a Baseball Annie, and the worst of it is, they'd win" ("Pinch Hit" 15).[10]

On the whole, Bulger's Rube more closely parallels the actual Rube Marquard in the second piece, as he has Vick tell his own story in a first person narrative reflecting Marquard's urban upbringing. Bulger has his Rube looking to supplement his insufficient salary in both stories, but Vick demonstrates the character to eventually do the right thing each time. In "Pinch Hit," he steps aside to make room for a pair of real vaudeville performers, even though it costs him $1,500 a week (which was what Marquard earned on the stage in real life). Bulger addresses the labor issue with stronger language in the later story when he has Rube's wife claim he could make as much as $10,000 if he could get away from New York, where he is "tied up like a slave" ("Major League" 8).[11] One unscrupulous friend goes so far as to suggest that Rube fake an injury to convince New York to trade him, but Rube's mother-in-law speaks as the voice of cultural authority in the story, encouraging him to follow the Victorian values of honesty, loyalty, and industry: "but I never yet have seen anybody succeed at anything without giving their best effort to the work they had undertaken" (9).

When the manager of the Grays (a thin veil for the actual New York Giants) asks Rube if he's up to pitching in Game 7 of the World Series, Bulger makes use of *Bildung* narrative and the Big Game. Choosing to pitch will probably lose Rube the vaudeville contract, while it might earn extra money for his teammates. To help Rube decide, his mother-in-law returns to her role as the mouthpiece of Victorian values, declaring that "the chance very seldom comes to a man to sacrifice his own future for the benefit of those who are depending on him" (10). In choosing the nineteenth century values of honesty and self-sacrifice over the vaudeville fame and personal gain of the twentieth century, Rube is rewarded with the ultimate validation from his mother-in-law: "I knew you were a real man" (11) and he goes on to thank her for "helping me make a man of myself" (78). This ending—along with the Americanism of virtue rewarded when Rube receives an offer to appear on the vaudeville stage anyway—is the most consistent with George Horace Lorimer's project of promoting the self-made man and the Victorian values of the nineteenth century to help guide the middle-class readers of the *Post*.

Conclusion

Although early twenty-first century American cultural voices would proclaim otherwise, sport in general and baseball in particular have not always been as popular as they are today with the middle class. The current bonds between sport, media, and culture were not forged overnight, nor were they historically destined to conjoin. While there were calls for baseball as America's pastime as early as the nationalistic 1850s, the means to elevate the game to that preeminent position did not exist until printing technology, governmental policies, and journalistic practices intersected. This combination gave rise to urban daily newspapers and mass market magazines, which appealed to audiences large enough to achieve a critical mass of supporters. Even then, the popularity of sports in general, and baseball in particular, benefited from the Physical Culture movement and the Social Gospel of the YMCA. These validated participation in athletic activities, separated them from the taint of gambling and rigged contests, and made them appropriate uses of the limited time of hard-working and industrious Americans.

Even with this outside support, someone had to write the game into American culture and further promote it to the middle class. The baseball fiction of Charles Van Loan, Ring Lardner, Bozeman Bulger, and other sports-journalists-turned-fiction-writers served as one avenue for bringing the game to George Horace Lorimer's "average American" and the readers of other mass market magazines. These writers packaged the game in a way that would make it palatable to a reader who was trying to make his or her way in the world of business. Using the *Bildung* narrative, they collectively illustrated how baseball players could follow the American path to the maturity of the self-made man — and to a lesser extent self-made woman — through the process of getting a job, getting ahead, and getting married. In this way, they helped create the middle-class ideology of the *Post* and other mass market magazines, while also holding up baseball players as models — both to emulate and otherwise — and ultimately portraying baseball and sport as worthwhile endeavors.

As the history of American popular culture reveals time and again, the support of the middle class is essential for commercial success and longevity. Positioned between the development of separate sections for sports reporting in the newspapers of the late nineteenth century and the development of radio reporting and broadcasting of sports in the 1920s and 1930s, the baseball fiction of Van Loan, Lardner, Bulger, and a number of other short fiction writers thus played a significant role in bringing the game to the middle class and writing it into American culture.

Notes

1. Hemingway identified dialogue as "the supreme trick," but there were other tricks, such as the first person vernacular narrator used routinely by Lardner and other baseball fiction writers (333).

2. According to Saxton, the original vernacular heroes "simultaneously championed the national identity against foreign detractors and egalitarianism against pretensions of the upper class" and were "implicated in the Jacksonian upsurge" of the 1820s and 1830s (113, 119–20). Unlike these original heroes who entered American culture through comedy and farce, the Western vernacular hero developed through fiction (184).

3. In contrast, two stories published elsewhere by Van Loan do not use the same plot or techniques. "The Golden Ball of the Argonauts," which appeared in Munsey's in September of 1909, is a nostalgic piece and "Too Much Pepper," which was published in Everybody's Magazine in June of 1915, features an anti–Bildung narrative of a baseball player who uses violence to make his way in the world.

4. The use of "swelled-up" and "ain't" (along with "'em") are examples of the vernacular sprinkled throughout the story. Van Loan uses just enough to create the sense that the narrator has modest origins.

5. According to Buckley, the phrase "makes good" is a euphemism for "makes money" within the context of American Bildung narrative (21).

6. Thus, when Ron Shelton has Crash Davis tell the hitters what is coming in the 1988 hit movie *Bull Durham*, he uses a formula element that is at least 70 years old.

7. In a situation similar to Van Loan's publishing record, both of Lardner's stories that appeared in other magazines did not contain Bildung narratives. Appearing in McClure's in August of 1915, "Harmony" is about an older player's efforts to maintain a singing quartet on his team, and "Back to Baltimore," which appeared in Redbook in November of 1914, contains an anti–Bildung narrative of a college graduate looking for an easy position on a team stocked with college players to make the game more "gentlemanly."

8. By contrast, other Post stories by Lardner feature Bildung narratives that are darker or problematic because their Bildungshelds are not being held up as models for behavior. "My Roomy" and "Sick 'Em" show the dark side of personalities and the willingness of teams to use their personalities to get ahead-even at the expense of the player's health. Stories like "Horseshoes" and "Good for the Soul" contain the Bildung narratives of baseball players who use violence or dishonesty to get ahead in the world.

9. Two other Bulger stories, "Big League Promise," which appeared in McClure's (another mass market magazine aimed at the middle class) in 1916, and "The Logansport Breeze," which appeared in the Post in 1920, feature strong female characters and more direct attention to social issues than either Van Loan or Lardner, marking Bulger as more of a politically conscious writer. In particular, the protagonist of "Big League Promise" tries to improve the social standing of ball players in a stratified southern town and fails in his effort to make the major league team.

10. Also of note here is the early use of "Baseball Annie" to describe female baseball fans.

11. The language used in this quote replays the rhetoric that of the Brotherhood War of 1890 when the players formed their own league in an attempt to break the Reserve Clause and control their own contracts.

Works Cited

Alden, Patricia. *Social Mobility in the English Bildungsroman: Gissing, Hardy, Bennett, and Lawrence*. Ann Arbor: UMI Research Press, 1986. Print.

Anderson, William B. "Crafting the National Pastime's Image: The History of Major League Baseball Public Relations." *Journalism and Mass Communications Monographs* 5.1 (2003). Print.

Appleton, Louise. "Distillations of Something Larger: The Local Scale and American National Identity." *Cultural Geographies* (2002): 421–447. Print.

Bakhtin, Mikhail. "The *Bildungsroman* and Its Significance in the History of Realism" *Speech Genres and Other Late Essays*. Trans. Vern W. McGee. Austin: University of Texas Press, 1986. Print.

Blain, Neil. "Beyond 'Media Culture'; Sport as Dispersed Symbolic Activity." *Sport, Media, Culture: Global and Local Dimensions (Sport in the Global Society)*. Eds. Alina Bernstein and Neil Blain. New York: Routledge, 2002. Print

Buckley, Jerome. *Seasons of Youth: The Bildungsroman from Dickens to Golding*. Cambridge: Harvard University Press, 1974. Print.

Bulger, Bozeman. "A Big-League Promise." *McClure's Magazine* 47 (1916): 30–2. Print.

_____. "The Logansport Breeze." *The Saturday Evening Post* 19 June 1920: 30, 32, 35, 82, 85. Print.

_____. "A Major League Mother-in-Law." *The Saturday Evening Post* 17 June 1916: 8–10, 78. Print.

_____. "A Pinch Hit in Vaudeville." *The Saturday Evening Post* 15 Sep. 1915: 15–17, 45–46. Print.

Castle, Gregory. *Reading the Modernist Bildungsroman*. Gainesville: University Press of Florida, 2006. Print.

Cohn, Jan. *Creating America: George Horace Lorimer and* The Saturday Evening Post. Pittsburgh: University of Pittsburgh Press, 1989. Print.
Edelman, Rob. "Baseball, Vaudeville, and Mike Donlin." *Base Ball: A Journal of the Early Game* 2.1 (2008): 44–57. Print.
Hilton, George W. "Introduction." *The Annotated Baseball Stories of Ring W. Lardner, 1914–1919*. Stanford: Stanford University Press, 1995. Print.
Kazin, Alfred. *On Native Grounds*. New York: Harcourt, 1942. Print.
Knight, Bill. "Heywood Broun." *Dictionary of Literary Biography* 171: 31–43. Print.
Lardner, Ring. *The Annotated Baseball Stories of Ring W. Lardner, 1914–1919*. Ed. George W. Hilton. Stanford: Stanford University Press, 1995. Print.
Lears, T.J. Jackson. *Fables of Abundance: A Cultural History of Advertising in America*. New York: Basic Books, 1994. Print.
O'Connor, Richard. *Heywood Broun: A Biography*. New York: Putnam, 1975. Print.
Ohmann, Richard. *Selling Culture: Magazines, Markets, and Class at the Turn of the Century*. London: Verso, 1996. Print.
Orodenker, Richard. *The Writer's Game: Baseball Writing in America*. New York: Twayne, 1996. Print.
Pendergast, Tom. *Creating the Modern Man: American Magazines and Consumer Culture*. Columbia: University of Missouri Press, 2000. Print.
Peterson, Scott D. "Do You Know Me Now: Cultural Reflection and Resistance in Ring Lardner's *You Know Me Al*." *Nine* 18.2 (2010): 38–48. Print.
Riess, Steven. "Sport and the Redefinition of American Middle-class Masculinity." *The International Journal of the History of Sport* 8.1 (1991): 5–27. Print.
Saxton, Alexander. *The Rise and Fall of the White Republic: Class Politics and Mass Culture in Nineteenth-Century America*. London and New York: Verso, 1990. Print.
Sharnhorst, Gary. "Demythologizing Alger." *Ragged Dick*. Ed. Hildegard Hoeller. New York: W.W. Norton, 2008. Print.
Tassin, Algernon. *The Magazine in America*. New York: Dodd, Mead, 1916. Print.
Tebbel, John, and Mary Ellen Zuckerman. *The Magazine in America, 1741–1990*. New York and Oxford: Oxford UP, 1991. Print.
Tolchin, Karen. *Part Blood, Part Ketchup: Coming of Age in American Literature and Film*. New York: Rowan & Littlefield, 2007. Print.
Trachtenberg, Alan. *The Incorporation of America*. New York: Hill and Wang, 1982. Print.
Van Loan, Charles. "The Bone Doctor." *The Saturday Evening Post* 4 July 1914: 8–10, 2–3. Print.
_____. "The Busher." *The Big League*. Boston: Small, Maynard, 1911. Print.
Wilson, Edmund. *The Shores of Light*. New York: Farrar, Straus & Young, 1952. Print.

"Disgraceful employment": The Gentleman Amateur in Eric Rolfe Greenberg's The Celebrant

MARK BRESNAN

When Eric Rolfe Greenberg's historical novel *The Celebrant* appeared in 1983, major league baseball had suffered through five work stoppages in the previous twelve years. While three of the five incidents were resolved by the beginning of the coming season, the most recent stoppage, a player strike, resulted in seven weeks of missed games during June and July of 1981. In the weeks after that strike began, furious fans wrote to *Sports Illustrated*, which had announced the stoppage with a cover reading "STRIKE!: The Walkout the Owners Provoked." While some wrote in support of the players, most printed letters had a decidedly less charitable tone. One fan cited Lou Gehrig as an exemplar of all that baseball used to represent: "[Gehrig] was typical of the men who played when baseball was America's *game*.... Today the game is a shame, and the overpriced, egotistical, self-indulgent players with their batteries of agents, lawyers and accountants have dulled my interest to the point where I'd rather watch reruns of *Father Knows Best*" (Ocel 66). Another claimed that he did not miss the major leagues at all, having spent his time watching the minors: "In one week, I saw eight exciting games, played by men who obviously love the sport for the game itself, not for the money they are being paid" (Park 82).

While *Sports Illustrated* covered the strike itself in detail, with a feature story from James Kaplan when the strike began and another when it ended, the magazine took the opportunity granted by the work stoppage to cover the allegedly purer version these letter-writers seemed to crave. The July 6 issue featured a spread on the Cape Cod summer college league, with eight pages of photos by Frank White and a brief but approving essay by Steve Wulf. Wulf begins by listing the famous alumni of the Cape Cod league but quickly digresses: "The greater truth is that these towns live for their teams, and these players live with the townspeople" (18). He commends outfielder Jim Sherman for postponing his professional contract offer from the Chicago Cubs in order to return for another summer on the Cape. In both word and image, the article presented the league as a pastoral, Edenic alternative to the fallen Major Leagues. In the following issue, Ron Fimrite's rapturous feature on two minor league games played at major league stadiums was ironically titled "Baseball Comes Back to the Big Time"; the content of the article made it clear that the joke was on striking ballplayers who did not think that fans would show up to see less-skilled (and lower-paid) substitutes.

Situated within this historical context, Greenberg's novel, featuring Christy Mathewson as its subject, might seem a similarly nostalgic gesture, no different than the baseball fans pining for Lou Gehrig or the sportswriter's encomium to college ballplayers. However, the novel explores the notion of nostalgia itself, implicitly critiquing those archaic notions of amateurism that fans invoked during the 1981 strike, while also explicitly critiquing the amateur ideal as it operated in early-twentieth century American culture. Commenting on his characterization of Mathewson in a 1989 interview, Greenberg claimed that the fictional pitcher's tragic flaw was that he "believed too much in his own image" (Nathan 12). As many readers have pointed out, one of the most powerful iterations of this image is Mathewson's self-perception as a Christ–like savior. The novel's title is just one of its many religiously suggestive tropes; critic Allen Hye locates *The Celebrant* in a long tradition of journalistic and literary baseball narratives, pointing out "dozens of religious images and allusions" and arguing that the novel enacts "something of a passion play ... with Mathewson assuming the role of the suffering—and ultimately avenging—messiah" (44). However, Mathewson trades on his identity as a gentleman athlete who lives by the ideals of amateurism despite his professional status, invoking nostalgic ideals within the novel's grimly profiteering environment. His aristocratic class position, secured by his college education and his family's wealth, enables Mathewson to pursue a lucrative career in baseball without sacrificing his image as a gentleman amateur. The novel's plot, in which Mathewson becomes involved in the 1919 Black Sox scandal, explores the contradictions inherent in this image. As an example of what Linda Hutcheon has termed historiographic metafiction, *The Celebrant* draws attention not only to the contradictions of the amateur ideal as constructed in early-twentieth century America, but also to the anxieties regarding professionalization that continued to shape sports culture in the 1970s and '80s.

In *A Poetics of Postmodernism*, Hutcheon argues that a primary characteristic of postmodern fiction is its impulse to "open itself up to history" despite the fragility and falsity of historical knowledge (124). In defining historiographic metafiction, she argues that the conscious incorporation of historical intertexts enables postmodern fiction to challenge the empiricist authority of historical narrative (128). She develops this concept in a discussion of E.L. Doctorow's *Loon Lake* (1980), describing the novel in terms that aptly apply to *The Celebrant*: "This is not documentary realism: it is a novel about our cultural representations of the past..." (136). Mirroring Doctorow's interest in historical representations, Greenberg explores both the class-inflected construction of the amateur ideal and the nostalgic reconstruction of baseball's pre–World War I past. In foregrounding the weaknesses and gaps in these parallel constructions, Greenberg offers a more nuanced reading of the professional athlete's world (for which Mathewson functions as exemplar), while simultaneously demonstrating the stubborn cultural power of the amateur ideal.

As voiced by narrator Jackie Kapp, *The Celebrant* reflects the ideals and fantasies of a Jewish immigrant and baseball fan living in New York City at the turn of the twentieth century. Properly named "Yakov," Jackie receives his name on the baseball fields he discovers with his brother Eli immediately upon their arrival from Europe. As Eric Solomon notes, *The Celebrant* shares its plot of acculturation through baseball with a long tradition of Jewish-American writing, including work by Roger Kahn, Irwin Shaw, and Philip Roth (99). However, Jackie's integration is complicated by a widespread cultural suspicion of "mercenary" professional ballplayers. A left-handed pitcher with enough promise to receive a minor league tryout at the age of seventeen, he quickly realizes his parents will never let him sign a contract. With designs on securing their status in the upper-middle class, the Kapps are wary of professional athletes, which Jackie explains translates to "prizefighters, jockeys, ballplayers," each of whom they deem undesirable:

> Club fighters were neighborhood heroes, yet the unspoken assumption was that they fought because they were unfit to do anything else.... Some professional ballplayers were locally bred, but an increasing number were itinerants from distant farmlands who lived out of cardboard suitcases in back street boarding houses [13].

Jackie emphasizes that the class issues regarding professional sports transcended financial concerns; even if he were to earn one of the lucrative salaries that had recently been awarded to the best ballplayers, "professional athlete" was not a career path for a middle-class Jewish immigrant. As he succinctly puts it, "We had not crossed the ocean to find disgraceful employment" (14).

The Kapps' suspicion of professionalism is partly informed by late-nineteenth-century baseball's identity as a game populated by the immigrant working class; as historian Jules Tygiel writes, Irish and German immigrants dominated professional baseball in the 1880s and '90s (40). Jackie's emphasis on "breeding" in the above passage indicates Greenberg's awareness of these racialized constructions; Jackie also notes that most jockeys were African American and therefore in the same conceptual category as their horses (13). However, their distaste for professionalism also echoes the emphasis placed on social class during the mid-nineteenth century institutionalization of sports, not only in the United States, but also in Great Britain and continental Europe.

As sports historian Allen Guttmann demonstrates, the first British sporting institutions were class-based organizations that strictly defined amateur athletics as a gentleman's pursuit. Rowing clubs and regattas explicitly excluded the working class: organizers of the 1879 Henley Regatta formulated a definition of amateurism barring "not only anyone who rowed for money but also anyone who had ever been employed in manual labor of any sort whatsoever" (Guttmann 96). British amateur athletics (track and field) clubs demonstrated equal exclusivity; when middle-class tradesmen were admitted to the London Athletic Club in 1872, sixty members resigned in a show of disdain (98). Similar class anxieties informed the inception of the modern Olympics in 1896. The rebirth of the Olympic Games institutionalized an amateur ideal developed and celebrated by Frenchman Pierre de Coubertin, who wrote extensively about the connection between amateurism and gentlemanly society. The invitation to the 1894 Paris International Athletic Congress (a key moment in the organization of the modern Olympics) emphasizes the social implications of amateurism:

> Above all, it is necessary to preserve the noble and chivalrous character which distinguished athletics in the past, in order that it may continue effectively to play the same admirable part in the education of the modern world as the Greek masters assigned to it. Human imperfection always tends to transform the Olympic athlete into a circus gladiator. We must choose between two athletic formulae which are not compatible. In order to defend themselves against the spirit of lucre and professionalism that threatens to invade their ranks, amateurs in most countries have drawn up complicated rules full of compromises and contradictions; moreover, too frequently their letter is respected rather than their spirit [trans. in MacAloon 166–7].

This strict division between amateur and professional remained an integral tenet of the Olympic Games until the 1950s. Helping to promulgate this binary opposition between amateur and professional through class and morality, De Coubertin equated class division with moral distinction, as made clear by the invitation's use of terms such as "chivalrous character" and its railing against "the spirit of lucre and professionalism."

Similar assumptions about social class and amateur athletics informed American sports culture during the turn-of-the-century era in which *The*

Celebrant is set. As a series of eligibility controversies at Harvard, Princeton, and Yale accompanied college football's growth in the 1890s, *Harper's Weekly* editor Caspar Whitney used his regular column to pose an ultimatum: "We had rather see football forbidden by the university faculties than pained by the exhibition of our college boys, sons of gentlemen, resorting to the intrigues of unprincipled professionals" (qtd. in Oriard 154). Whitney's identification of college students as "sons of gentlemen" reflects the elite nature of the universities where football was first played. Their elite status, Whitney argues, is threatened when players enter any system of exchange, either by accepting scholarship money or transferring to another school (sometimes at midseason) specifically to play football. As Michael Oriard argues, "Whitney did not object to professionalism itself; instead, he criticized any commerce at all between amateurs and professionals. As he wrote in early 1899, 'There are no degrees of amateurism'" (155).

In contrast to football's historical association with the elite Ivy League campuses where it was first organized, baseball has been extensively mythologized as a fundamentally democratic and rural sport. In 1905, a commission assembled by Albert Spalding proclaimed that the game had been invented in Cooperstown, New York, in 1839 by Civil War general Abner Doubleday. The agrarian nature of this creation myth (Doubleday purportedly held the first game in a cow pasture) established it as a counter-narrative to the class-based elitism of European sports, especially the British games of rounders and cricket from which baseball actually derived. As cultural historian Nicholas Dawidoff writes, "Americans wanted baseball to be from the rural heartland, and to be all theirs, and they willed it be so" (7). In *America's National Game*, published in 1911, Spalding eagerly differentiated baseball from British cricket, arguing that the latter is "a genteel game" whereas a baseball player "says goodbye to society [and] doffs his gentility" when he steps on the field (7). Despite the seeming disparities between them, however, both these rural baseball players and their gentlemanly counterparts on the football field were culturally constructed as pastoral subjects. Both were shown as free from the constraints of industrial capitalism, which defined the ideals of athletic amateurism in *fin-de-siecle* urban America. The same desire for upward social mobility that fueled the novels of Horatio Alger was deemed unacceptable on the athletic field, where the spirit of fair play held sway over the pursuit of economic gain.

While this celebration of pastoral amateurism may seem a relic of the first decades of the twentieth century, fan reactions to the 1981 baseball strike demonstrate that the amateur ideal remained stubbornly powerful in the years before *The Celebrant*'s publication. While the fans writing into *Sports Illustrated* might not necessarily have represented the views of the general public, their language clearly evoked the pastoral rhetoric of de Coubertin, Whitney, and Spalding. As fan Philip Schacca wrote: "Historians may one day record that grown men once played a little boy's game, with many of them being paid millions of dollars to hit a ball with a bat and run around a diamond, until they decided to go on strike" (87). Another fan expressed consternation that a sports magazine would devote so many pages to the financial details of the strike: "If I had wanted to subscribe to a business magazine, I would have.... I hope this will be the last issue where negotiators and mediators turn a clean, healthy sport into an obscenity" (Kramer 66). As de Coubertin believed over eight decades earlier, many *Sports Illustrated* readers clearly voiced suspicions towards the "filthy lucre" generated by professional sports.

As such, *The Celebrant* speaks to both the historic promulgators of the amateur ideal and to the contemporary fans who continued to see professional athletes through a pastoral lens. In a clear dig at baseball's agrarian creation myth, an early scene in the novel features Jackie's father-in-law Richard Sonnheim telling him about meeting Alexander Cartwright, the game's true founder and a member of the New York Athletic Club (76). More important, however, is the novel's exposing of the false nostalgia of athletic amateurism. Historicizing fan's suspicions towards professionalism — a phenomenon *The Celebrant* suggests has dogged the game ever since the late nineteenth century — Greenberg demonstrates the untenable artificiality of the amateur ideal. For example, Jackie reports that his aristocratic father-in-law was hesitant to attend a Giants game because he held the professional leagues in disdain; when Sonnheim finally relents, he buys tickets in a box in the upper grandstand and brings his opera glasses to better see the field (75–77). While Sonnheim's wealth and elevated social status distinguish him from the vast majority of fans (he also reports attending polo matches at the private field of *New York Herald* publisher James Gordon Bennett), this distaste for professionalism was not limited to the moneyed class. On a trip through the Midwest with his brother Eli, a salesman for the family jewelry business, Jackie frequently encounters reservations towards professional baseball: "Many of our clients were frankly disgusted with big-league ball," which had transformed from battles for local pride "into a disquieting brawl among mercenaries" (40–41). Even among the striving middle-class store managers Eli and Jackie work with, professional ballplayers remain an anathema.

These social mores help explain the extraordinary attention directed towards Giants pitcher Christy Mathewson, both as depicted in Greenberg's novel and as recorded during his playing career. A former student at Bucknell University (where he was class president before leaving to pursue his baseball career), Mathewson is frequently referred to in *The Celebrant* as "college boy" and "collegian." While watching Mathewson pitch a no-hitter in St. Louis, Jackie "wondered why a true collegian would choose the life of a professional ballplayer" (22). After the game, when Eli describes the hurler as "a bit too marvelous for my blood," Jackie points to his class status as evidence of his worth: "He doesn't even belong on a baseball field, a college man with money of his own. He could be a doctor or lawyer or stockbroker, but there he is, pitching for the Giants. It's a miracle" (37). Although he is describing one of professional baseball's first superstars, Jackie's emphasis on Mathewson's economic disinterestedness has more in common with historical constructions of the amateur athlete. In the fan culture depicted in *The Celebrant*, Mathewson's ability to earn money in other professions renders the fact that he *actually* earns it as a baseball player irrelevant, and he enjoys both the cultural prestige of the amateur and the pecuniary rewards of the professional.

Jackie's investment in this amateur image helps explain his decision to give the rings he makes for Mathewson as gifts, never accepting money from the wealthy pitcher. As Ronald Kates writes, Jackie's relationship with Mathewson represents a "gift-exchange economy" uncontaminated by market forces, and Jackie takes pains to make certain that it stays in that realm (62). As such, Jackie transcends the role of casual fan; not content to merely follow his hero's exploits, he eagerly takes an active role in shaping Mathewson's identity. Given Jackie's own frustrated attempt to play professional baseball, his celebration of the pitcher is displaced wish fulfillment; as an Anglo-American born in Pennsylvania, Mathewson appears to enjoy options that a Jewish immigrant does not.

While the novel makes the personal nature of this transference clear, Jackie's admiration of Mathewson iterates the almost universal high esteem with which the pitcher has been historically regarded. In an interview conducted by Daniel Nathan, Greenberg confesses astonishment that his research failed to unearth any negative accounts of Mathewson by his contemporaries. Indeed, Mathewson has appeared frequently in baseball literature, usually portrayed as both fan favorite and American hero. When he is announced as starting pitcher in William Carlos Williams's novel *White Mule* (1937), the crowd roars with approval; in fact, his popularity is so universal that it spurs a disgusted reaction from at least one fan: "All you hear now is Mathewson. I'll admit he's a good ball player but you'd think to hear some of them talk it was him invented the game" (277–79). Mathewson's iconic status extends to the many lists that claim to rank baseball's all-time greatest players, wherein he usually lands among the top ten or twenty players. His legacy was institutionalized in 1936, when he was inducted into the Hall of Fame's inaugural class alongside four men (Babe Ruth, Ty Cobb, Honus Wagner, and Walter Johnson) universally cited among baseball's ten best all-time players. However, an objective look at Mathewson's accomplishments suggests that, while he was without doubt a great player, his extraordinary cultural status must have owed itself to something beyond the field of play. For instance, although baseball historian Bill James recognizes Mathewson as his era's "Most Admirable Superstar," he ranks the pitcher only forty-second in a statistical analysis of the game's greatest players: "Mathewson, as I see it, was the fourth-best pitcher of his generation.... I just don't think one year as the best pitcher in baseball is enough to rank him among the twenty greatest players of all time" (364–65).

Indeed, the cultural impact of both the historical Mathewson and his fictional counterpart go well beyond on-field achievements. Mathewson's service in World War I, where he was exposed to mustard gas and developed an ultimately fatal case of tuberculosis, helps to explain his high historical reputation. However, it does not account for his tremendous popularity during his playing career. (To cite just one counterexample, military service did nothing to burnish the reputation of Ty Cobb, who served in Mathewson's unit.) In the Nathan interview, Greenberg argues that the esteem directed towards the pitcher was a function of his unique class position: "Mathewson was just another class of individual at a time when America was much more class conscious than it is now" (13). As Greenberg points out, contemporary major league baseball players come from a wide variety of social classes, but "[t]hat was not the case in 1898. At all. Mathewson broke a mold. He was something brand new" (13). Indeed, the brief inscription on Mathewson's Hall of Fame plaque makes special note that the "charismatic and popular" pitcher was "college-educated," still a rarity among professional ballplayers in 1936, over a decade after his untimely death.

Mathewson's characterization in *The Celebrant* reflects the interdependence of his heroism with his status as a gentleman amateur, as without his class positioning, the novel suggests, Mathewson would have been just another ballplayer. He first appears in the novel while throwing a no-hitter against St. Louis; in its final scenes, he helps a journalist expose the involvement of gamblers in the 1919 World Series. In between, the novel devotes several scenes to an exploration of Mathewson's social status, most notably in a dinner at Richard Sonnheim's posh private club. As Jackie accompanies Mathewson to the meeting with his father-in-law, he takes note of the pitcher's regal bearing, particularly how he seemed "no less at ease in black tie than in his playing togs ... not so much fit[ting] into his surroundings as defin[ing] them" (83). Indeed, Mathewson consciously celebrates his gentility and economic disinterest, explaining to Sonnheim and Jackie that he could have embraced several other careers after college: "Had I never pitched an inning, there were still great worlds open to me by reason of my family and upbringing" (91).

However, Greenberg foregrounds several counter-narratives complicating the gentlemanly amateur ideal that Mathewson exemplifies. While his insistence to Jackie and Sonnheim that he does not "need" the sport is arguably true, it conveniently marginalizes both the financial wealth and the social capital increasingly realized by professional baseball players. As Jackie notes when visiting the opulent Upper West Side building in which Mathewson, Giants manager John McGraw, and catcher Roger Bresnahan all kept apartments, "Ballplayers were gaining respect if landlords of such buildings would accept their signatures on leases" (68). The pursuit of player endorsements by the Kapp's expanding jewelry business further underlines the ability of professional baseball players to generate extra income with little more than a signature. Jackie specializes in designing a line of rings inspired by Mathewson, items that rank among the company's top sellers (172). While Mathewson buys into the views of his contemporaries, who viewed him as a gentleman amateur, he was in fact one of the earliest beneficiaries of the professional system.

The commercial success of Mathewson's ghost-written autobiography, *Pitching in a Pinch*, continued to reinforce the ideals of amateur athletics even as it cemented his status as one of professional baseball's first true superstars. Jackie confesses his dismay at the spotless depiction of Mathewson constructed by his ghostwriter, John Wheeler: "There wasn't a word of the broken contract with Mack or the hostilities of McGraw's early years," or how Mathewson's aggressive pitching style had "kept batters wary" (175). Having earlier expressed his admiration for Mathewson's embodiment of gentlemanly ideals, he criticizes the book's failure to acknowledge the complications inherent in these. He points to gaps in both the economic and moral narratives by which the pitcher has been constructed, wishing Mathewson would sincerely explain his broken contract and rough pitching style, rather than obfuscating any details that complicate his idealistic mythology.

As with most of the novel's historical elements, *Pitching in a Pinch* is a real book, and a closer reading of the 1912 autobiography helps explain why Greenberg chose the historical Mathewson as the source for a fictional character who could not conceive of his professional status. In his discussion of fellow pitcher Grover Cleveland Alexander, Mathewson describes the "ideal way" to develop a superstar. He notes that Alexander was picked up on waivers for a minimal contract and received little attention until he performed well for several months with the Philadelphia Phillies. Mathewson reads the small salary as a decided advantage, claiming that Alexander could focus on pitching without worrying about being criticized for making too much money: "If he didn't last, the newspapers wouldn't laugh at him, and the people wouldn't say: '$11,000, or $22,500, for a lemon.' That's the dread of all ball players"

(Mathewson 34). The "dread," for Mathewson, lies not in a failure on the field but in the economic shame of a player being compensated beyond his worth. "Philadelphia was lucky," he adds with regret, "it's hard to get stars now without paying enormous prices for them" (34).

The historical Mathewson's fictional counterpart is equally unable to identify himself and his sport within the capitalist system of exchange, an inability that leads to *The Celebrant*'s key tragedy — not the simple fact of Mathewson's death after exposure to mustard gas, but his decision to enlist in the military as an act of penance for his perceived complicity in a gambling ring. Shortly after retiring from his playing career, Mathewson returns to the game in order to manage the Cincinnati Reds. When compelling evidence surfaces that one of his players (Hal Chase) is betting against the club, Mathewson does nothing. As Jackie's brother Arthur says, "He is either the most credulous man in America or its greatest model of Christian forgiveness. Perhaps both" (219). Both this credulity and forgiveness are a function of Mathewson's inability to see his players as autonomous professionals. When the situation comes to public attention, he resigns, casting himself in his statement to the press as an inattentive father figure, claiming "a manager has a responsibility to protect his players from such contacts [with undesirable elements], and evidently I have failed in that regard" (222).

Mathewson notably describes the crisis in moral rather than economic terms. He perceives himself as a paternal figure, one responsible for protecting his players from corrupting elements. In an earlier conversation with Jackie and Eli, Hal Chase offers a far different narrative of his decision to throw games: "'Professional means only one thing.... I do it for money, and if there's more money in losing than in winning, shit if I care" (172).

The Celebrant neither endorses Chase's amoral attitude towards baseball nor criticizes Mathewson for idealizing the game. Instead, the novel demonstrates the consequences of Mathewson's inability to recognize baseball as a professional enterprise, fully enmeshed in a capitalist system of exchange. Greenberg juxtaposes Mathewson's statement with the managerial strategy of McGraw, whose team signs Chase the following year. As Carl Kapp tells it, McGraw recognized Chase's complete lack of shame and therefore controlled his behavior with intimidation and bravado: "He told Chase that at the first sign of any funny business he'd brain him with a baseball bat" (225). McGraw's brash manner is not the only marker differentiating him from Mathewson. Earlier in the novel, the pitcher notes McGraw's working class roots in explicit contrast to his own social position, as for the manager, "baseball wasn't one way out, but the only way out. He had nothing but baseball, and he still believes that, absent baseball, he is nothing" (91). Indeed, McGraw fully invests in the sport in a way that Mathewson deliberately avoids, and is depicted throughout the novel as the antithesis of the gentleman amateur. Further, McGraw's success in managing Chase highlights the clash between Mathewson's idealized self-image and the economically-driven world in which he can no longer sustain a career.

In addition to resigning his managerial position, Mathewson responds to the Hal Chase fiasco by enlisting in the military. In a formal statement, Mathewson cites his own integrity as the primary factor both in his decision to enlist and in the relative tardiness of that decision. While important, his duty to country did not initially supersede his commitment to manage the Reds (222–23). As he tells Jackie later, though, his rationale for joining the Army was not a function of his sudden availability; instead, he hoped to die as punishment for his failure. Hye identifies the messianic quality of this impulse, suggesting that Mathewson performs penance not only for himself but also for all of the players on his team (47). While Greenberg unmistakably uses Christ–like imagery, especially as Mathewson speaks to Jackie on his deathbed, the pitcher's earlier decision to enlist also reveals his desire for the same sort of escape from the social world he once thought baseball provided. Early in the novel, Mathewson separates the rules of baseball from those of life, telling Jackie's father-in-law that, "Baseball is all clean lines and clear decisions.... Oh, for a life like that, where every day produces a clear winner and an equally clear loser, and back to it the next day with the slate wiped clean and the teams starting out equal" (86–87).

Throughout the novel, Mathewson idealizes the game as a pure meritocracy in which a player's worth can be judged with epistemological certainty. As Tim Morris writes in *Making the Team: The Cultural Work of Baseball Fiction*, many novels make this connection between baseball and meritocracy; he describes the baseball novel genre as fundamentally "a defense, and a mythology, of meritocracy" (110). However, when Mathewson's experience managing the Reds disabuses him of this notion, he turns to the military, where he tells Jackie he felt he was fated to die in defense of the United States (262). Sadly, his ultimately fatal exposure to gas takes place not on the battle field, but during a training exercise, and Mathewson ironically loses the opportunity to prove his worth on the battlefield.

In the novel's final chapter, Greenberg further critiques nostalgia narratives of baseball's past by using the 1919 World Series as Mathewson's moment of redemption rather than as a symbol of the sport's loss of innocence. Many writers and historians, including Nelson Algren, Eliot Asinof, and James Maxwell, have cited the Black Sox scandal as a moment that transcended baseball and corresponded with America's fall from grace after World War I. The scandal even appears in F. Scott Fitzgerald's *The Great Gatsby* in the form of gambler Meyer Wolfsheim, a character loosely based on Arnold Rothstein, who was charged but not convicted in the Black Sox scandal. In his reading of Fitzgerald's novel, John Lauricella argues that the casual association between Wolfsheim and Gatsby signals the latter's irredeemable corruption, especially given Gatsby's professed distaste for the game: "[I]n the iconography of American culture, a boy playing baseball participates in an honest, wholesome means of self-improvement, whereas the man who bends the game to force-fit capitalism's profit motive destroys its integrity and makes himself a thief" (49). In his interview with Nathan, Greenberg acknowledges this interpretation of the Black Sox scandal while noting its self-reinforcing quality, arguing that the sheer repetition of the idea that the 1919 World Series destroyed American innocence ultimately makes it so (17). The prevalence of this myth makes *The Celebrant*'s invocation of the 1919 Series even more remarkable, as Greenberg deploys the scandal as an opportunity for Mathewson to redeem himself by finally acknowledging the economic forces at work in his sport. When rumors swirl about a possible fix, journalist Hugh Fullerton invites him to watch the game from the press box and evaluate the White Sox play.

Indignant at first, Mathewson repeats the naïve belief in his team's players that prevented him from identifying Chase's complicity with gamblers: "[T]here's not a man on [my team] I wouldn't trust with my life" (255). Only when Fullerton promises that the rumors concern only the Chicago club does Mathewson relent. Finally, he acknowledges both the involvement of gamblers in the Series and the desire for economic gain that drives many of his professional colleagues. No longer willfully naïve, he lectures Jackie about the obviousness of the fix: "It takes no profound knowledge of the game" to see the ways in which the White Sox deliberately misplayed the field (260).

In his reading of the novel, Solomon identifies the corruption of the game by gambling interests as evidence of the novel's late-Marxist bent:

> Greenberg is talking about kinds of labor, the economic labor of Jackie the jeweler and the originally joyous, non-alienated labor (play, actually) of Christy the pitcher. Both these work ethics, foregrounded early in the fiction, shift as gambling ... allow[s] the business society to take hegemonic control over the game and its players [85].

However, *The Celebrant* makes clear that baseball and business became inextricably enmeshed from the moment professional teams were organized. Gambling on the game takes place throughout the novel and drives one of its major narratives, the bankruptcy and eventual suicide of Jackie's older brother Eli. From the novel's first baseball scene, in which Mathewson throws his first no-hitter as Eli takes bets from his clients, Greenberg suggests that nostalgic narratives depicting the Black Sox scandal as the game's fall from grace ignore the economic realities of turn-of-the-century sports culture. Even more revealing are the frequent references to the elevated wealth and social status afforded to professional baseball players. In this context, Mathewson's inability to see the fundamental connection between Jackie's labor and his own is revealed as hopelessly naïve.

The Celebrant exposes Mathewson's view of professional baseball as pure play, a luxury available only to college-educated gentleman. Ironically, only when Mathewson acknowledges the profit motive at work in professional baseball can he live up to his own iconic status. This new vantage helps him to expose one of the game's most troubling episodes, rather than remaining complicit by maintaining his silence. The novel depicts a culture that shunned the economic dimension of professional sports even as it ravenously consumed them; writing from the historical vantage point of the early 1980s, Greenberg suggests a continuity between the cultural suspicion of "mercenary ballplayers" in the early 1900s and fan reactions to the 1981 baseball strike. Of course, this cognitive dissonance is not unique to professional baseball or even to sport itself. However, the extent to which baseball has cultivated the idealized image of amateurism, which legitimized the game for a middle class audience in the early 1900s, and which endures today, makes it an especially important subject for *The Celebrant*'s critique. The novel's tragic plot reveals the tenuous nature of Mathewson's construction as a gentleman amateur impervious to the lures of commercial reward; simultaneously, it demonstrates the power of that ideal. As the motivating force behind the novel's key moments, his amateur status both sparks Jackie Kapp's initial attraction to Mathewson and animates the pitcher's heroic fall. Greenberg presents the resilient appeal of this amateur ideal, suggesting a profound and pervasive cultural ambivalence towards the very same economic forces that have helped make American sports so popular.

Works Cited

Dawidoff, Nicholas, ed. *Baseball: A Literary Anthology*. New York: Library of America, 2002. Print.

Fimrite, Ron. "Baseball Comes Back to the Big Time." *Sports Illustrated* 13 July 1981: 22–27. Print.

Greenberg, Eric Rolfe. *The Celebrant*. Lincoln, NE: Bison Books, 1993. Print.

Guttmann, Allen. *Sports Spectators*. New York: Columbia University Press, 1986. Print.

Hutcheon, Linda. *A Poetics of Postmodernism: History, Theory, Fiction*. New York: Routledge, 1988. Print.

Hye, Allen. "The Baseball Messiah: Christy Mathewson and *The Celebrant*." *Aethlon* 7:1 (1989): 41–49. Print.

James, Bill. *The New Bill James Historical Baseball Abstract*. New York: Free Press, 2003. Print.

Kaplan, James. "Let the Games Begin." *Sports Illustrated* 10 August 1981: 14–19. Print.
_____. "No Games Today." *Sports Illustrated* 22 June 1981: 17–21. Print.
Kates, Ronald. "Rings Born of Impulse: Gift-Exchange Economies in Eric Rolfe Greenberg's *The Celebrant*." *NINE: A Journal of Baseball History and Culture* 17:2 (Spring 2009): 58–69. Print.
Kramer, Joel. Letter. *Sports Illustrated* 6 July 1981: 66. Print.
Lauricella, John. *Home Games: Essays on Baseball Fiction*. Jefferson, NC: McFarland, 1999. Print.
MacAloon, John. *This Great Symbol: Pierre de Coubertin and the Origins of the Modern Olympic Games*. Chicago: Chicago University Press, 1981. Print.
Mathewson, Christy. *Pitching in a Pinch*. New York: Grosset and Dunlap, 1912. Print.
Morris, Tim. *Making the Team: The Cultural Work of Baseball Fiction*. Urbana: Illinois University Press, 1997. Print.
Nathan, Daniel. "Touching the Bases: A Conversation with Eric Rolfe Greenberg." *Aethlon* 7:1 (1989): 10–19. Print.
Ocel, William. Letter. *Sports Illustrated* 6 July 1981: 66. Print.
Oriard, Michael. *Reading Football: How the Popular Press Created an American Spectacle*. Chapel Hill: North Carolina University Press, 1993. Print.
Park, Andy. Letter. *Sports Illustrated* 13 July 1981: 82. Print.
Solomon, Eric. "'Memories of Days Past' or Why Eric Rolfe Greenberg's *The Celebrant* is the Greatest [Jewish] American Baseball Novel." *American Jewish History*. 83:1 (1995): 83–107. Print.
Schacca, Phillip. Letter. *Sports Illustrated* 29 June 1981: 87. Print.
Spalding, Albert. *America's National Game: Historic Facts Concerning the Beginning, Evolution, Development, and Popularity of Base Ball with Personal Reminiscences of its Vicissitudes, its Victories and its Votaries*. New York: American Sports Publishing Company, 1911. Print.
Tygiel, Jules. *Past Time: Baseball as History*. Oxford: Oxford University Press, 2000. Print.
Williams, William Carlos. *White Mule*. 1937. 6th ed. New York: New Directions, 1967. Print.
Wulf, Steve. "'And Somewhere Children Shout.'" *Sports Illustrated* 6 July 1981: 12–19. Print.

Rings Born of Impulse: Gift-Exchange Economies in Greenberg's The Celebrant

RONALD E. KATES

A number of critics of baseball literature reserve *The Celebrant* a place on the short list of the best baseball-themed fiction. Indeed, Eric Rolfe Greenberg's narrative of Jewish immigrant jeweler Yakov Kapinski's relationship with baseball and Hall of Fame pitcher Christy Mathewson, for whom he crafts a series of commemorative rings, provides a depth not commonly seen in sports fiction. Critics have provided a number of interpretative strategies for reading the work, including viewing the novel as an assimilation narrative, a text guided by religious symbolism, a tale of lost innocence, an awareness of what Eric Solomon terms "the ever-darkening business ethic" (89) and the role art plays in Kapinski's transformation from baseball fan to "'the celebrant of [Mathewson's] works'" (Greenberg 195). In "'It's a player's place, not mine': Vicarious Living, Learning, and Teaching in *The Celebrant*'s Converging Narratives" I discussed how the assimilated Jackie Kapp creates what Howard Becker terms an "art world," which forms "when it brings together people who never cooperated before to produce art based on and using conventions previously unknown or not exploited in that way" (310), yet subsequent readings of *The Celebrant* have led me to consider other elements *within* this art world that in turn impact how I consider—and teach—Greenberg's novel. Not only, as Solomon suggests, does *The Celebrant* investigate how "growth of a business threatens early family solidarity and a pure art" (90), but also, as I have discovered, a reader must also consider the role gift exchange economies play in re-considering Jackie (the artist and fan), Mathewson (the pitcher and artistic inspiration), Jackie's brother Arthur (the businessman and unsentimental pragmatist), and John McGraw (the user of men and, as Solomon calls him, "a pagan devil" [102]).

In *The Gift: Imagination and the Erotic Life of Property*, Lewis Hyde thoroughly discusses the dichotomy the artist commonly faces: to create works that explore the depth of the human condition, emotions, or perceptions; or to fashion pieces that will appeal to potential buyers. Hyde declares, in the third paragraph of his introduction, that "a work of art is a gift, not a commodity," in that "a gift is a thing we do not get through our own efforts. We cannot buy it; we cannot acquire it through an act of will. It is bestowed upon us" (xi). Indeed, as Hyde qualifies further on in his text, "a gift establishes a feeling-bond between two people, while the sale of a commodity leaves no necessary connection" (56).

This gift vs. commodity conundrum reappears throughout *The Celebrant*, particularly once Jackie's younger brother Arthur seizes control of the newly-renamed Collegiate Jewelers and pushes Jackie to adapt to creating mass-produced pieces, as well as commemorative works designed to "make a down-payment" on the future services of such budding stars as Giant pitchers Rube Marquard and Jeff Tesreau (177), a request to which Jackie replies, "The point is that I haven't the impulse to design for Marquard and Tesreau. The Mathewson rings, those early ones, were never assigned or commissioned. They were done on impulse (178). This impulse closely parallels Hyde's suggestion that "an essential portion of any artist's labor is not creation so much as invocation. Part of the work cannot be made, it must be received" (143). In accepting the work — and often also understanding the process of invocation or impulse that goes into the creative process— the recipient enters a collaborative community with the artist/giver that Hyde terms the "gift sphere" (276).

Hyde's definition of the gift-sphere certainly parallels the dilemmas Jackie faces throughout the text to balance art and the market, family and baseball, and business responsibilities and the impulse to create. In developing a gift-sphere, Hyde maintains, "the artist who sells his creations must develop a more subjective feel for the two economies and his own rituals for both keeping them apart and bringing them together. He must, on the one hand, be able to disengage from the work and think of it as a commodity ... and he must, on the other hand, be able to ... serve his gifts on their own terms" (276). From the moment Jackie's connection with Mathewson begins, as he watches the Giant pitcher throw a no hitter against St. Louis on July 15, 1901, he also embarks on a nearly two-decade process of first building, and then sustaining the gift-sphere he and the pitcher share.

As he observes Mathewson work through the St. Louis lineup, Jackie draws the association between the pitcher's successes and his own failure to pursue a life in baseball, in the process transposing his own ambitions onto the hurler: "I watched Mathewson, and he became my youth" (26). The Jewish immigrant Jackie, bound to his family's old-world sensibilities and responsibilities, takes on the obligation of working so his younger brother Sam could pursue his education because he "had not the wherewithal to resist [his] parents" (14) and accept the contract offered him by "the Altoona club of the New York-Pennsylvania League" (13). As Greenberg's narrative unfolds, the family responsibility motif creates a bond between Mathewson and Jackie, but at this particular moment, in the aftermath of Mathewson's first great career achievement, Jackie's confronts his first impulse to create *art* rather than jewelry to sell in department stores nationwide. On the train to Chicago, Jackie stops on the way to the dining car to check out "the sounds of raucous festivity" he hears in an adjacent car (28). When he peers through the window, he sees the Giants celebrating, "serenading Mathewson," as "the whole cart rocked with applause and shouts" (29). Despite the connection Jackie had felt with Mathewson during the pitcher's no hit performance earlier that day, Jackie stands transfixed as he "watch[es] him through [his] own mirrored image in the glass and sens[es] an immense distance from him," lamenting "there was a gulf between us that I felt I must not cross. I had nothing to offer him" (29). Disappointed that he could not muster the appropriate words or courage to approach Mathewson in the midst of the celebration, Jackie returns to his car to sketch a ring commemorating the no hitter, creating a strong design, yet with an "overall effect [that] lacked vibrancy" (30). Waking up in the early morning Midwestern heat, Jackie feels a new inspiration and recreates the design with "a polished ruby, red with fire" as the centerpiece (30), his first experience with artistic inspiration.

Hyde asserts that "most artists are brought to their vocation when their own nascent gifts are awakened by the work of a master. That is to say, most artists are converted to art by art itself. The future artist finds himself or herself moved by a work of art, and, through that experience, comes to labor in the service of art until he can profess his own gifts" (47). Inspired by Mathewson's performance, Jackie bridges the gulf he perceives between himself and the pitcher through a gift born of *impulse* rather than demand, an act he repeats with crafting rings to commemorate Mathewson's second no-hitter and the Giants 1905 World Series championship. While Mathewson reciprocates the gift of the rings with a simple wedding gift, a more subtle reciprocity echoes throughout the rest of the book, as each man draws inspiration from the art of the other, in the process further refining the diligence with which they approach their respective arts of pitching and jewelry design. As Mathewson tells Jackie during the second of their three actual meetings, receiving the first ring, the red ruby, brought about a profound emotional impact:

> The no-hit game was the peak, the last out intensely fulfilling, and yet within an hour it was fading, within a month it was a distant memory, and by season's end, with the club in the cellar, it was almost forgotten.... After my last turn of the

season, when I'd won and it hardly mattered that I'd won, when I was giving some considerable thought to whether I'd play again the following year, out of nowhere came this marvelous piece of work. It made the moment real again, and I never wear it but that I feel it anew [89].

To Hyde, "we come to painting, to poetry, to the stage, hoping to revive the soul. And any artist whose work touches us earns our gratitude.... It is when art acts as an agent of transformation that we may correctly speak of it as a gift" (47). Jackie and Mathewson clearly both undergo professional transformations as a result of providing artistic inspiration (a gift in itself) to one another at critical junctures in their respective careers, but they must also struggle with the attending conflicts and responsibilities that come with the gift giving and receiving processes.

For Jackie, the greatest conflicts derive from his responsibility to design rings for the family business, to try "to guess what ten thousand people are going to want to buy for grandma next Christmas" (37), as well as the realization that he could not expect his brothers "to understand the nature of an offering" (66). Jackie clearly feels the conundrum Hyde outlines when he proposes that "every modern artist who has chosen to labor with a gift must sooner or later wonder how he or she is to survive in a society dominated by market exchange" (xiii), and he laments several times that his inspiration has faded in the face of market-driven concerns. Michelle Marder Kamhi further delineates the contrast between the artist and the commercial artist:

> A work of art is the product of an artist's personal engagement with the subject matter at hand, and the process of making it is painstakingly selective, searching, and relatively fluid.... During the creative process, an artist is concerned first and foremost with getting the work right by his own judgment. Although he may refer to such things as aiming to please God or the gods, the work is nonetheless governed by his own conception of what will best achieve that end. At every stage of the work, the implicit question is, Does this say what I think it should?
>
> In contrast, the commercial artist typically focuses on the client's needs. Because the primary purpose of commercial art is the selling of a product or an idea to a third party, the artist's main concern is with how others will view the image. The artist is therefore more detached and less emotionally engaged. He aims to get the job done to satisfy others [27].

Just as Mathewson draws emotional strength and inspiration from the rings Jackie crafts for him, so too does Jackie from the design processes that bring about these rings. Throughout the text Jackie refers to the drawings as inspirational touchpoints, even going so far as to hang in his home office only the drawings of the ruby ring and the triple diamond ring he designed for Mathewson to commemorate the 1905 World Series victory.

Throughout *The Celebrant* Jackie continually confronts the artistic conflicts Kamhi discusses above, and virtually all of these instances relate to Mathewson or to baseball in general, thus challenging the sanctity with which Jackie views his offerings to the pitcher. For instance, Jackie's brothers Eli and Arthur, as well as his Uncle Sid, who runs the family jewelry business, perceive Jackie's connection with Mathewson as one that they should exploit for the benefit of the family—as Uncle Sid asserts, "'If it's good business, I got a responsibility to do it!'" (120). Jackie refuses to craft commemorative rings for Marquard and Tesreau, yet Collegiate Jewelers lands a contract that effectively corners the commemorative jewelry market with a deal that will enable the company enter every city with "an officially endorsed line, locally promoted, locally manufactured, locally retailed" (245). After all, as Arthur notes, "'every city has its heroes'" (245). Jackie disdains Arthur's suggestion that he fit his designs to the machine, yet within four years the Collegiate has, "as a matter of economy," moved to a system of designing championship rings where "'there's a basic model [of championship ring], the changes from year to year are microscopic…. We try to use the dies we've already cut'"(171). In the aftermath of the meeting that effectively marginalizes Eli's role as a functioning member of the family firm, Uncle Sid wisely tells Jackie, "'Yakov, failure got no problems. If we fail we got no problem with Eli, no problem with anything. We just curse and cry and go to the next thing. But success! Success got a million problems, new ones all the time. So? We do what we got to do. For the family'" (190–191). While Collegiate's success raises the expectations for Jackie to continue to produce products with wide consumer appeal, the success the Giants and Mathewson enjoy during the first decade of the 20th century similarly increases Jackie and the firm's association with the team, a connection that continually threatens the gift-exchange economy Jackie and Mathewson maintain.

While attending the banquet celebrating the Giants 1904 National League championship, Eli has an epiphany that eventually leads to a series of challenges to Jackie's attempts to separate art from business: "'Rings! Championship rings, one for everybody on the club!... We'll sell them, sport. At cost, but we'll sell them to the club'" (60). While this realization eventually leads to the commemorative memorabilia monopoly noted above, it also poses a significant challenge for Jackie: to create art or art for the masses, an element Hyde addresses in determining how an artist inclined to craft art as a gift can also function in a commercial arena:

> How, if art is essentially a gift, is the artist to survive in a society dominated by the market? Modern artists have resolved this dilemma in several different ways, each of which, it seems to me, has two essential features. First the artist allows himself to step outside the gift economy that is the primary commerce of his art and make some peace with the market…. And then—the necessary second

phase — if he is successful in the marketplace, he converts market wealth into gift wealth: he contributes his earnings to the support of his art [274–275].

Once Eli gains approval from Giants President John Brush and Uncle Sid to craft the 1904 commemorative rings, he and Jackie — to Jackie's intense dismay — travel to the apartment of Giant manager John McGraw to discuss design. As Jackie learns from this and subsequent encounters with McGraw, the manager is clearly more market-centered than art centered. Even before Jackie discusses the ring design with him, McGraw forcefully and rudely asserts his preference for diamonds in the rings, causing Jackie to retort, as he lays out a number of sapphires from smallest to largest, "'there's a meaning beyond the gemstone or its cost which is what everyone means when they ask the size of a diamond. This is not a diamond ring, it's a world championship ring'" (70). McGraw then charges out of his apartment, with Jackie and Eli in tow, to go upstairs to Mathewson's apartment to take a closer look at the ruby ring. Besides learning, in this first meeting with Mathewson, of the pitcher's admiration of his work, Jackie also gains an appreciation of Mathewson's artistic sensibilities, which starkly contrast with those held by his manager. Mathewson positively responds to Jackie's sketch — asking, "'I wonder if I might have this drawing when you're done with it.... I think your work is extraordinary'" (74) — yet also diffuses McGraw's demand for diamonds with a curt "'If Master Kapp designed it for a sapphire, a sapphire would be best'" (73). At this moment, Jackie has managed to salvage some artistic integrity in the face of market demands, in effect making peace with the market Hyde alludes to above. Seemingly innocuously, however, Eli assuages McGraw's demands by offering to "make one with a diamond for [him] and do the rest in sapphires" (73). This concession later leads to an artistic conflict between Jackie and McGraw, a conflict that eventually turns him away from the team he has followed and loved.

Following the Giants 1905 World Series triumph, Jackie designs Mathewson a ring different from those given to the rest of the club: "It was simple and bold, in the experimental style then emerging from German schools: three diamonds set flush on a thin band of platinum, without embellishment of engraving and filigree ... nothing like the old-fashioned pieces thick with swirls and curlicues that McGraw had commissioned for his champions" (107). Three years later, following two Chicago Cubs pennant victories, McGraw re-builds the Giants with "a brace of anxious rookies: Fletcher, McCormick, Herzog, Merkle, Snodgrass. With these, McGraw expected, his next title would be won" (107). By 1908, Jackie, too, had confronted professional and personal changes. With increasing pressure from Arthur, Eli, and other family members to transform his relationship with Mathewson into a purportedly mutually-beneficial endorsement opportunity, Jackie faces an artistic crisis where "everything took a diamond shape, nothing had worth. Designing the company line had become as routine as the ride to work on the 'el'" (118). While the success of the re-vitalized Giants and the dominant Mathewson (who had arguably his finest year in 1908) engulfs the city in the tension of the pennant race with the Cubs, Jackie does not embrace the team with the same fervor as he did as a young fan, perhaps because Collegiate's business concerns have infringed so greatly on his ability to enjoy baseball as a pastime rather than a lifeblood of the company. Indeed, as Arthur points out to Jackie, "'As best I can tell the whole business is subsisting on your designs and the reputation of the New York Giants'" (110), a clear indication of how others perceive the indelible ties between Jackie's art and the game that offers *artistic* and not market-based inspirations.

Two curt retorts to his brothers provide further evidence of Jackie's growing disillusionment that he had "staked [his] fortune on the vagaries of the game" (175). When Eli asks, "'Hey, sport, you're really somewhere on the moon these days. There's more to life than a pennant race'" (123), Jackie replies, "'That's what I'm thinking'" (124). The following day, Arthur tells Jackie, "'The truth is that I have some appreciation of the artistic temperament, and for that reason I make allowance for your behavior,'" to which Jackie responds, "'Don't call me an artist. It's a job'" (126). Clearly Jackie at this moment faces what Hyde refers to as "an irreconcilable conflict between gift exchange and the market," where "as a consequence, the artist in the modern world must suffer a constant tension between the gift sphere to which his work pertains and the market society which is his context" (273).

Jackie carries this conflict with him to that day's Giants-Cubs game, the infamous "Merkle's Boner" game where Giant rookie Fred Merkle's failure to touch second base following Al Bridwell's apparent game-winning single costs the Giants the game, and eventually the 1908 pennant, and must directly confront the gift-market tension with Eli and then McGraw. As Eli frantically searches for information on the game's outcome at the Ansonia Hotel, he begs Jackie to call Mathewson to try to learn any inside information: "'It would look like the big, wide world, Jackie,'" he implores, referencing the money Mathewson would earn through the impending endorsement contract, "'We've been scratching Matty's back for years. How many rings have you done for him? How many gifts? It's time we got a little something back'" (146). Jackie rebuffs Eli, and they "stared at one another, surprised with [them]selves and sensing the danger in another word" (147) before McGraw enters with Merkle and five others and calls Jackie to his table to make a request. In an attempt to lift the dismayed Merkle, McGraw proceeds to applaud the efforts of the team's rookies, insisting, "'No, we wouldn't be close without these kids,'" and then making a request of Jackie that quickly transforms to a demand: "'I want a class ring, if you get my drift, for the Class of 'Aught-Eight. I think something with seven diamonds on it, doesn't that sound right? Charge whatever you want. And I want them by the end of the season, so I can give them to the boys before we play the World Series'" (148). When Jackie demurs citing the time frame and his workload, McGraw's tone changes: "'Oh, come on, son, this is for John McGraw and the New York Giants. Drop everything else.... I want those rings on the last day of the season, son'" (149). As Jackie notes, "the order might be a mere gesture, but McGraw's whole force was behind his words. I felt his power" (149), yet he chooses not to fulfill the request, a decision that carries significant later ramifications.

McGraw clearly perceives the rings Jackie has created and given to Mathewson as a form of economic cultivation as opposed to gifts based on impulse. As a result, McGraw can justify his request to the man and company whose jewelry has become commonly associated with the Giants, as a business proposition rather than a request for an object of artistic merit. Even though Merkle declares at the Ansonia table that "'I wouldn't wear such a ring'" (149), McGraw consciously (and *not* impulsively) conceives of the rings as a heavily motivated gift designed to bring about a particular response. He, in effect, requests art for business sake, believing that the rings would therefore inspire Merkle and his fellow rookies to play harder, help the Giants win the pennant, and push on to the World Series. Yet McGraw fails to see the communal nature of gift giving that Jackie has entered into with Mathewson, nor does he understand, to reiterate Hyde's point, that "a gift is a thing we do not get through our own efforts. We cannot buy it; we cannot acquire it through an act of will. It is bestowed upon us" (xi). Three years later, McGraw refuses to allow Jackie and his young son into the Giants clubhouse following his son's first game at the rebuilt Polo Grounds, relaying a message to the policeman at the door, "'You don't get in 'til [I see] the rings'" (173), effectively ending his close association with the team, but also pushing him closer to an artistic awakening and re-creation.

Earlier that season, while designing the pieces Mathewson would endorse for Collegiate Jewelers, Jackie finds "it impossible to express [him]self in studs and pins for his endorsement," declaring, "My initial drawings satisfied no one, least of all myself," and then creating designs in which he "took no pride ... [and] as the project grew in scope, so did my low opinion of it" (167). Yet just as Jackie had inspired Mathewson at the time when the pitcher questioned his art a decade earlier, the arrival of the ghost-written Mathewson autobiography *Pitching in a Pinch* provides Jackie with similar motivation during the winter of 1911–1912. Finishing the book in his workroom, Jackie

> stared at the drawings on the wall, envying their youthful energy and clean direction. In creating them, I'd felt myself an instrument of Mathewson's own

genius ... [yet] through the years of accident and frustration I'd become like [the ghost-writer], exploiting rather than glorifying the hero. I scanned my current work, and I was ashamed; I realized that I needed new inspiration and could not look to Mathewson to provide it [175].

Jackie subsequently "stayed away from the Polo Grounds in 1912," choosing instead to frequent "the museums and galleries," as well as other "attractions of the city that [he'd] always ignored in favor of a ballgame" (175–176). While the 1905 championship ring is the final material gift Jackie gives Mathewson, the pitcher's aura clearly drives Jackie to seek artistic re-birth, a gift Jackie receives without he nor Mathewson realizing the pitcher has offered it. As Hyde relates, the *process* of gift-giving can supercede the material value of any items offered or exchanged: "The nourishment flows both ways. When we have fed the gift with our labor and generosity, it grows and feeds us in return. The gift and its bearers share a spirit which is kept alive by the motion among them, and which in turn keeps them both alive" (36). While Mathewson only physically *gives* Jackie the single material gift mentioned above, the pitcher clearly provides Jackie with the inspiration to develop and maintain a successful artistic career balanced between the gift and the market economies. The balance, however, shifts when Jackie visits the dying (though he would live another six years) pitcher in a Chicago hotel room during the infamous Black Sox World Series of 1919. Following an encounter with Hugh Fullerton during which the famed sportswriter relates Mathewson's disgust with the efforts of the Black Sox to throw the 1919 World Series, Jackie agrees to visit the pitcher alone in his hotel room. The conversation, which begins with Mathewson offering condolences to Jackie for the death of his daughter, quickly changes in tone when Jackie mentions Eli's name. During the resulting exchange, Jackie admits that he has in his pocket $40,000, money he plans to lay on the Reds in order to save Eli from a betting catastrophe and financial ruin, and asks Mathewson, "'I must know if these rumors are true ... if the Series were honest I'd let Eli fall of his own misjudgment, but if he's caught up in foul play...'" (260). Rather than providing Jackie with a straight answer, Mathewson, "almost wallowing in religiosity" (Solomon 105), launches into a monomaniacal diatribe where he confesses his own failings on the field in 1908 and 1912, his inability to control Hal Chase's influence on the Reds, and finally casts himself as a Christ–figure.

This exchange, particularly Mathewson's bizarre response, threatens and ultimately destroys the gift-sphere that has bound together pitcher and jeweler for nearly twenty years, in the process re-conceiving the relationship into one based on profit seeking. Jackie admittedly comes to Mathewson's Congress Hotel room to seek what amounts to inside information, yet quickly puts aside his request in the face of the pitcher's adamant reaction. Rather than attempting to dissuade Jackie from placing the bet, Mathewson instead infers that Jackie has a *duty* as "celebrant" to forsake his brother in order to preserve the already-compromised integrity of the game. By requesting — nearly *demanding*— that Jackie cast aside his familial bonds and perceived duties, Mathewson basically becomes no better than McGraw in seeking to "acquire [this gift] through an act of will" (xi), a stark departure from his gracious acceptance of Jackie's earlier gifts. In insisting that Jackie has a duty to forsake his brother, Mathewson displays a consciousness of his own market value and status as a commodity.

Interestingly, in an interview with Daniel A. Nathan, Greenberg points to this exchange as an element of the text he would change: "'I wish that I could bring back the last couple of pages of that novel and re-do them. Because I don't think I got it quite right. If I had to write it again, I'd just have Mathewson asleep and let Jackie play out the whole dialogue in his mind. I wouldn't have Mathewson say a word'" (12). Mathewson's silence at this moment, perhaps, would have reciprocated both the rings and the adoration he perceives Jackie as giving him, in effect making a silent offering or gift: the opportunity for Jackie to reconcile his relationship with baseball and Mathewson against the familial bond and make a decision without coercion, instead of reorienting it toward a more communal basis for interaction. Unveiling Mathewson's madness as he does in the existing text enables Greenberg to more fully develop the Mathewson-as-Christ-like-savior-figure motif and provide Jackie a certain *sense* of choice of action, yet can he realistically — from the reader's standpoint — deny the dying Mathewson's implication that helping save Eli would be the equivalent of dicing for Christ's robe "while He suffered on the cross?" (263). By allowing Mathewson to speak, Greenberg not only alters the gift-exchange economy the pitcher and Jackie have shared, but also destroys the illusion that has provided Jackie with an artistic identity.

Jackie, who maintains he is "not an educated man" (260), displays an awareness that belies both his self-image as well as Solomon's characterization of him as "a naïve immigrant jeweler" (85). This awareness of boundaries not only keeps him from setting foot on a major league field but also enables him to ascertain the finality of the hotel room exchange with Mathewson, maintaining in *The Celebrant's* Epilogue, "It was my happiness to celebrate his perfection" (269). Thus Jackie demonstrates a willingness to accept the emotional toll brought forth from participating in a gift exchange economy, as well as an awareness that gifts, according to Hyde, "*must always move*" (4).

Jackie certainly benefits from building a gift exchange economy wherein he gives material gifts in exchange for the intangible inspiration he receives from watching Mathewson pitch, yet while Jackie "moves" his gift by in turn producing jewelry that theoretically brings joy to people across the country (who may well offer a purchased piece as a gift to a loved one), Mathewson takes his rings to the grave, "the triple diamond on his finger and the others in the leather box at his feet" (268). Throughout *The Celebrant*, Jackie displays a prescience that the gift-sphere he constructs lacks permanence, an ironically market-driven perspective given Arthur's declaration in 1918 that "'we haven't done business with Mathewson for nearly six years'" (222), and one that echoes Becker's caution that "no art world can protect itself fully or for long against all the impulses for change, whether they arise from external sources or internal tensions" (300). Jackie's gift-sphere, then, as a product of a gift-exchange economy, fittingly cycles through the same process as art worlds, which "are born, grow, change, and die" (350), a fitting parallel given baseball's inherently cyclical nature and the transformational process Jackie undergoes throughout the text.

Works Cited

Becker, Howard S. *Art Worlds*. Berkeley: University of California Press, 1982. Print.
Greenberg, Eric Rolfe. *The Celebrant*. Lincoln: University of Nebraska Press, 1983. Print.
Hyde, Lewis. *The Gift: Imagination and the Erotic Life of Property*. New York: Vintage, 1979. Print.
Kamhi, Michelle Marder. "Rescuing Art from Visual Culture Studies." *Arts Education Policy Review* 106.1 (2004): 25–31. Print.
Kates, Ronald. "'It's a player's place, not mine': Vicarious Living, Learning, and Teaching in *The Celebrant*'s Converging Narratives." *Baseball/Culture: Biennial Essays: 2002– 2003*. Jefferson, NC: McFarland, 2004. Print.
Nathan, Daniel A. "Touching the Bases: A Conversation with Eric Rolfe Greenberg." *Aethlon* 7.1 (1989): 9–19. Print.
Solomon, Eric. "'Memories of Days Past' or Why Eric Rolfe Greenberg's *The Celebrant* is the Greatest [Jewish] American Baseball Novel." *American Jewish History*. Baltimore: American Jewish Historical Society, 1995: 83–107. Print.

Playing the Field: Rube Marquard's Performance of Class Identity in Early Twentieth Century Baseball and Vaudeville

ANDREW FRIEDMAN

In August of 1908, Rube Marquard lied to the *New York World*. Recently purchased by the New York Giants for what was then the largest fee in baseball history, Marquard sent a letter of introduction to his waiting New York sports fans. The pitcher used his public statement to concoct a fictional account of his ethnicity, familial structure, and social and economic class. Marquard's portrayal of himself as a working class farmer would have a lasting impact on his career in both baseball and vaudeville. The letter appeared in the August 1st edition of editor Joseph Pulitzer's *New York World*, the nation's largest circulating conglomerate newspaper, boasting a daily run of roughly 600,000 copies (Topping). Pulitzer's success stemmed from "defining New York's working class as consumers, with leisure time and dollars to spend ... help[ing] to create markets that were vital to the health of a rapidly expanding capitalist economy" (Steele 596). Because of the paper's connection with the *World*'s middlebrow readers, Rube's claim to working class roots was just the type of news that Pulitzer's behemoth publication was eager to print.

However, interest in the working class was not isolated to Pulitzer and his readers. The plight and edification of the working class and immigrant populations was a central concern of the United States during the Progressive Era roughly between 1890 and 1920. Baseball and vaudeville businessmen seized upon this preoccupation, advertising their entertainments as instructive for both working class audiences and participants. According to Steven A. Riess, baseball advocates claimed their sport "promoted sound morality, developed good character, enhanced public health, and provided a substitute for the lost world of small-town America" (*Base* 12). Vaudeville advertised itself along similar lines, as an institution that Robert W. Snyder in *The Voice of the City* argues, provided an opportunity for upward mobility for New York's various ethnic communities while educating diverse audiences in middle-class expectations of social behavior.

In 1911, one such audience at Brooklyn's Alhambra Theatre watched vaudevillian Mabel Hite reveal a series of celebrity photographs as part of her routine. As a *Variety* reviewer noted, "one [photograph] showed Rube Marquard and the gallery was ready to tear up the seats" (Jess 18). The crowd's enthusiasm was understandable, given Marquard's fast rising fame. Just a month earlier he had helped lead the New York Giants to the World Series. Later that same year, Marquard parlayed his baseball celebrity into a successful vaudeville career. By 1913, Rube could be seen either performing skits before more than 1,700 spectators at the Palace Theatre or pitching for the New York Giants before 36,000 fans gathered at the Polo Grounds (Snyder 88, Mansch 137). By the end of his baseball career (1908–1925), Marquard had amassed a won/loss record of 201–177, and a career ERA of 3.08, for which the Veterans Committee elected him to Cooperstown in 1971. This was a significant honor for an athlete whom Bill James, baseball's foremost statistician, later identified as "the worst starting pitcher in the Hall of Fame" (170). Even at the height of Rube's vaudeville career, a critic from *Variety*, reviewing his performance in *The Suffragette Pitcher*, wrote that he was primarily "a curiosity by reason of his Giants connection" (Mark 19).

Marquard's symbolic performance of working class mobility, a narrative central to the popularity of both baseball and vaudeville in early twentieth century New York, was celebrated and promoted by both audiences. Marquard's assumed working class identity functioned as a type of currency within the marketplace of both baseball and vaudeville, demonstrating what twentieth century French theorist Pierre Bourdieu termed "symbolic capital." Randal Johnson explains that "symbolic capital refers to a degree of accumulated prestige, celebrity, consecration or honour and is founded on a dialectic of knowledge and recognition" (qtd. in Bourdieu 7). The working class, essential to the popular narratives of edification and upward mobility used to promote sports and entertainment at the turn of the century, possessed the essential element of "symbolic capital" needed to negotiate class boundaries. According to Bourdieu, this abstract capital is typically cultivated into economic capital through its owner's opportunistic maneuvering. Marquard's alleged working class background availed to him a symbolic currency that he converted into cash through achievements in baseball and vaudeville. Marquard's claim to this form of capital highlights the eagerness of both baseball and vaudeville audiences to embrace the symbolic function of class.

Examining Rube's fashioning of this working class background highlights his awareness of its symbolic power and demonstrates the ability of athletes and entertainers to satisfy the class conscious imperatives of the cultural marketplace. However, the value of symbolic capital is never uniformly applied. Although the working class was an object of fascination throughout the Progressive Era, this symbolic capital was not always convertible to economic capital or even recognized as valuable in other industries. Even so, Marquard's falsified persona was of particular value to both vaudeville and baseball, two entertainments that promoted themselves as directly linked to the welfare of the working class.

As vaudeville impresario Tony Pastor implemented a strategy for popularizing vaudeville by "cleaning house" to accommodate upper and middle-class tastes, baseball's expanding audience also required certain middle class refinements without diluting the game's essential function "to demonstrate the continued relevancy of old values and beliefs in an increasingly modern urban era" (Riess, *Base* 7). These "values" and "beliefs" were exemplified, according to Riess, by the three *myths* central to the popular conception of baseball: that the sport was "agrarian" in origin, "democratic" in its recruitment, and "integrative" in its ability to mix various classes and ethnicities within its fans and players (7). Ultimately illusory, these romantic perceptions of the game's roots and the opportunities it offered to the working classes were nonetheless valuable to early twentieth century America's democratic perception of itself as the country was transformed by industrialization, urbanization, and waves of immigration. And so, by exemplifying these "values" and "beliefs," Marquard increased his value within the industries of baseball and vaudeville.

The collective values of an industry, like baseball or vaudeville, amount to what Bourdieu terms as "fields." David Swartz summarizes fields as "areas of production, circulation, and appropriation of goods, services, knowledge, or status, and the competitive positions held by actors in their struggle to accumulate and monopolize these different kinds of capital" (117). The term is useful for understanding how the symbolic capital of class was valued as "knowledge, or status" within the seemingly disparate entertainment industries of baseball and vaudeville. By tracing Marquard's career from the baseball diamond to the vaudeville stage, I argue that his success in both fields was aided by a symbolic capital, "a form of power that is not perceived as power but as legitimate demands for recognition, deference, obedience, or the service of others" (Swartz 90). Marquard garnered this form of power through his assumption of a working class identity.

Since its professionalization in 1869, baseball has traveled a path similar to that of vaudeville, as both experienced rapid growth during the first decade of the twentieth century. From 1901 to 1908, attendance at Major League games doubled to over 7 million, while attendance at minor league games saw even greater increases (Riess, *Base* 5). This rapid growth revealed the statistical realities behind baseball's myths. The professionalization of the game not only attracted new audiences of middle class men and women but also radically changed the demographic of the players. In 1855 a dozen nonprofessional teams existed in New York City, three-fourths of which were comprised of middle class, white-collar workers. With the sport's growing popularity, however, teams recruited talented players from various class backgrounds; as a result, middle class participation dropped two-thirds, and low-level, non-manual laborers came to outnumber higher class players by a ratio of 2 to 1. This ratio stayed consistent for roughly the next fifteen years, except in the most industrialized cities (Riess, *Games* 34–36).

Meanwhile, through expansion and professionalization, baseball was becoming a potentially lucrative industry for athletes. Player salaries rose from an average of $600–$2,000 per year in 1869 to $1,400–$4,000 annually in 1901 (Dreifort 36, 38). Despite the economic gains of players, the behavior on and off the field of some of these alleged "lower class" players led critics to question the game's cultural value. The concern over the moral character of baseball players is succinctly captured in an 1872 *New York Times* editorial that contested the game's status as the nation's pastime, concluding that "in every point of view, he [the ballplayer] is an eminently undesirable person and he ought to be peremptorily and completely suppressed" ("Professional" 4). Baseball businessmen, fearing the loss of prestige and revenue, sought to rebrand their institution from the bottom up through the unionization of players, and from the top down through owners who levied fines for disreputable behavior.

The most effective method of curbing these disturbing patterns of player behavior was through the recruitment of middle class, college educated men. Managers found these athletes capable, disciplined, educated, and, equally important, emblematic of middle class values. By the turn of the century, players were rewarded for their middle class behavior with upper middle class salaries. The shift in player demographics continued until 1910, as by then 75 percent of ballplayers had attended high school and 25.8 percent attended college. Nationally, less than 5 percent of college-aged Americans attended post-secondary school in 1910 (Riess, *Base* 173). Not only were fewer players from the lower or working classes, but a survey of their fathers' occupations found that the number of non-manual laborers was double that of the national average (172). The cleaning up of baseball had succeeded, but at the expense of excising those working class players whom spectators expected to see realizing the American dream on the field.

Likewise, the demographic of the fan base had changed drastically. Despite Albert G. Spalding's assertion that baseball was played and watched by "a cosmopolitan people, knowing no arbitrary class distinctions, acknowledging none," the grandstands had become as exclusionary of the working class as the playing field" (6). The sport's ties to the working class were wearing thin, as those fans were increasingly prohibited from attending games due to rising ticket prices and late afternoon start times of contests. By 1920, tickets ranged, on average, from $0.50 to $1.65, while twenty years earlier the standard price of admission was only 25 cents (Riess, *Base* 41–43). Turn-of-the-century games began between three and four o'clock in the afternoon and were not played on Sundays, when skilled and unskilled laborers had the day off. These start times were scheduled to accommodate the white collar work schedule and were planned so that the game would end with enough time for fans to make it home for dinner. Baseball's expansionism, appeals to the middle class, and resulting economic gains had threatened to undermine the sport's claim that it continued to embody agrarian values and democratic inclusiveness.

Eight months prior to the *World*'s publication of Rube Marquard's false biography, baseball told its largest and most enduring falsehood. In an attempt to resolve a dispute over the origins of baseball, former player, team owner, and sporting goods magnate Albert G. Spalding assembled a commission to render a decision on the game's roots. Named after National League president A.G. Mills, the Mills Commission, was comprised of two United States senators and various baseball officials, businessmen, and players. The Commission concluded that firstly, "Base Ball had its origin in the United States;" and secondly "that the first scheme for playing it, according to the best evidence obtainable to date, was devised by Abner Doubleday, at Cooperstown, New York, in 1839" (qtd. in Spalding 19). Though founded on speculative and erroneous evidence, which was later disputed, "[t]his genesis immediately became part of the conventional wisdom" (Riess, *Base* 16). The Commission's findings were instrumental not only in ensuring substantial wealth for its members, all of whom had a vested interest in the game's continued success, but their conclusions also helped to solidify the sport's symbolic capital during a period of flux within American culture. At the start of the twentieth century, nearly 75 percent of New York City's inhabitants were foreign born (Riess, *Games* 93). The confirmation that baseball, an instrument thought capable of disseminating American values to this new population, was rural, domestic in origin, and founded by a Northern Civil War General, strengthened the sport's symbolic value as an authentically American pastime, capable of assimilating and producing model Americans in line with emerging national cultural norms.

Long before the downtown editorial rooms of the *New York World* Building opened in 1890, Joseph Pulitzer's working class consumers had begun to congregate uptown in the burgeoning vaudeville theatres of Times Square. Between 1865 and 1875, Tony Pastor, a New York singer and songwriter performing in downtown saloons, legitimized variety acts by staging shows that appealed to men and women of different classes. By moving his theatres further uptown over time (from the Bowery to Union Square to Broadway), Pastor attracted new middle class audiences while continuing to cater to working class demographics through newspaper advertisements, which included maps to the theatres' new locations. Alcohol, prostitution, smoking, and other perceived vices were eliminated or, in some cases, hidden in backrooms, giving his theatres an air of respectability, while offering a welcoming venue to middle class men and women (Snyder). The content of Pastor's variety performances walked the line between "providing 'hearty, genial, racy' entertainment," enjoyed by his downtown working-class crowd and acts that attracted women and families. Other than relocating his theatres to draw a new demographic of customers, Pastor's transformation was primarily cosmetic. Snyder asserts that Pastor essentially switched "from running a saloon that presented variety theatre to running a variety theatre that served drinks on the side" (18).

At the turn of the century, vaudeville had largely replaced variety, by wholly divorcing itself from its vices and origins in downtown saloons. Vaudeville simply retained the structure of its previous variety form, presenting "a series of individual acts strung together to produce a complete bill of entertainment" (Snyder 12). The governing principle was to "stage shows with something for everyone"; therefore, any given vaudeville program presented a diverse style of talents in hopes of appealing to an equally broad public (xiii). A typical evening's entertainment included musical numbers, acrobatic stunts, comic sketches, short dramas, celebrity appearances, and animal tricks. Peaking in the first decade of the twentieth century, vaudeville's prominence was all but extinguished by the Great Depression.

Vaudeville's transformation into a middle class entertainment, begun by Pastor, was fully realized through the efforts of B.F. Keith and Edward F. Albee. A pair of New England entrepreneurs who met while working in P.T. Barnum's circus, Keith and Albee appeased moral reformers and courted middle class families by imposing strict limits on the material presented within their theatres. These reforms earned their network of theatres the moniker "The Sunday School Circuit" (Snyder 28). The two vaudeville entrepreneurs enforced their brand of middle class entertainment by using placard-carrying ushers, who instructed audiences not to stomp their feet or canes, laugh too loudly, and to otherwise remain silent during the performance (32). These rules conformed to middle class expectations of social behavior that were still deeply rooted in Victorian notions of etiquette.

Keith and Albee's model stretched nation-wide with their creation of The Association of the Vaudeville Managers of the United States. The Association nearly monopolized the vaudeville circuit, becoming the primary and centralized intermediary between performers and venues. Although this organization gave rise to performers' unions such as the White Rats, the broader effect was to homogenize vaudeville in line with middle class ethics and norms. The transformation was rapid and stark. Vaudeville in the 1880s "was created largely by people from immigrant and working class backgrounds who supplied both its talent and audiences"; by 1916 it was serving mass audiences through a national circuit of over 906 theatres and 20,000 performers whose routines were selected by Keith and Albee to appeal to middle class tastes (43, 76).

Although subject to the same reforms and expansions that transformed baseball, vaudeville preserved some of its symbolic value by remaining a career path open to immigrant and working class populations. Even while courting middle class audiences, vaudeville continued to provide opportunities for upward mobility to New York's various ethnic communities, with top acts receiving as much as $2,500 per week. Vaudeville wages offered an increase from the earnings of domestic workers and manufacturers who netted between $538 and $1,293 annually. This romantic notion of class mobility through performance, however, should be tempered by a starker reality: that while there may have been upwards of 9,000 jobs, there were, at any given time, roughly 20,000 vaudevillians looking for employment (Snyder 45–47).

Even though performance opportunities were more democratic in vaudeville, success on the stage, like on the baseball diamond, was still contingent on one's ability to produce. For both performers and athletes of the era, "[t]heir capital was in their bodies and their craftsmanship," yet appraisal of each was dependent upon particular class-bound criteria (Snyder 52). The majority of performers were "beyond the pale of native-born, middle class society," which must be understood as one of the symbolic values of the medium (44). Within vaudeville theatres, working class performers were presented with economic opportunities, while middle class audiences saw entertainers who represented the egalitarian values of American democracy and inclusiveness achieved through class mobility. Posturing as a democratic institution, baseball had turned away from working class aspirants; in contrast, vaudeville maintained an inclusiveness that was evident to the widest base of patrons. This inclusiveness was especially true with respect to women and African American performers, who outside of the stage had little opportunity for economic mobility. Those limited opportunities were epitomized by the then-segregated and still exclusively male world of Major League baseball. Therefore, the story of Rube Marquard was essential to the egalitarian image that professional baseball wished to project

Playing for the minor league Indianapolis Browns, Marquard proved himself to be an athlete ready to make the leap to the highest professional level. However, without free agency, the Browns controlled Marquard's contract and access to professional baseball. His talents were on display June 30, 1908. Before an estimated crowd of 5,500 and representatives from teams vying for his services, Rube pitched a complete game shutout (Mansch 29). Shortly thereafter the sale of Marquard's contract to the New York Giants netted the Indianapolis Browns' owner W.H. Watkins $11,000, the highest price paid for a player in the history of the sport, eclipsing the previous peak of $10,000, spent in 1887 on Mike Kelly, a ten-year veteran of the game and "baseball's first superstar" (31). Perhaps more unusual was that other well regarded minor league players of Marquard's time were routinely sold at prices ranging between $2,000 and $3,000 (31).

Larry D. Mansch, Marquard's biographer, cites two likely reasons for the unprecedented price paid for Marquard's contract. Firstly, the New York Giants were determined to win the 1908 National League pennant, and secondly, the Giants saw an opportunity to win the loyalty and financial support of New York Yankees fans, a group frustrated by their underperforming ball club. Giants management gambled that the high profile signing of Marquard would help them win games and keep the turnstiles clicking. While the Giants would fail to achieve their first goal in 1908, they saw their attendance figures jump from 538,350 to 910,000 thanks to a competitive pennant race and the well publicized signing of Marquard (Mansch 33–35).

However, the anticipation of Marquard's début resulted from more than his high asking price and previous minor league success. More importantly, he epitomized the popular image of the baseball player, and affirmed the mythos of baseball's origins through his fictitious identity. Indeed, he symbolized the "important ideals of those native-born Americans who looked back nostalgically to an idealized, pristine past and were worried about the future of their society [...] [and] suggested a way to secure that society" (Riess, *Base* 7). Through his talent and his deft attention to the cultural desires of the sport, Marquard embraced the symbolic capital necessary to embody the sport's most popular myths.

Soon after his purchase by the Giants, Marquard made two contradictory statements to his future fans. The first, in an interview with sportswriter Sid Mercer from the New York *Globe*, focused on the negotiation process to determine Rube's salary. Addressing the topic of his economic value, Marquard claimed that "if I'm worth that much to the New York club, I should get a good salary [...] when I start in fast baseball, I want a salary that will make it worthwhile" (qtd. in Mansch 36). Less than a month later, in his letter of introduction to the city of New York, written with the assistance of Sid Mercer and his former manager Charlie Carr, Rube downplayed his interest in money.

In expertly distancing himself from his exorbitant contract fee, Marquard embodied a crucial component to Bourdieu's concept of symbolic capital. Indeed, Swartz explains that for Bourdieu, people or activities "gain in symbolic power, or legitimacy, to the extent that they become separated from underlying material interests"; therefore, the less interest Rube showed in money the greater his value increased (90). This equation is completed, for Bourdieu, when the accumulated symbolic wealth is later exchanged for cold hard cash.

In the letter he co-wrote with Mercer, Marquard feigned disinterest in his salary negotiations, stating he was the last to know of his sale or the price paid, despite attending at the negotiations. Unlike his interview, Marquard's letter focused on his biography. He claimed that both of his parents were first generation French immigrants who died when he was a child and although he attended some schools in Cleveland, he "got most of [his] education on ball fields" (qtd. in Mansch 36). Although he had actually received payment from a local team before being hired by the Indianapolis Browns, Marquard had stated that he owned and operated a chicken farm outside of Cleveland to support himself. He claimed that this occupation paid better than baseball, but "the game had a fascination for [him], and [he] could not keep out of it" (qtd. in Mansch 36). Of his personality, Rube noted he was an "exponent of the simple life" and had tried "'living high'" once until his friends heckled the pretentions out of him. In closing, Rube promised "to show New York they were not 'gold-bricked' when they got [him]" (qtd. in Mansch 36). Despite largely avoiding the subject of his contract, Rube repeatedly emphasizes his disinterest in money, even suggesting that his decision to give up his chicken farm was guided not by greed, but by his "fascination" of the sport. Marquard's false statements frame him as the epitome of the idealized baseball player of the Mills Commission's report. The character he portrayed was a self-made son of immigrant parents who, as a working class farmer, had spun adversity into economic success, which he put aside to pursue his love of the American pastime. Even his nickname, "Rube," the origin of which is unknown, connotes an unsophisticated pastoral existence personifying the American dream.

Interviewed by Lawrence Ritter more than three decades after his retirement from baseball, Rube told a more truthful version of his life story with regard to his class status and upbringing (1–19). In actuality, Rube was the son of middle class second-generation German immigrants. His father, Fred

Marquard, was the Chief Engineer for the Building Inspector Department of Cleveland and lived until Rube was fifty-nine years old (Mansch 202,9). Rather than leaving his education to the ball field, Rube's father fully expected that his son would attend college. Marquard would ultimately choose the pitcher's mound over a college degree, but the option alone placed him within the top 5 percent of the nation who had access to a post-secondary education (Riess, *Base* 173). The intentions behind Rube's fabrications are unknown, but the involvement of keen baseball insiders Charlie Carr and Sid Mercer in shaping the letter's content and high profile publication suggests a carefully considered publicity campaign. What is certain, however, is that the letter, as Mansch sums it up, "was filled with falsehoods and wild concoctions and was designed to endear Rube to the fans" (36).

And so Marquard quickly cashed in, having been paid $300 for the final month of the 1908 season, in which he made a single mound appearance (Mansch 37). Despite his limited on field activity, Giants' manager John McGraw displayed Rube for the appraisal of New York's sports writers, who marveled at his height and build. In this final month, Marquard's abilities were secondary to his storied existence; as the New York *American* noted, he "may or may not prove to be a big league star, but if he falls short, it won't be because he is lacking in genuine nerve and boyish self-confidence" (qtd. in Mansch 44). Ultimately, for McGraw and for the Giants, Rube's value was evident even before he took the mound. The *Chicago Tribune* noted the strategic use of Marquard during a double-header against the Cubs. McGraw had Marquard warm up before each game as if he would be the starting pitcher, and once had his "$11,000 beauty [...] walk out on the diamond just as the game was to start," only to replace him at the last moment (qtd. in Mansch 44). McGraw's trick failed to help the Giants win either game, but the very appearance of Rube was prominent enough to warrant coverage in the newspaper, despite the fact that he spent both games on the bench.

Despite this buildup, Marquard's career with the Giants started slowly. Indeed, over his first three seasons, Rube managed to win only nine of the twenty-seven games he pitched, but these early failings were obscured by the team's success. Even with Marquard's failure to win any of the games he pitched in during the team's 1910 World Series defeat, Marquard still was able to launch a vaudeville career. Baseball players had crossed over into vaudeville for at least a decade prior to Marquard's transition. Mike Donlin, a teammate of Marquard and early ball player turned vaudevillian, advised Rube to cancel a contract he had signed to act in the play *Way Down East*, a serious piece of drama (Mansch 97). Donlin recommended that Rube first try vaudeville before tackling more serious dramatic roles. Importantly, vaudeville routines allowed Marquard to represent himself as a ball player, rather than assume the position and responsibilities of an actor playing a role. Of the numerous players crossing over from the ball field to the stage, Mansch notes that "most performed monologues, offering 'inside stuff' on the great plays they had made or famous games they had been in." To that end, "the titles of most ballplayer acts had a baseball connotation" (96). As long as Marquard traded on the reputation he had garnered on the playing field and from his persona as an idealized baseball man who crossed class boundaries, he would remain insulated from more serious criticism of his stage performances.

The danger in straying too far from the persona of the ball player became evident in Rube's first performance. When paired with vaudevillian Annie Keat for a duet and dance routine, one *Variety* reviewer quipped, "[b]aseball players are no longer stellar attractions in New York vaudeville.... Rube took one step to each three of Miss Keat's" (qtd. in Mansch 99). Marquard's decision to perform a song and dance skit minimized his celebrity, and left audiences and critics "puzzled that Rube and his partners had decided to forego the sure thing—baseball-related material." As a result, the Hammerstein's Victoria Theater "declined to renew the group's contract after their first week of performances" (Mansch 98). As a corrective, the following year Rube teamed with vaudeville agent Joe Sullivan and writer C.H. Kerr to create *Baseball Mad* with Annie Keat, which was booked at the Orpheum Theater in Brooklyn and paid Rube $1,500 per week (99). The show, well received, transferred to the Colonial in January of 1912 for two weeks. Once there, *Variety* assessed the fundamental element to the show's success, noting that the "act passed because Marquard undoubtedly is a popular young man in baseball circles, around New York, anyway" (qtd. in Mansch 99). By evoking baseball, he could convert his celebrity into economic capital within the field of vaudeville. Conversely, using the reputation he had amassed as a celebrated vaudevillian, Marquard successfully renegotiated his baseball contract with the Giants, guaranteeing himself an annual salary of $5,000 for three years (100).

Rube performed in two more successful vaudeville shows at the conclusion of the 1912 and 1913 seasons. *Breaking the Record, or the 19th Straight* (1912) and *The Suffragette Pitcher* (1913) both featured Marquard performing as himself and playing baseball. Both shows were critical and commercial successes, which traveled the national touring circuit after opening in New York. As his monthly vaudeville salary eclipsed his annual baseball pay, Marquard wielded his popularity in a final renegotiation of his contract. Using the media as his mouthpiece, Rube threatened to continue in vaudeville if he was not paid $10,000 a year for his remaining seasons with the Giants. Cornered, the Team's ownership consented to an annual salary of $7,500 (Mansch 125). The strategy had worked again, with Marquard once more trading on his symbolic capital for a bigger paycheck.

In an editorial for *The Sporting News*, W.A. Phalon sarcastically took Marquard to task for what was perceived as his mercenary bargaining tactics, asking, "[w]hat on earth could the game have done without Mr. R. Marquard? Can you imagine base ball groping, stumbling, staggering along from April to October without Mr. Marquard? There would have been nothing but empty stands and grass-grown bleachers" (qtd. in Mansch 99). Phalon's sarcasm alludes to a larger question: what would happen to baseball should it lose its symbols and myths? This question has consistently dogged the sport.

In recent decades, baseball's symbolic capital, malleable by nature, has allowed the game to rebound from its many exposed hypocrisies and adapt to the tastes of new audiences. For example, when the symbolic integrity of baseball was shattered by the vision of greedy players and owners during the 1994–95 strike, the game rebounded with home runs and staggering statistics, emphasizing power and age-defying athleticism. Close to a decade later, Jose Canseco's public unveiling of the systemic use of steroids and other performance enhancing drugs once again floored the sport, forcing both ownership and the players union to plot a new course to move public perception away from the now-blighted long-ball era.

Ultimately, baseball's symbolic capital has proven fluid through the game's history. Characteristic of baseball's ability to remake itself, atonement for the steroid-era now seems all but guaranteed with known users, so far, systematically snubbed on the immortalizing Hall of Fame ballot. Luckily, Major League Baseball, with the aid of an impressive 2010 season, is currently embracing the symbolic power of the game through pitching, epitomized by the rotation heavy Philadelphia Phillies and San Francisco Giants with young ambitious players or newly anointed superstars like Cliff Lee who heroically "left money on the table" in his 2010 high-profile contract negotiations. In 1913, as Phalon contemplated the impact Rube's retirement might have on baseball's symbolic capital, a new embodiment of baseball's myths emerged. As if frightened of Phalon's satiric prophesy that without someone like Rube the sport would become irrelevant, the following season Major League Baseball embraced another rags-to-riches biography that epitomized its mythic narratives, when the Boston Red Sox signed George Herman Ruth, the truant son of a Baltimore saloon keeper. Like Rube, he too came with a nickname that suggested a romanticized and uncorrupted American character. For short, they called him "the Babe."

Works Cited

Bourdieu, Pierre. *The Field of Cultural Production.* Ed. Lawrence D. Kritzman. New York: Columbia University Press, 1993. Print.

Dreifort, John E., ed. *Baseball History From Outside the Lines.* Lincoln: University of Nebraska Press, 2001. Print.
James, Bill. *Whatever Happened to the Hall of Fame: Baseball, Cooperstown, and the Politics of Glory.* New York: Fireside, 1995. Print.
Jess. Rev. of *Character Songs. Variety* 14 Oct 1911: 18, Print.
Jolo. Rev. of *Baseball Mad. Variety* 16 Dec 1911. Print.
Mansch, Larry D. *Rube Marquard: The Life and Times of a Baseball Hall of Famer.* Jefferson, NC: McFarland, 1998. Print.
Mark. Rev. of *The Suffragette Pitcher. Variety* 7 Nov 1913: 19. Print.
"The Professional Player." *The New York Times* 8 Mar. 1872: 4. Print.
Riess, Steven A. *City Games: The Evolution of American Urban Society and the Rise of Sports.* Chicago: University of Illinois Press, 1989. Print.
_____. *Touching Base: Professional Baseball and American Culture in the Progressive Era.* Westport: Greenwood Press, 1980. Print.
Ritter, Lawrence S. *The Glory of Their Times.* New York: Vintage, 1966. Print.
Snyder, Robert W. *The Voice of the City: Vaudeville and Popular Culture in New York.* Chicago: Ivan R. Dee, 2000. Print.
Spalding, Albert G. *America's National Game.* Lincoln: University of Nebraska Press, 1992. Print.
Steele, Janet E. "The 19th Century World Versus the Sun: Promoting Consumption (Rather than the Working Man)." *Journalism Quarterly* 67.3 (1990): 592–600. Print.
Swartz, David. *Culture & Power: The Sociology of Pierre Bourdieu.* Chicago: University of Chicago Press, 1997. Print.
Topping, Seymour. "Pulitzer biography." Pulitzer Prize Official Web site. Web. May 14. 2009.

"The Old College Try": Eddie Collins and the 1919 Black Sox

Warren Tormey

Historians of the Black Sox scandal of 1919 quickly acknowledge that Eddie Collins, the college-educated superstar, stood apart from his less-polished teammates. In the contemporary imagination, the most vivid illustration of this difference comes in the memorable courtroom scene from John Sayles' cinematic version of the Eliot Asinof historical novel, *Eight Men Out*. Pressing the second baseman to admit knowledge of his teammates' conspiracy, a prosecuting attorney sneeringly exhorts his witness to "give it the college try." In reply, the self-assured Collins flatly states that he "had [his] differences" with his teammates and publicly denies any knowledge of their gambling. Played with cool patrician flair by actor Bill Irwin, Sayles' Collins contrasts markedly with his rough-hewn Black Sox mates. Focused largely on the gradual and tragic corruption of reluctant conspirators, pitcher Eddie Cicotte and outfielder Joe Jackson, and the tainted innocence of third baseman Buck Weaver, the movie also highlights the maneuvering of the scandal's architects, first baseman Chick Gandil and shortstop Swede Risberg, and established fixers Arnold Rothstein and Sport Sullivan. Shown as the narrative's most significant "operators," they cash in most profitably on the opportunities that the Series offers to line their pockets.

Even though he plays a reduced role in Sayles production, Collins still stands apart notably. Sayles had much to draw on in portraying the college-educated Collins' detachment from his working class teammates. Asinof's most explicit comment about their derision of the second baseman is supplied early in his account. Discussing the cliques that had formed by 1919 in Charles Comiskey's bunch in the previous two seasons, Asinof notes that one group's ringleader was, of course, Gandil. The aging first baseman had taken the much younger, more impressionable Risberg under his wing, as, despite their Midwestern roots, both could claim a background in the "wilds of California" (Asinof 18). Shoeless Joe Jackson, acquired from Cleveland during the 1915 season, came to identify with their "undisciplined toughness" and fell in with them. His fellow poorly educated Southerner Lefty Williams also joined in, as did another rural Midwesterner, Happy Felsch. The other clique, led by Collins, was more "somber and subdued" (18) and included ballplayers whose competitive streaks burned more inwardly, with the exception of Ray Schalk, the "fiery little catcher," who was "hardly the sociable type" (18). Gandil and his bunch hated Schalk, who "had no trouble despising them back" (18). Rounding out this more subdued group were pitchers "Red" Faber and the youngster Dickie Kerr. Over time, these two groups established clear social demarcations on this talented, dysfunctional ballclub that continued to win despite these constantly simmering tensions.

However, Gandil's crew reserved their strongest antipathy for Collins, whom Asinof describes as "recently of Columbia University, New York City bred," and "smart enough to have his $14,500 Philadelphia salary written into his contract when Comiskey bought him" in 1915 (18). Asinof credits the friction between these groups to "clashes of temperament that grew to serious rifts" as much as to "sectional prejudices" (18), such that "Collins could legitimately complain that there were times when he didn't get a chance to feel the ball unless Ray Schalk threw it to him" (18). Even as Collins scarcely exchanged words with his infield mates, "it was incredible that, with all the bitterness and dissension, they could continue to win ball games" (18). With this description, Asinof speaks to the class differences that enabled Collins to stand apart as his teammates bristled at their parsimonious owner's ways.

Yet Collins' involvement in the Black Sox scandal merits fuller consideration, as critics generally understate his role. The perception of Collins as aloof, detached, and unconnected with the rest of his Sox teammates endures with good reason. Collins was no conspirator against Comiskey, as both were aligned by a common entrepreneurial mindset ultimately traceable to their common middle class origins and experiences of upward mobility. Despite the spotless reputation he cultivated and capitalized on throughout his playing career, Collins remains an overlooked and unwilling catalyst in the scandal, a role shaped by differences with his teammates in his social positioning and entrepreneurial savvy. In this way, his place in the story of the fixing of the 1919 World Series remains similarly understated. Like Gandil, Risberg, and other game-fixing teammates, however, Collins also importantly claims status as an "operator," one who rose above the rampant game-fixing culture among major league ballplayers of that era. Understanding his teammates' dealings more so than he ever let on, Collins turned a blind eye to them, and traded on his educated background and higher class affiliations to keep his reputation — and his "operation" — intact as the scandal broke. The writer James Farrell echoes the sentiments of many in holding Collins in the highest regard (Nathan 41–44; Anderson 91–92), and his view was not singular. Historian Daniel Nathan observes that, in coming from Philadelphia to Chicago as a three-time series champion, "Collins was, and was cast by the media as, a powerful role model. Not surprisingly, then, when the scandal was revealed, Collins emerged as the foremost of the 'Clean Sox' or 'Square Sox'" (Nathan 44). Distinguished by his talents and achievements, Collins also understood the importance of managing his image in a way that distinguished him in terms of class, background, and professional ethos from his teammates and from other major leaguers.

Collectively, Asinof and Sayles do much to portray the Black Sox within the contemporary imagination as a talented bunch on the brink of establishing their own dynasty. The enduring image of the conspirators as underpaid roughnecks and country rubes who chafed at their owner's well-known penny pinching habits justifiably endures as a convenient stereotype, as does the idea that "Cocky" Collins, the college-educated and quietly self-promoting star, struggled to adapt to his decidedly working class teammates. By 1913, when he still played for Philadelphia, Collins' reputation within the game was set. In a preview of the 1913 World Series written on October 2, *The Day Book*, a Chicago–based periodical, forecasted the position matchups for the upcoming World Series between the Giants and Athletics (which the A's won in five games). The article's anonymous writer offers both glowing tributes to Collins' ability and guarded comment about the self-advocating nature of his temperament, "generally conced(ing)" that he is "the best second baseman now in the game, considered from every angle" (9). Recounting some "big wonderful fielding" from the 1910 series, the article cites Collins' "brainwork," in conjunction with his "grand, mechanical ability," to break up a Cubs rally "with a remarkable stop toward first and throw to second for the forceout" to lead the A's to victory. Despite Collins' successes, however, the writer shows wariness toward the second baseman's character, as he "is of the high-strung type." Even so,

> his nerves never reach the breaking point. He does not become overzealous or hysterical. He has ability, knows it and wants everyone else to know it. Some people call this having the swelled head. But ballplayers refer to it as the quality that makes diamond stars [9–10].

And these habits of mind, coupled with his supreme physical skills, translated into well-honed entrepreneurial abilities. Any consideration of Collins' role within the Black Sox scandal requires a return to the beginning of the 1914 season, when the seeds of the Sox's 1919 rebellion were really planted. As an established star, Collins had used the leverage afforded by the prospect of a Federal League offer to dictate the terms of the contract he signed during 1914 season. Collins and his decorated teammates, architects of a dynasty as winners of three of the previous four World Series, were also using their bargaining power to wrest bigger salaries from Connie Mack,[1] the eternally cost-conscious manager, general manager, and newly-installed part-owner of the Philadelphia Athletics. Collins secured from Mack an uncharacteristically generous contract for between 11,500 and 14,000 dollars, "the club's protection against a jump to the Feds" (Jordan 71), in mid-season negotiations as his team loped toward the pennant. More importantly, he managed to have the reserve clause stricken from his contract which gave him an autonomy and bargaining power realized by few other players of his age.

Resentments simmered within the 1914 Athletics as the inevitable spoils of success; select teammates, notably catcher and team captain Ira Thomas, came to resent Collins' increasingly vocal temperament and cool autonomy, and the occasional demonstration of that "swelled head." They also reacted to his growing "operation," his increasingly lucrative ancillary endorsements, and especially his scribal duties with the *Philadelphia Evening Ledger*. In a climate where brand identification was in its infancy, Collins took advantage of only select endorsement and profiteering opportunities, as well as timely press coverage, which fed into his reputation as a "brainy" player. In this way, he realized a sort of "brand" status as an established star who, trading on the capital of his class background and education, gradually realized an earning potential well-beyond that available to most players. Gradually, he outgrew the role Mack envisioned for him as a superstar fixture on the A's who seemed destined for the management track, and saw increasing income-earning opportunities that would enhance his popular appeal in ways closed off to the less fiscally inclined working class ballplayers of his generation.

That 1914 season ended in disappointing fashion for the star second baseman and the rest of the American League Champion Philadelphia Athletics. After building a substantial lead early in the season, the team inexplicably seemed to lose interest and limped into the post-season. There they were humiliated in the World Series in four straight by George Stallings' scrappy and mouthy bunch of "Miracle" Braves of Boston. With the season over, Connie Mack's team headed into a winter of turmoil, as teams from the newly established Federal League continued their bidding war for the game's biggest stars. Believing that he had stockpiled enough young talent on his roster to keep his team competitive at a lower cost, Mack was content to let his All-Stars go. With the unexpected retirement of third baseman "Home Run" Baker and the sale of Collins and outfielder Eddie Murphy to the White Sox,

Mack began the process of gutting his famed "$100,000 infield" as the 1915 season rolled around. This early foray into "moneyball" strategies would prove disastrous for Mack's franchise, resulting in a decade and a half recovery period. Collins joined Holy Cross graduate Jack Barry and Gettysburg College graduate Eddie Plank as the team's most successful examples of stars who found greener pastures with the franchise's downturn.

On December 8, 1914, the *Philadelphia Evening Public Ledger*, the onetime forum for Collins' self-composed feature pieces, announced that the second baseman would be leaving Mack's crumbling American League dynasty.[2] Sold in a cost-cutting move to Charles Comiskey's crew for the 1915 season, Collins was allegedly slated for a playing manager's position. And mindful of his $50,000 price tag, the Middletown, New York, native, Columbia University graduate, and three-time series winner was also aware of the leveraging power he brought to his new team. He used this position to leverage a $15,000 contract from the notoriously penny-pinching White Sox owner, the deal placing him behind only superstars Ty Cobb and Tris Speaker in salary. Echoing the observations above, the article itself offers a prescient comment on Collins' dealings with his new team. Initially noting the "steadfastness" of the star's contract, which required that Collins approve any efforts to trade him, the anonymous writer then reasserts the second baseman's preeminence as one of the game's greatest stars. He then accounts how Collins' name has become a "by-word for baseball efficiency," citing no less of an authority than Giants' manager John McGraw to confirm this judgment. As "the world's foremost exponent of the national pastime" Collins' abilities "in all-round play" show his "quick thinking" and supreme skill in the "'headwork' end of the game" ("Sold" 3).

Despite these attributes, the article then alludes to "Cockie" Collins habit of polished self-advocacy. Although he "displays as much 'pep' as any man that ever played the game" and "is not what is commonly known as a 'crab,'" he is still "always ready to look to his own rights and to the rights of his fellow players" not by "vulgarly protesting" an umpire's bad call, but rather by "putting up a logical, though spirited argument" ("Sold" 3). Playing further to Collins' image as a player of skill and intelligence, the *Ledger's* writer also alludes to his Columbia background and praises Collins' distinctive newspaper accounts of past Series, written for that same publication. In these accounts, the second baseman was able

> to give the public a remarkable account of several world's series [sic.] besides special analytical articles, which were at once technical and interesting, a rare combination. Collins is one of the few "player writers" who does his own "stuff." He operates a typewriter rapidly and does all of his work at his home in Landsdowne ["Sold" 3].

The article concludes by reporting that Collins is slated to manage his new team with "no interference in the selection of his players" from his pennant-hungry owner ("Sold" 3).[3] In total, the article maintains that Collins had not only achieved a sort of "brand" status as an established star, but had also realized his place as a baseball entrepreneur among baseball players. Over time, his enterprises would grow from the standard endorsement deals that star players enjoyed with cigarette and sporting goods sellers. Beyond his writing about the game (in a manner worrisome to select A's teammates), they included serving as his own agent (in an era when few players brought significant leverage to salary negotiations), as well as his investing in the business side of the game while still a player. Eventually, with his playing days over, he assumed a seemingly natural place as baseball executive. He was autonomous in a way that few players in the reserve era could be — an entrepreneurial "operator" whose ventures generated some envious suspicion. But these ventures were generally cloaked in a veil of legitimacy, speaking to Collins' unique class standing in the world of professional baseball.

Having secured his reputation and accompanying salary in his final days with Mack, Collins dictated the terms of his employment in ways that few other players enjoyed. Mack's predilection for college-educated ballplayers had been well established, as he ascribed to the philosophy that those who "knew their Greek and Latin and their algebra and geometry and trigonometry" would put their "intelligence and scholarship into the game" (qtd. in Jordan 20). This bias served him well throughout the pennant winning years of the early teens, when his rosters featured the college-educated stars Plank and Barry as well as Collins. However, the culture of the team Collins joined for the 1915 season contrasted markedly with the comparatively highbrow contingent of teammates he played with during the Mackmen's glory years. One can easily oversimplify that culture clash, assuming immediately that the divide across salary and class must have only intensified despite the team's success in the years during and after World War I. The 1915 Sox were a team on the rise, with a new manager, a promising young roster, a core of young talent, and a tight-fisted owner uncharacteristically ready to spend. The year began well, but a mid-season swoon prompted Comiskey to spend again for talent, first drawing from Mack's housecleaning, but also from other clubs to supplement his outfield. He wrested Nemo Leibold, Oscar ("Happy") Felsch, and Shoeless Joe Jackson[4] from other clubs during that important season, in addition to the signings of Collins and Murphy. Despite reports that Comiskey would name him manager, Collins was initially passed over even as team captain after A's teammate Danny Murphy joined him in Chicago and was assigned the honor.

With the crumbling of Mack's White Elephants, Collins' new team would emerge, along with the Red Sox, as the class of the junior circuit as World War I approached. Fans and followers of Chicago's South Siders quickly pinned their hopes on their new stars as Collins, and soon after, Jackson quickly settled in with their new mates. The remade club finished a respectable but distant third place to the World Champion Red Sox. As his 1915 and 1916 dealings demonstrate, Comiskey earned a reputation for spending for talent to improve his club, but few players brought Collins' star power and negotiating talent to the table to bargain for salary. And despite this deliberately cultivated image of an owner willing to spend, Comiskey's parsimony toward select players was soon to become evident.

By 1916, Collins had emerged as the star and leader of this up-and-coming bunch, the team's changing dynamics reinforcing his reputation as a thinking player whose brains complemented his talents. Having finally been appointed team captain, Collins had also taken additional measures to supplement his baseball revenues, venturing into the realm of ownership while acquiring a share of the minor league Baltimore Orioles franchise in March, 1916. On July 27, 1916, *Day Book* writer Mark Shields credited Collins brainy play for guiding his team into the thick of the pennant race, in particular the confidence and skill in pitch selection of the "South Side Keystoner." Shields noted also:

> When Collins gets on first base the aliens confront a man who can move around the paths with intelligence and speed, a combination that is not too frequent on the South Side. Some members of the cast have speed but lack brains, while others have the thought waves, but lack the legwork [10].

Beyond his growing reputation as a smart player standing out on a roster of uneducated roughnecks, Collins also represented the best demonstration of Comiskey's public largesse and willingness to win.

Those 1916 White Sox missed winning the American League pennant by two games, but by 1917 they were contenders again. When Gandil arrived after a season in Cleveland, allegedly slowed by injuries but filling a key gap at first, he brought important dimensions. A former player in outlaw Mexican mining leagues and part-time bare-knuckle boxer, he embodied the rough-hewn working class personality that counterbalanced Collins' college-educated polish. Sportswriters reinforced this contrast by portraying most of the other team members as working-class rubes, and in this way Gandil's mere presence accelerated Collins' separation from his teammates. More importantly, he was an "operator" of a different sort, having contacts with gamblers on other teams. Although less "connected" than the notorious Hal Chase, Gandil still gave the underpaid Sox an established "fixer" to help them line their pockets.[5] As the 1917 Series approached, Hugh Fullerton, writing for the *Washington Times*, would again reinforce this divided image of the

White Sox, calling them "an uncertain, thoughtless, almost brainless, arratic [sic] team," talented but with "very little knowledge of the generalship of the game" ("Dope" 8). And two days later, the esteemed sportswriter singled Collins out for special criticism, praising his mechanical skills but suggesting that the star had adopted a "safety first" approach to the game, avoiding "chances when those chances involve possible injury of himself" because he "evidently realizes the value of such high class live stock" ("Far Ahead" 15). Fullerton's comments capture the resentments of many within the game toward Collins' assertive habits and entrepreneurial mindset, which exacerbated the increasingly toxic atmosphere of the Sox clubhouse. With Collins frequently singled out by the media for his entrepreneurial self-determinacy, Gandil and his cohorts inevitably came to see him in quasi-management terms, as a well-connected and better-paid company man who existed in a separate category from his teammates and was destined to fill the manager's role (in fact, beginning in 1926, Collins did manage the rebuilt Sox to two consecutive winning seasons).

Collins' biographer, Rick Huhn, notes the distinctive features of Collins' and Gandil's contrasting personalities. Put simply, "Chick Gandil did not like Eddie Collins" (141). In 1912, Collins had broken the first baseman's nose as the latter tried to break up a double play, and the relationship only deteriorated from that encounter. Huhn casts their contrast primarily as functions of temperament, salary, and success — or in other words, differences in class background that played out in income potential. Given the vast gulf separating their background and experience, a personality like Gandil's, Huhn explains, was bound to clash with Collins'. Those in Gandil's faction — including Risberg, Weaver, Jackson, Williams, and Felsch, earned between $3,000 and $6,000, and generally resented their more decorated, better paid, entrepreneurially-inclined teammate. If, as Huhn suggests, the resentments of Weaver, Gandil, and Collins seem "out of proportion to Collins' alleged conduct," in his successes they saw constant reminders of their own limitations:

> Gandil, Weaver, and the others were really condemning Eddie for what they all sought — top dollar for their performance on the ball field. The fact that Collins achieved that goal, their goal, and they had not, made him a "company" man in their eyes. Commy's "man," so to speak. The fact that he was college-educated and by nature somewhat reserved and aloof only added to the image, further separating him from that faction of his team. In reality, Collins was not Commy's "boy." The two respected each other at least in their early relationship but were never close [142].

Moreover, having "wisely negotiated a lucrative long-term contract for himself," Collins' salary with the Sox was "public knowledge," as was the fact that he was "locked in until 1920." Cobb and Speaker made more, but played on clubs more appreciative of their star power.

In contrast with their rivals, the Sox were a contentious, divided bunch whose "makeup" managed to "breed serious discontent" in a post–Federal League marketplace where player salaries were "shrinking, not rising" (Huhn 141–42). And yet, "Collins was no fool. He felt the rising animosity on the White Sox squad" (142), and by 1918 he would be well aware of their frustrations, associations, interactions, and schemes, as well as their feelings of exclusion via income differences, public stature, and class boundaries. In that "non-essential" season he took advantage of a late-season opportunity in August to enlist in the service, sparing himself the scorn reserved for Jackson, Weaver, and others who only belatedly helped in the war efforts. According to a piece in the January 4, 1919 *Chicago Eagle*, Collins was publicly considering retirement, likely wary of returning to the dysfunctional culture of his ballclub ("Retire" 7).

However, that divisive clubhouse culture only grew as the season's opening approached. On April 5, 1919, the front page of the *Eagle's* sports section featured a story that once again made public the income disparity between Collins and his mates. The piece notes that while Comiskey "has been charged by baseball fans with underpaying his ballplayers," his largesse toward his star second sacker "does not make it appear as if the players on the South side were poorly paid" ("Retire" 7). Decades later, Gandil remarked that the "sharp contract" that Collins had "finagled" with his owner made him "happier with Comiskey than we were" ("My Story" 64). Thus, as the season began, the talented, successful, chronically underpaid Black Sox once again projected their frustrations onto their second baseman, who in reply pointed to his already significant achievements, and also possessed the sufficient reserve, self-assurance, and salary, and — perhaps most importantly — the public image to handle their scorn.

In this light, one might also infer that unlike his rough-hewn teammates, Collins was ahead of his time, a baseball entrepreneur among baseball players. Leaving Philadelphia for Comiskey's rougher crews, Collins joined a roster of baseball players who depended on management for wages and salary. Ultimately, Collins sense of affinity toward Connie Mack's Athletics differed from that he felt toward Comiskey's Sox. The star second baseman might have felt some measure of class and moral kinship with the A's dynasty of the early 1910s, a prospect reinforced by his return to Mack's roster as a player-coach at his career's end. In contrast, he felt only a perfunctory connection toward the rowdier Sox bunches of the later teens, wearing the same uniform but approaching the game with a more mercenary mindset. For his part, it seems unlikely — if not impossible — that Collins had no interaction with the other members of that White Sox infield, a prospect borne out by the sheer impossibility of taking the field, sharing the clubhouse, and hitting the road with his teammates over the course of three full, albeit interrupted seasons.

Throughout these years, Collins grasped the importance of silently staying above the fray. A participant in the established practice among major leaguers, he compensated opposing players for well-timed victories over contending rivals. Even within this under-the-table reward system, he knew to cover his bases. Huhn reports that as early as 1917, Collins contributed to a Gandil–organized "collection," later maintaining that he wanted to reward the Tigers for sweeping the surging Red Sox in a mid–September series that allowed his team to claim the flag. In courtroom testimonies in the middle 1920s, Collins testified that this 1917 "donation" was meant to reward Hughie Jennings and his team for the key wins, and he even produced an old check with Gandil's name on it, properly dated in accordance with that series, to "prove" his innocence (Huhn 166). However, the testimonies of other players suggested that the payment allegedly compensated the Tigers not for the key wins, but instead for throwing four contests to the Sox over the Labor Day weekend that year. Late in the 1919 season, the Sox returned the favor. Having already won the flag, they allegedly laid down against the Tigers, who in turn received first division monies for their late season surge.

By the time the 1919 Series rolled around, Collins had shared roster space with the Black Sox conspirators for the better part of three seasons, and likely knew their schemes better than he ever let on. He also knew enough to preserve the appearance of professional loyalty and kept that public image intact, giving his best "College Try" while his conspiring teammates sputtered indecisively against that underrated 1919 Reds team. More importantly, Collins understood the importance of keeping an image of relative cohesiveness with his teammates, maintaining his silence as fix rumors flew, and knowing not to clamor publicly about teammates who had involved him marginally in previous fixes. He kept his mouth shut and hit a woeful but honest .226. Privately, he must have realized that he could not control the fact that his poorly-paid Black Sox mates were scheming to throw the Series. He had his own "schemes" going as endorser, commentator, and franchise partner, enterprises that projected entrepreneurial legitimacy and upper middle class stability. If he missed out on the winner's share of the 1919 Series, he would, unlike his teammates, make that money back in other ways.

Put simply, Eddie Collins did not hunger to win the 1919 Series, nor did he need to throw it. His poor hitting escaped close scrutiny, and his silence helped to preserve the thin veneer of cohesion despite the Sox's suspicious play. In the immediate wake of the scandal, his unscathed reputation—credited to his educated background and higher class affiliations—endured. Writing for the *Atlanta Journal*, writer Morgan Blake "surely spoke for many fans" (Nathan 44) in declaring,

> It is gratifying to note that Eddie Collins emerges from the scandal unscathed. Eddie was really the most popular member of the team and greatest second baseman of all times. He is a college man, who was trained in college athletics where a man would rather lose his life than throw a game [qtd. in Nathan 44].

Collins already earned back the losses he'd take by collecting the loser's share of the 1919 Series through his higher wages and with his ancillary business ventures. In retrospect, neither his Sox teammates nor Comiskey could fully appreciate such a figure, a superstar "college man" who used his stardom and salary as entrepreneurial springboards into other profiteering opportunities. His chronically underpaid Sox teammate, pitcher Eddie Cicotte, had grown up believing that "it was talent that made a man big" (Asinof 257). At the top of his game, however, he learned otherwise, grasping the fact that "the men who ran the show and pulled the strings and kept it working" had "fed off him (and) used him" "while pay(ing) him peanuts," and would eventually "dump him" (257), while a whole range of others made big money off his right arm. According to Asinof, Cicotte's great epiphany in the 1919 affair came when he realized that he wasn't an "operator," and those that "knew how to operate"—Gandil, Burns, Comiskey, etc.—were those who beat the system (257). Among ballplayers, Collins was arguably the best operator of all, a college-educated entrepreneur and occasional clubhouse lawyer who knew when to advocate on his behalf and when to keep quiet. He kept his "operation" above board, understanding his "Old College Try"—his policy of strategic inaction as his teammates threw the Series—would serve him well, only enhancing his public image in games, jobs, and ventures down the road.

Unlike Cicotte, Collins was sufficiently well-traveled and immersed in the business of the game to know that strains of crookedness were inevitable, and that players were responsible for supplementing their incomes with other options. Benefiting from the associations others projected onto his college background and middle-class origins, Collins thereby escaped the suspicions that ultimately exposed his less-educated, working class teammates. As the fallout from 1919 extended into the middle 1920s, Collins had the smarts and the resources to cover himself whenever his name resurfaced in later hearings about the Black Sox and the games' other gambling scandals.

So Collins operated as an ethical negotiator who knew how to play on his business instincts and class background to endure in a game that was notoriously unkind to those who lacked basic business acumen. A product of the educated upper middle class, Collins stood out on a talented Sox team otherwise dominated by working class personalities. To them, the game offered wages, whereas to him it offered social stability and income potential. As a result, he stayed in the game for another decade, drawing an increasingly higher salary and finally returning to the Mackmen to close out his career as a player-coach on a pair of championship-winning teams. Within two years, he would become an essential cog in the front office of Tom Yawkey's Red Sox franchise as the team began its re-ascent to relevance in the later 1930s.

However, in this executive role, Collins' class affiliations and background would figure in a later, more shameful chapter of the game, one in which he would negotiate the status quo through a policy of strategic inaction, standing pat as the winds of change and controversy swirled. The instincts that enabled his enduring the ever-present scorn of the 1919 Sox conspirators also allowed for his survival as a baseball executive into the late 40s when, with owner Tom Yawkey's "blessing," and as contributing architect of the Doerr-Pesky-Williams Red Sox, he presided over an organizational culture of ingrained racism that resisted change. Pressured to organize a tryout in 1946 for a trio of black prospects, including Jackie Robinson and Sam Jethroe, Collins demonstrated the same unwillingness to confront facts publicly, responding with calculated indecisiveness to the reality of "race as an emerging and ultimately unavoidable factor in the game" (Bryant 43). In fact, the tryout was a sham. And under their venerated general manager, that organization would "adopt the characteristics of a southern team, and naturally the environment would be considerably unfriendly to blacks" (Bryant 44). Although he would later claim credit for the great Sox teams of the late 1940s, he would also ignominiously stand pat as his team passed on Robinson and Jethroe as the prospect of integration loomed, a choice credited as the "real" curse of the Boston franchise.

In both 1919 and 1946, Collins' silence spoke volumes, showing that he was no innovator, or decrier of massive injustice, nor agent of social transformation. Instead, he was a solidly middle class man of entrepreneurial bearings who knew how to flourish within the context of his times. Facing two culture-shifting moments of epic proportions, he met both with genial silence and inaction, preserving climates in which he quietly held an upper hand. This policy served him well with the Comiskey White Sox of 1915–19, but would come to tarnish his legacy with the Yawkey Red Sox of the 1940s, whose inaction with Robinson, Jethroe, and later, Willie Mays, would facilitate an almost two-decade slide to the middle and later, lower rungs of the American League. Just as it was not to his benefit to call out Gandil, Risberg, and their Series-throwing cohorts for gambling in 1919, it was also not in his interests in 1946 to advocate for dramatic change in a Red Sox organization that, according to many, was defined by its culture of institutional racism into the early 1990s. Collins was a skilled talent who was distinguished by his achievement, a survivor who knew how to use the game to suit his needs, a businessman who knew how to advance his own interests, and, over time and as a result of his own efforts, a representative of a privileged economic position who knew when to keep his power intact by keeping quiet and not making waves. True to the understated, solidly middle class habits of his origins and background, he has left it to historians to shed light on this carefully crafted effort to maintain his public image, and to illuminate the contradictory nature of select moments across the career of this important baseball lifer.

Notes

1. His loyalty to the AL and Mack remained strong even as his awareness of his own emerging fiscal autonomy was enhanced. Biographer Rick Huhn writes that "the Federal League in its pursuit of him presented him an opportunity, through increased bargaining power, to increase his earnings and he took it" (Huhn 105). In this way Collins was not different from the other stars of his era, including Walter Johnson, Hal Chase, Joe Tinker, Ed Reulbach, Three Finger Brown, and teammates Eddie Plank and Chief Bender, all of whom sought bigger money by negotiating (if not signing) Federal League contracts. But Collins was one of the few players who understood the bargaining power afforded by merely negotiating with the new league, and he also understood his value to Mack's franchise beyond his ball playing accomplishments.

2. Mack's willingness to sell his star players in these two years to American League rivals can be read as an effort to keep the league afloat in the face of the threats posed by the Federals. Shortstop Barry would be gone 54 games into the dismal 1915 season, sold to the eventual World Series champion Red Sox. Unsigned pitching aces Plank and Chief Bender signed for higher wages with the new league. Only 24-year-old first baseman Stuffy McInnis remained with the A's, enduring awful 1915 and 1916 seasons, but his stint in baseball purgatory mercifully ended with a mid-season trade in 1918 to the eventual World Series Champion Boston Red Sox.

3. Even though Collins wouldn't manage the Sox until the 1926 and 1927 seasons, the remark suggests that given Collins' salary, reputation, background, and insight, Comiskey may have consulted him when making personnel decisions and other matters relating to the pursuit of a pennant, a goal the Old Roman was eager to realize.

4. Signed originally by the A's, Jackson had proved to be a bad fit with Mack's teams in his early years. The illiterate southerner found himself mostly among college-educated teammates who made him feel insecure even as they embraced his talent. Jackson later emerged as a bona-fide star with the Cleveland Naps, who by 1914 had retreated to the lower reaches of the second division. By 1915, the renamed Indians, having jettisoned their manager, Napoleon Lajoie, to Mack's sinking ship, were also willing to sell their star outfielder for whatever Comiskey was willing to pay, for, as reported in Chicago's Day Book of August 21, 1915, the Sox owner had "[given] up a healthy wad of money. The Cleveland club is in financial difficulties and need[ed] coin badly" ("Sports" 22).

5. Gandil himself spoke to this perception in an interview published in the 17 September 1956 issue of Sports Illustrated, stating that "I have often been described as one of the ringleaders of the Black Sox scandal. There's no doubt about it. I was" ("My Story" 64). He also noted that ballplayers and gamblers had "mixed freely" in those bygone years, sitting "in lobbies and bars" and "gabbing freely" ("My Story" 64). Claiming to have known Sport Sullivan since his days in Washington in 1912, he "never figured the guy as a fixer but just one who played for the percentages" ("My Story" 64). Although Gandil also identifies Cicotte as less a victim and more a principal in the scandal than Sayles' movie lets on, it is safe to say that the first baseman's connections gave the gambling underworld greater access to that divided, disgruntled Sox clubhouse.

Works Cited

Anderson, Andrew. "James T. Farrell's *My Baseball Diary*." *Baseball/Literature/Culture: Essays 1995–2001*. Ed. Peter Carino. Jefferson, NC: McFarland, 2003. Print.
Asinof, Eliot. *Eight Men Out*. 1963. New York: Holt, 2000. Print.
"Baseball—Sports of All Sorts—Boxing." *The Day Book* [Chicago] 2 Oct 1913, 9–10. Chronicling America. *Library of Congress*. Web. 8 July 2011.
"Baseball—Sports of All Kinds—Boxing." *The Day Book* [Chicago] 21 Aug 1915, 22. Chronicling America. *Library of Congress*. Web. 8 July 2011.
Bryant, Howard. *Shut Out: A Story of Race and Baseball in Boston*. Boston: Beacon Press, 2003. Print.
"Collins to Write Big Series for Evening Ledger." *Philadelphia Evening Ledger* 17 Sep 1914, 12. Chronicling America. *Library of Congress*. Web. 8 July 2011.
"Eddie Collins May Retire from Game." *Chicago Eagle* 4 Jan 1919, 7. Chronicling America. *Library of Congress*. Web. 8 July 2011.
"Eddie Collins One of High Paid Stars." *Chicago Eagle* 5 Apr 1919, 7. Chronicling America. *Library of Congress*. Web. 8 July 2011.
"Eddie Collins Sold By Mack to White Sox." *Philadelphia Evening Ledger*. 8 Dec 1914, 3. Chronicling America. *Library of Congress*. Web. 8 July 2011.
Eight Men Out. Dir. John Sayles. Perf: D.B. Sweeney, Bill Irwin, David Strathairn. Orion. 1988. Film.
Fullerton, Hugh. "Fullerton Finds it Difficult to Dope Out This Year's Big Series." *Washington Times* 24 Sep 1917, 8. Chronicling America. *Library of Congress*. Web. 8 July 2011.
_____. "Fullerton Puts Collins Far Ahead of Herzog When Second is Covered." *Washington Times* 26 Sep 1917, 15. Chronicling America. *Library of Congress*. Web. 8 July 2011.
Gandil, Chick. "This Is My Story of the Black Sox Series." Interview with Mel Durslag. *Sports Illustrated*. 17 September 1956. Microfilm.
Huhn, Rick. *Eddie Collins: A Baseball Biography*. Jefferson, NC: McFarland, 2008.
Jordan, Robert. *The Athletics of Philadelphia*. Jefferson, NC: McFarland, 2004.
Nathan, Daniel. *Saying It's So: A Cultural History of the Black Sox Scandal*. Urbana: University of Illinois Press, 2005.
Shields, Mark. "Eddie Collins Big Factor in Recent Sox Successes." *The Day Book* [Chicago] 27 Jul 1916. Chronicling America. *Library of Congress*. Web. 8 July 2011.

The "Lost Art" of Baseball: James Weldon Johnson, the Negro Leagues and the "Black Bohemia" of the Harlem Renaissance

DANIEL ANDERSON

For most of the leaders of the Harlem Renaissance, the baseball diamonds of the Negro Leagues, like the saloons and nightclubs of New York, seem to have suggested an unseemly netherworld that was best left unexplored. Other intellectuals of the era celebrated the idea of Harlem as the capital of black counter-culturalism — the flourishing "Black Bohemia," according to James Weldon Johnson. Yet they ignored sports generally and baseball in particular. Only in the decidedly bourgeois African American press did professional baseball and popular culture co-exist on the printed page. For writers with a Marxist bent, such as Claude McKay, professional sports were too easily conflated with capitalism, even when their organizers made pragmatic appeals to the anti-elitist sentiments of the middle class. For other self-proclaimed Bohemians, such as Langston Hughes, sports may simply have seemed more middlebrow and authoritarian than they could bear. As a result, the presence of sports in the everyday life of the Renaissance remains largely unexamined and creatively untouched in the literature of the period, even in those depictions of Harlem in which writers aimed for social realism and class consciousness.

Johnson, however, stands out as the exception to these many rules. In the early 1930s, at the end of the Renaissance era, Johnson paid homage to the game in two works that stand as the most extensive treatments of baseball by a major Renaissance writer. Devoting a chapter of *Black Manhattan* (1930) — his "impressionistic history" of African American culture in New York — to the athletes, their achievements, and their fame, Johnson placed ballplayers and "sportsmen" on a par with performing artists and other cultural dignitaries. For Johnson, baseball in particular was a form of popular entertainment. As such, he aligned it with the ethos of a Black Bohemia that accepted its subcultural status and resisted pressure to assimilate to the tastes of the growing African American middle class of the 1920s. In his autobiography, *Along This Way* (1933), the sport became for Johnson not a sociological subject but an art form, as he recounted his experiences as a young ballplayer. Like the minstrel tradition that gave rise to popular musical theater, African American baseball in both *Black Manhattan* and *Along This Way* emerges as a unique folk art; in these sketches, Johnson defines athletic performance as creative, indigenous, and distinctively racial.

Paradoxically, while serving as the head of the National Association for the Advancement of Colored People from 1920 to 1930, and as an elder statesman in the Renaissance movement generally, Johnson also argued for integration and assimilation in his serious critiques of the social significance of athletics. In these instances, Johnson ignored baseball almost entirely, despite the fact that the professional Negro Leagues formed in the '20s, coinciding precisely with the rise of the Harlem Renaissance. Just as a multitude of African American ballclubs competed in New York City, Johnson followed his compatriots in both the Renaissance intelligentsia and the Bohemian art world and looked beyond the game. Johnson's emphasis on integrated cultural institutions, even as he argued for the overlapping historical significance of the early, distinctive artistry of African American baseball and theater, has left him open to later criticism, especially from the more radical critics of the 1960s and '70s. Most forcibly, Harold Cruse, in *The Crisis of the Negro Intellectual* (1967), found Johnson's two strains of argument incompatible, even incoherent. "The analytical flaws in James Weldon Johnson's treatment of the Harlem Renaissance developments," Cruse argued, "reflected the lack of a definitive cultural philosophy characteristic of the other Harlem intellectuals" (Cruse 37). Cruse specifically blames Johnson and other leading intellectuals for failing to support the cause of African American theater in Harlem. His provocative questioning — "Without an ethnic theater how can there be a cultural renaissance? Or better — what is the cultural renaissance for?" (36) — could easily expand to include Negro League baseball, as it emerged and was ignored by intellectuals in the Renaissance.

Ultimately, the extent to which African American athletes managed to challenge institutional racism seems to have been of primary importance to Johnson. As a committed integrationist, he measured the social impact of professional sports by their success in achieving mainstream recognition — a principle that probably explains his apparent lack of regard for Negro League baseball in the Renaissance years. Moreover, the disappearance of a distinctively African American style of play, significant in his construction of cultural history and capable of generating romantic reminiscences in his autobiography, apparently diminished Johnson's interest in the game. Still, the attention Johnson paid to sports was not anomalous, even in the Black Bohemia he helped to name and to nurture: for Johnson, the prominence of sports in Harlem was something to celebrate, if only imaginatively and nostalgically. While the formation of the Negro Leagues in the 1920s failed to catch his fancy or attract his support, the rich history of black baseball, with its mythological aura and its connections to the worlds of nightlife and entertainment, gave the game a central role in his sketches of life and art in Black Bohemia.

Johnson's interest in athletics was evident, if not predominant, throughout his writing career. As a columnist for the *New York Age* between 1914 and 1922, he wrote periodically on sporting issues, though rarely about baseball. Frequently in those years, Johnson turned his attention to boxing—a sport he claimed never moved him—because of its demonstrable cross-cultural appeal and growing mainstream popularity; writing as a public intellectual, Johnson used his forum to argue for the appeal of interracial bouts. However, in his longer, more ruminative works, published after he had resigned from his official position with the NAACP in 1930, baseball displaced boxing as Johnson's topical sport of choice. Immediately upon his departure from public life, Johnson published *Black Manhattan* and traced the history of African American baseball in New York from its early roots in popular entertainments, such as vaudeville and minstrelsy, through its more serious and pragmatic manifestation in the Negro Leagues.

The African American press took notice of Johnson's attention to sports, even if most artists and intellectuals did not. Reviewing *Black Manhattan*, the *New York Age* observed: "Mr. Johnson is at his best in his description of the growth of the race along artistic, sporting, and theatrical lines" (Review 4). Meanwhile, the conservative critic George Schuyler, noting the "almost total absence" of references to labor and business in Johnson's book, complained in the *Pittsburgh Courier*: "It strikes me that Mr. Johnson has given a little too much space to the New York Negro's activities in the sporting and theatrical worlds: the realm of entertainment.... One feels that much of the space so utilized could have been better filled with more sociological and economic information" (Schuyler 4).[1] From a contemporary perspective, it is primarily in *Black Manhattan* that one finds any evidence that the writers of the Renaissance were aware of the history being made by the pioneering ballplayers—something well-known by the press and the people of Harlem.

By the time Johnson published *Black Manhattan*, New York City had joined Chicago and Philadelphia as one of the hotbeds of Negro League baseball. In 1920, Rube Foster organized the first African American league, the Negro National League, which consisted entirely of clubs in Midwestern cities.

The Eastern Colored League formed in 1923, including teams in Harlem (the Lincoln Giants) and Brooklyn (the Royal Giants); in addition, the Cuban Giants—still considered something of a barnstorming club despite their membership in the organized leagues—were based in New York City.[2] (A sister operation, based in Cincinnati, competed in the Negro National League.) As a testament to the popularity of Negro League ball in New York, the Bacharach Giants of Atlantic City also played occasional home games there.

Despite this flurry of activity, Johnson alludes only briefly in *Black Manhattan* to the organized clubs that achieved great popularity in the 1920s. Instead, he concentrates almost exclusively on the independent teams that played in the nineteenth century. He concedes that with the formation of the leagues, the clubs "have become better organized" and that they "play very good ball and are quite popular," but he emphasizes to a much greater extent the early barnstorming teams and "baseball comedy" (74). For Johnson, baseball is above all a form of entertainment, and, as such, it has much in common with popular theater. Indeed, in *Black Manhattan* he discusses the history of both as interrelated, central elements of New York's "Black Bohemia."

While Johnson's interest in African American baseball was unusual among the writers of the Renaissance, his designation of sports and popular theater as kindred elements of African American cultural history was not. Former boxers owned many of the saloons in the "black Tenderloin" district west of Midtown that predated the migration uptown to Harlem in the 1910s, while jockeys and other well-known athletes frequented the clubs.[3] In 1902, Paul Laurence Dunbar described one such nightclub as "a social cesspool, generating a poisonous miasma and reeking with the stench of decayed and rotten moralities" (as qtd. by J. Anderson 17).[4] By the time of the Renaissance, however, amid the fervor of Modernism and the emergence of the New Negro movement, that "stench" had been widely absorbed by the Bohemian aesthetes, and the question of whether the saloons were social cesspools or creative nerve centers became an issue of literary and intellectual debate (J. Anderson 17). To Johnson, the answer seems to have been clear and unambiguous: the clubs were places where the spirit of the Renaissance took root at the turn of the century. While writers such as Claude McKay, especially in his novel *Home to Harlem* (1928), wrote of the gamblers and sportsmen who reigned in Harlem's cabarets in terms described as both shocking and realistic, Johnson's portrait of the Bohemian subculture in *Black Manhattan* seems comparatively genteel and bourgeois. He describes not a teeming underworld, as W. E. B. DuBois saw (and reviled) in *Home to Harlem*, but a world of cultural achievement and racial pride, much like the Black Bohemia that Johnson had previously depicted in his novel, *The Autobiography of an Ex-Colored Man* (1912).

In *Black Manhattan,* Johnson quotes from his own novel extensively to portray the clubs of the early Black Bohemia, citing the *Autobiography* as "a fresher picture of these places and the times than anything I might now write" (*Black Manhattan* 75). In the *Autobiography,* Johnson had described a night club situated above a Chinese restaurant. The walls are adorned with pictures of jockeys and boxers, stage celebrities, and Frederick Douglass; the illegal bar is hidden in a closet; and the clientele consists of both black and white patrons:

> No gambling was allowed, and the conduct of the place was surprisingly orderly. It was, in short, a center of colored Bohemians and sports. Here the great prize fighters were wont to come, the famous jockeys, the noted minstrels, whose names and faces were familiar on every bill-board in the country; and these drew a multitude of those who love to dwell in the shadow of greatness [*Autobiography* 76].

The "Club," as it is simply called, constitutes a world — a subculture — that brings together artists and athletes as socially significant figures, on the basis of their comparable popularity. This use of "subculture" is informed by Raymond Williams, who classifies subcultures in two groups: "residual," which have been appropriated by the mainstream culture or which oppose the dominant culture only in novel or archaic ways; and "emergent," which arise as substantially alternative or oppositional to the mainstream culture (Williams 121–23). Peter Donnelly, analyzing sport within Williams's framework, points out that subcultures can be both residual and emergent, as in the case of boxing, which evolved from its leisure-class, "gentlemanly" origins into a marginalized subculture — even as it grew in popularity (Donnelly 127–29). While Williams and Donnelly focus on subcultures from a British perspective, their seemingly contradictory definitions of residual and emergent subcultures are clearly suited to the marginalizing of African American popular entertainment. In particular they cite baseball, as it aims for mainstream, middle-class acceptance, and attempts assimilation with the dominant white major leagues, only to marginalize itself out of existence.

Therefore, this kind of popularity, as exemplified by the Club and its denizens in Johnson's novel, is not simply "subcultural." Significantly, in Johnson's depiction, the artists and athletes are popular entertainers who draw "crowds of admirers, both white and colored" (77). What marks this underworld as subcultural is not only its racial makeup, but also its ironic popularity in mainstream culture. By the 1920s, this subculture had been entirely marginalized or utterly subsumed, as wealthy, white voyeurs from midtown Manhattan and points beyond turned Harlem's nightclubs into tourist attractions. According to critics and observers such as Langston

Hughes, the actual participants abandoned the scene as a result: "As for all those white folks in the speakeasies and night clubs of Harlem — well, maybe a colored man could find some place to have a drink that the tourists hadn't yet discovered" (Hughes 229).

Significantly, Johnson's unnamed narrator, an accomplished pianist, first encounters ragtime music at the Club. He notes that the piano players at the Club "knew no more of the theory of music than they did of the theory of the universe, but were guided by natural musical instinct and talent" (73). Despite — or in light of — the narrator's own awareness of music theory, he acknowledges the "alembic genius" of ragtime, which is proven by its international appeal. However, he also notes that the popularity of an art form can relegate it to subcultural status: "Whatever new thing the *people* like is pooh-poohed; whatever is *popular* is spoken of as not worthwhile" (73, emphasis in original). Ragtime, like the Club, can thus command the respect of artists and attract a widespread audience without winning elite approval.

Similarly, the appeal of the Club for Johnson lies in its ability to attract white patrons without compromising its original character. Much as ragtime appeals to "not only the American, but the English, the French and even the German people," the Club is "well known to both white and colored people of certain classes" (73, 75). While some clubs draw patrons with gambling and dancing, the "professional clubs," as Johnson calls them, are distinguished from "gambling-clubs" and "honky-tonks" by the talents of their performers. In *Black Manhattan*, Johnson elaborates:

> New York's black Bohemia constituted a part of the famous old Tenderloin; and, naturally, it nourished a number of the ever present vices; chief among them, gambling and prostitution. But it nourished other things; and one of these things was artistic effort. It is in the growth of the artistic effort that we are here interested; the rest of the manifestations are commonplaces [74].

In the *Autobiography*, Johnson praises the "natural" talents of popular musicians, admiringly contrasting their ignorance of musicology with his own more specialized knowledge. Describing a ragtime pianist, Johnson's narrator muses:

> I began to wonder what this man with such a lavish natural endowment would have done had he been trained. Perhaps he wouldn't have done anything at all; he might have become, at best, a mediocre imitator of the great masters in what they have already done to a finish, or one of the modern innovators who strive after originality by seeing how cleverly they can dodge about through the rules of harmony and at the same time avoid melody. It is certain that he would not have been so delightful as he was in ragtime [74].

While Johnson's praise for the musician's natural talent could be considered reductive, it remains nonetheless in the realm of the aesthetic: in the end, the ragtime musician is inarguably an artist. However, Johnson was rare among the intellectuals of the Renaissance era in distinguishing between cultivated and natural talents.

Even though the performers are more frequently patrons of the Club than players on its stage, their professionalism is the essence of Johnson's Bohemia. At the Club, minstrels perform scenes from Shakespeare on demand, while successful jockeys buy bottles of champagne by the dozens— and waiters are instructed to leave the empties on the table as free advertising that the celebrated athlete is drinking a particular brand (77–78). In both *Black Manhattan* and the *Autobiography*, Johnson emphasizes the ability of these professionals to draw crowds of admirers of both races. Some of the white patrons are voyeurs, while others are performers who play in blackface and come "to get their imitations first hand"; but all are lured by talents that are original and distinctively African American.

Johnson's history of African American baseball in *Black Manhattan* revolves almost exclusively around the "original character" of the black game. He emphasizes the popularity it achieved and, especially, the widespread coverage it attracted in the white press. "One of the main reasons why they were such good copy," Johnson writes of the nineteenth-century Cuban Giants ballclub, "was the fact that they brought something entirely new to the professional diamond; they originated and introduced baseball comedy" (*Black Manhattan* 64). Many of Johnson's ensuing descriptions are striking to the reader of today: he refers to the players' "constant banter," "pantomime," and "monkey-shines," making their performances seem close minstrelsy, something like those of the later Harlem Globetrotters. Johnson notes that, with very few exceptions, this style of play "never gained much headway" with white ballclubs, which played in a manner he describes as "dignified and rather grim" (65). The Negro League teams of the 1920s, he points out, largely adapted their style of play to compete with that of the white major leagues, leading Johnson to observe that no black team since had played in the style of the early Cuban Giants. With a hint of disapproval, he adds: "And it is probable that the clubs of today do not wish to be quite their equals" (65).

Unquestionably, the teams that the Negro clubs wished to "equal" were the big-league teams, and, despite the lure of celebrity in the subculture of Black Bohemia, they saw professionalism as the key to this goal. Under the leadership of founder Rube Foster, the Negro Leagues adapted the hierarchical structure and disciplinary approach of the historically black colleges, creating a culture of professionalism that exceeded that of their original model, the white major leagues.[5] In most oral histories of the Negro Leagues, for example, the players inevitably refer to the sense of purpose they felt upon donning their uniforms, which they called "suits" (Rogosin 71).

In the Renaissance years, this emphasis on professionalism and discipline alienated many self-proclaimed Black Bohemians. The poet Albert Rice, for example, cited his disdain for baseball in an autobiographical sketch that appeared in *Caroling Dusk* (1927), an anthology edited by Countee Cullen. After noting that he had migrated to Harlem from Washington, D.C., where his radicalism "could not become reconciled to the conservative bourgeois ideals around me," Rice called New York "an outpost of Europe," associating it with Latinate countries and contrasting it to the Germanic (Rice 176). Much as Claude McKay did in non-fictional works such as *The Negroes in America* and *A Long Way from Home*, Rice differentiates these two strains of Western culture on the basis of their tolerance for Bohemianism and on what he sees as their characteristic sports:

> Despite my radicalism I am religious. I admire the socialist form of government, and my favorite poet is Claude McKay. And some day I hope to flee the shores of this exquisite hell. My temperament is Latin. I abhor all things Anglo-Saxon. I'd rather live in the squalor of Mulberry Street, N. Y. (Little Italy) than at Irvington-on-the-Hudson. I love bull fights and dislike baseball games. I like dancing and dislike prayer meetings [177].

By beginning and concluding his dialectic with religious references, Rice defines cultural character as inherently ritualistic and deeply embedded. Similarly, Rice considers baseball a white, Protestant game, aligned with prayer meetings— provoking his disdain because it is distinctly American and therefore bourgeois–as contrasted to bullfighting, an entirely foreign sport.

Still, the worlds of professional sports and entertainment intermingled in Harlem. In their striving for equality, the ballplayers' professional approach matched that of the most successful African American entertainers, and at times, the two were directly related. When tap-dancer Bill "Bojangles" Robinson became a co-owner of the Harlem Stars in 1931, for example, the club changed its name to the New York Black Yankees and purchased old New York Yankee uniforms to wear.[6] While Robinson was known as "an avid Yankee fan" who sometimes danced atop the dugout during their games (Lanctot 453 fn38), the Black Yankees enjoyed a successful, 15-year run with Robinson as a symbol that connected them to both mainstream entertainment and the white major leagues. Although his official involvement with the Black Yankees was indirect and mostly ornamental (his manager, Marty Firkins, was the team's primary investor), Robinson's role in the team's success underscores the multifaceted connection between Negro League baseball and popular theater that runs throughout Johnson's cultural history in *Black Manhattan*.[7]

This association helps explain Johnson's apparent preference, throughout his writing on sports, to emphasize artistic performance and popularity over athletic achievement and results. Johnson's roots, like Robinson's, were in the popular theater: he had first gained fame as a writer of lyrics, sometimes in dialect, for songs composed by his brother, Rosamond. Indeed, Johnson's primary sources for the sports history in *Black Manhattan* came from the entertainment world. In his preface to the book, Johnson thanks William H. Foster, one of the earliest black filmmakers, and Irving Jones, a comedian and songwriter, for "furnishing and corroborating from their intimate knowledge of many of the facts regarding the era of professional sports and of Bohemian life in the eighties and nineties" (*Black Manhattan* xix–xx).

Johnson's interest in the history of baseball seems to have stemmed from his respect for the game's status as a broadly popular form of entertainment. The larger system of apartheid that kept the game segregated severely compromised the black baseball's social position in the first half of the twentieth century. In the Renaissance years, Johnson kept scrapbooks of clippings dealing with some sports subjects, including Jesse Owens's triumphs in the 1936 Berlin Olympics and the heavyweight championship fights of Joe Louis. In writing *Black Manhattan*, Johnson seems to have relied entirely on his personal recollections when describing the exploits of the early African American game. In his correspondence with William H. Foster, for example, Johnson specifically asked about baseball; but Foster's replies include only recollections of boxers and jockeys (JWJP, Box 7). No scrapbooks devoted to baseball exist in his collected papers; perhaps Negro League baseball's failure to reach a similar level of widespread popularity explains this absence.

While Johnson suggests in *Black Manhattan* that baseball's prominence in African American culture had faded by the 1920s, he invests the game with more lasting sheen in his memoir *Along This Way*. Even among his academic boyhood pursuits, Johnson declares: "Baseball was my game. I not only practiced steadily but studied assiduously" (36). Growing up in Florida, Johnson followed the major leagues by reading *Sporting Life*, a popular paper of the 1880s that was a forerunner to *The Sporting News*, the weekly baseball "bible," and he recounts learning to pitch under the tutelage of one of the Cuban Giants (whom he declines to name).

Johnson selectively describes his own exploits on the diamond—confined to a single game—in the same mythic tones that characterize much writing about baseball, especially accounts of the largely undocumented Negro Leagues. As a teenager, after garnering something of a reputation locally for his mastery of several trick pitches, Johnson is asked to pitch for the local semi-pro team, known as The Roman Cities, "in a big game with a formidable team from Savannah" (*Along* 37). The opposing pitcher throws with an elaborate motion, turning his back to the hitter and twirling his arm in a figure 8 as he delivers the ball. "It was an exhibition of the perfection of masculine grace," Johnson recalls. "Beautiful pitching like that is among the lost arts" (38). Despite this grace and artistry, however, this pitcher turns out to be no match for Johnson, who compares himself first to David facing Goliath and then to a "medicine man," dazzling the tribe with his conjures: "David used long-range artillery against a short sword, and I had up my sleeve what was practically a magic power, the power to make the ball suddenly change its course and dart out of the path of the on-coming bat" (38). Johnson's Jacksonville club wins easily as he strikes out sixteen batters. Most noteworthy in Johnson's description, however, is the effect his performance has on the large, vociferous, and biracial crowd. In Johnson's description, fans of both races understand and appreciate the "lost arts" on display.

Such brief moments of racial harmony are commonly invoked in appreciative sportswriting and memoirs, as geographical rivalries temporarily supersede the racial divide. Johnson notes that white fans in Jacksonville were ardent boosters of The Roman Cities, especially when they played a club from Georgia (37). In both *Along This Way* and *Black Manhattan*, he recalls that in the nineteenth century, African American teams in the South often drew as many white fans as black to their games; white southerners, he notes approvingly, were often "fierce partisans and strong supporters" of their local black teams (*Black Manhattan* 63). Lester Walton, a sportswriter and colleague of Johnson's during his tenure with the *New York Age*, held a similar opinion on the interracial support of African American baseball in the years before the organized Negro Leagues: "Just as the public like colored shows and acts, so it is fond of colored baseball players, which fact is borne out by the local and consistent manner in which white fans patronize colored semi-professional clubs" (Walton 6).

Johnson's description similarly appropriates not only the rhetoric of sport and its transformative effect on fans, but also that of popular entertainment as he characterizes the hero's enchantment of the crowd in many of the same terms he uses to describe mesmerizing musical or theatrical performances in New York City's Bohemian clubs. Fans of both races are spellbound by his performance, and, in turn, the ballfield is transformed into a vaudevillian amphitheater:

> As the game went on it assumed a humorous aspect. As many spectators as could do so crowded behind the catcher to watch the vagaries of the ball, and yells of derision greeted bewildered batters, especially when they lunged at the elusive wide-breaking out-curves.... My reward was a pretty full cup of the sensation of being a popular hero [38–39].

In his account, Johnson has become more than a baseball star. As the game assumes a "humorous aspect," its result becomes secondary to the entertainment that produces a protagonist with wide-ranging appeal. Johnson then goes one step further, by conflating theatrical performance and sport. He concludes his reminiscence by noting that after the game, a "colored sport ... said to be the best-dressed man in Jacksonville," challenges the validity of the performance by suggesting that Johnson's pitching depends on an optical illusion. Johnson declines to bet, but he demonstrates for free that his magic is the real thing. He throws the ball so that it moves around one tree and back out behind another (39). It's the stuff of a traveling carnival, folkloric and fabulous.

Like the impromptu challenge between unknown *wunderkind* and Ruthian hero that Bernard Malamud stages in *The Natural*, the sideshow recalls contests of strength and skill: it is mythic and unreal, but not a hoax in the Barnum tradition. In Malamud's novel, soon after the heroic Roy Hobbs boards a train to Chicago for his major-league tryout, he encounters the mythic Walter "The Whammer" Wambold, a star slugger reminiscent of Babe Ruth. At the next station stop, the two stage a contest of skill in which Roy uses an unusual motion ("a little like a dancer") to strike out his rival (22). The carnivalesque nature of the event upsets the vanquished star as much as the simple athletic contest does:

> Though he did not show it, the pitch had bothered the Whammer no end. Not just the speed of it but the sensation of surprise and strangeness that went with it — him batting here on the railroad tracks, the crazy carnival, the drunk catching and a clown pitching, and that queer dame Harriet, who had five minutes ago been patting him on the back for his skill in the batting cage, now eyeing him coldly for letting one pitch go by [Malamud 21–22].

Similarly, Johnson's baseball reminiscence, which begins with his reminding the reader that he had begun as a student of the sports pages, concludes firmly in the tradition of baseball lore. While affirming his appreciation for the basic skills of the game, Johnson adds elements of theater to the athletic performance. The significance lies in the interplay between theater and sports, in their broad-based popular appeal; Johnson draws on the black and white traditions of each.

While the magical realism of his memoir celebrates the potential of sports to erase the racial divide, Johnson's formal analyses of the color line take a decidedly different approach. His later sociological writings, like his earlier newspaper columns, reflect the moderate, pragmatic views concerning racial protest that were generally associated with the NAACP — and ignore the Negro Leagues and baseball altogether. A year after *Along This Way* appeared, he explained his viewpoints on the racial situation as he saw it and pointed to "the ways which, I believe, lead out" (*Negro Americans* vi). In his pamphlet *Negro Americans, What Now?* (1934), Johnson argued for increased, coordinated protests but took an ambivalent position on racial unity. He defended the political independence of the African American voter but cautioned against "voluntary isolation," which could only lead to "a permanent secondary status" (15). He further argued that even the achievements that had contributed the most to racial pride had been realized within the broader context of the dominant culture: "Our separate schools and some of our other race institutions, many of our race enterprises, the greater part of our employment, and most of our fundamental activities are contingent upon our relationship with the country as a whole" (15).

Emphasizing activities that are directly related to the "country as a whole," Johnson apparently left the Negro Leagues out of his social analyses and protest writings. By the 1920s, most of the African American athletes who had gained mainstream acclaim were boxers and jockeys; few of them played a team sport. A conspicuous exception was Paul Robeson, a football star at Rutgers who became more widely known as a singer, actor, and political activist. Indeed, in *Black Manhattan*, Johnson attributes the success of African Americans in horse racing and boxing to the individualist natures of those sports. The African American, he wrote, "never gets so fair a chance in those forms of sport or athletics where he must be a member of a team as in those where he may stand upon his own ability as an individual" (*Black Manhattan* 62–63). Although those athletes, like minstrel performers, were dangerously susceptible to subcultural marginalization and the demands (and whims) of popular opinion, they had singular opportunities to achieve mainstream popularity and to reap financial rewards. For Johnson, such popularity and rewards carried demonstrable importance in the pragmatic project of forcing change in American culture.

While Negro League baseball may have minimally impacted on mainstream American culture, it clearly helped to define the character of Harlem and other black population centers within the context of African American culture — with little or no outside capital. E. Franklin Frazier, a leading sociologist of the Harlem Renaissance era and later the author of *Black Bourgeoisie* (1951) — a seminal study of the African American middle class — noted that the social importance of sports in this group exceeded even that in American society at large (Frazier 170–72). No wonder: In the Renaissance era, Negro League baseball collectively formed the second-largest black-owned business interest in America, behind only the insurance industry (*Negro Leagues* 18). Beginning in the 1920s, team sports and organizations became influential, popular, and prevalent in African American society, although the forces of institutionalized racism, segregation, and economic discrimination stifled their roles as community-builders (Riess 109–10). Slowly and fitfully, however, Negro League baseball undoubtedly became one of the "race institutions" suggested by Johnson, working within the framework of segregation in hopes of forcing major-league baseball to integrate, whether by pragmatic or idealistic means.

Just as the game failed to capture Johnson's interest in his years of writing columns for the *Age*, however, baseball found no place in *Negro Americans, What Now?* Perhaps, amid the heady days of the early Renaissance, it carried for Johnson the taint of isolationism; perhaps, in the later days of the deepening Depression, the financial disintegration of the leagues had convinced him of their inefficacy. While the game remained ever capable of stirring his sense of artistic appreciation and cultural nostalgia, in the end organized Negro League baseball failed to move Johnson—as it also failed to move Renaissance intellectuals as disparate as Du Bois and McKay—to recognize its potential and to rally to its cause.

Notes

1. Schuyler, incidentally, was a finalist for that year's Harmon Award for Literature, for which Johnson was a judge. Chicago Defender sportswriter Frank A. Young was also a candidate, though his sportswriting was not mentioned in his dossier (James Weldon Johnson Papers; subsequent references to the collection will be cited as JWJP).

2. The Cuban Giants were the first all-black professional team, organized in 1888. Although based in New York City, they were, like many independent teams of the era, a barnstorming operation. They referred to themselves as Cubans because discrimination against Latin-Americans was thought to be not so strong as it was against African-Americans, while the Giants nickname seems to have been taken to align the club with the city's representative in the white National League, the New York Giants. In time, the "Giants" name became a codeword that indicated to fans that a particular barnstorming team was African American; most newspapers refused to print photos of black teams (James 180).

3. The boxers George Dixon, Joe Walcott, and Joe Gans all owned saloons on the West Side between Twenty-seventh and Thirty-third streets around the turn of the century (Anderson 15).

4. Anderson also cites the reminiscences of Sissle and Johnson, and quotes contemporary newspaper accounts regarding the character of the old Tenderloin clubs, but only Dunbar's takes a disapproving tone (15–18).

5. Donn Rogosin notes that Foster aimed to groom an elite "managerial class" of coaches and administrators (82). In many ways, this model of professionalism was designed to appeal specifically to the African-American middle class. See also my "'Minds of Fleetful Thoughts': Rube Foster, Dave Malarcher, and the Intellectual Project of Negro League Baseball." Baseball/Literature/Culture, eds. Ronald E. Kates and Warren Tormey (Jefferson, NC: McFarland; 2010), 57 & passim.

6. The Harlem Stars had operated for only one truncated, cash-strapped season after a long run as the Lincoln Giants. The Lincolns were founded in 1911 as a semi-pro team, playing "several times a week before crowds that often numbered in the thousands," sometimes against white all-star teams, at Olympic Field at 136th Street and Fifth Avenue (Peterson 70). By the 1920s, they had become Harlem's favored team, even though the Royal Giants of Brooklyn and the Bacharach Giants of Atlantic City also had strong New York City connections. After playing in the Eastern Colored League from its inaugural season of 1923 through its folding in 1926, the Lincolns became a powerful independent team, luring star players from weaker, poorer clubs.

7. In time, Robinson's involvement in baseball became more controversial. In 1943, Mayor Fiorello LaGuardia named Robinson to a subcommittee that was to study racial issues in the sport

and offer recommendations to major league baseball on the possibilities of integration. Several prominent African-American sportswriters, such as Rollo Wilson and Sam Lacy, objected to the inclusion of Robinson, who had come to be seen as a "largely apolitical racial symbol" (Lanctot 15, 276).

Works Cited

ARCHIVES & COLLECTIONS

James Weldon Johnson Papers. James Weldon Johnson Collection, Beinecke Rare Book and Manuscript Library, Yale University, New Haven, Conn.

BOOKS AND ARTICLES

Anderson, Daniel. "'Minds of Fleetful Thoughts': Rube Foster, Dave Malarcher, and the Intellectual Project of Negro League Baseball." *Baseball/Literature/Culture*. Eds. Ronald E. Kates & Warren Tormey. Jefferson, N. C.: McFarland, 2010. 50–63. Print.

Anderson, Jervis. *This Was Harlem: A Cultural Portrait, 1900–1950*. New York: Farrar, 1982. Print.

Cruse, Harold. *The Crisis of the Negro Intellectual*. New York: William Morrow, 1967. Print.

Donnelly, Peter. "Subcultures in Sport: Resilience and Transformation." *Sport in Social Development: Traditions, Transitions, and Transformations*. Eds. Alan G. Ingham and John W. Loy. Champaign, Ill.: Human Kinetics, 1993. 120–39. Print.

Frazier, E. Franklin. *Black Bourgeoisie: The Rise of a New Middle Class in the United States*. New York: Collier, 1962. Print.

Hughes, Langston. *The Big Sea: An Autobiography*. 1940. New York: Hill and Wang, 1993. Print.

James, Bill. *The New Bill James Historical Baseball Abstract*. New York: Free Press, 2001. Print.

Johnson, James Weldon. *Along This Way*. New York: Viking, 1933. Print.
_____. *The Autobiography of an Ex-Colored Man*. 1912. New York: Penguin, 1990. Print.
_____. *Black Manhattan*. 1930. New York: Da Capo Press, 1991. Print.
_____. *Negro Americans, What Now?* New York: Viking, 1934. Print.

Lanctot, Neil. *Negro League Baseball: The Rise and Ruin of a Black Institution*. Philadelphia: University of Pennsylvania Press, 2004. Print.

Malamud, Bernard. *The Natural*. 1952. New York: Avon, 1993. Print.

The Negro Leagues Book. Eds. Dick Clark and Larry Lester. Cleveland: Society for American Baseball Research, 1994. Print.

Peterson, Robert. *Only the Ball Was White*. New York: Oxford University Press, 1970. Print.

Rev. of *Black Manhattan*, by James Weldon Johnson. *New York Age*. 12 July 1930: 4. Print.

Rice, Albert. "Albert Rice." *Caroling Dusk: An Anthology of Verse by Negro Poets*. Ed. Countee Cullen. New York: Harper & Brothers, 1927. 176–77. Print.

Riess, Steven A. *Sport in Industrial America, 1850–1920*. Wheeling, Ill.: Harlan Davidson, 1995. Print.

Rogosin, Donn. *Invisible Men: Life in Baseball's Negro Leagues*. New York: Atheneum, 1985. Print.

Schuyler, George. "Shafts and Darts." *Pittsburgh Courier*. 19 July 1930: 4. Print.

Walton, Lester. "An Unwritten Law." *New York Age*. 17 June 1915: 6. Print.

Williams, Raymond. *Marxism and Literature*. New York: Oxford University Press, 1977. Print.

The Gentle Player: Baseball and the "Gentle People" in Irwin Shaw's Short Fiction

Nathaniel Valle

In his essay "Jews and Baseball: A Cultural Love Story," Eric Solomon asks what lies behind Jewish-Americans' complex relationship with America's pastime. This question is most often answered in a word: assimilation.[1] Baseball provided Jewish Americans with an imperialistic and social channel into the mainstream of American society.[2] During the 1920s, despite the presence of anti–Semitic sentiment,[3] urban Jews adapted to baseball as a means of connecting with American culture, despite the relatively short time they had spent within it. Burton and Benita Boxerman note that along with anti–Semitism, "the second trend affecting Jews and baseball was a growing obsession with the game. Acculturated second-generation Eastern-Europeans followed baseball almost religiously, attended more games, and often dreamed of being major leaguers" (75). Within the urban setting of New York City, baseball's allure was interestingly strong; the tight quarters of city life often made finding space for baseball impossible, yet it nonetheless remained a prevalent influence in the lives of immigrant Jews. The spatial limitations of the city might seem like a hindrance to organized baseball, but its unique place in the lives of immigrants ensured that baseball would eventually become viewed as the most American, if not most-played, sport in which a Jewish-American could participate[4]

Admittedly, boxing also occupied a large role in Judeo-American culture during the turn of the twentieth century, a point Allen Bodner makes in his work *When Boxing was a Jewish Sport*. Nonetheless, by the 1920s, baseball had largely replaced boxing as the preeminent sport of assimilation: "It was not until 1928 that the *Forward* [a prominent Jewish paper in New York City] printed another sports story, and then it did so every Friday for nearly a year ... [t]here was virtually no coverage of boxing, and when there was, it was usually not about Jewish boxers" (Bodner 17). Nowhere did this transition become more viewable than within the urban center of Judaism — New York City.[5]

Not surprisingly, Irwin Shaw, a twentieth century Jewish writer who lived from 1913 to 1984, embraced the issue of assimilation throughout his short fiction. To a much subtler and far less understood degree, he uses sporting motifs to depict a narrative of social, physical, and, in a very real sense, religious assimilation. Descriptions of sport resonate within his work, and he often employs the cultural symbol of a stadium — a physical space — to suggest that sports offer a more complete means of assimilating into American society than religion. Writing his fiction over a fifty year span (a point that he prided himself upon),[6] Shaw's stories consistently return to the idea of sport as representative of American culture and values. Even so, his use of baseball within his fiction is distinguished from his other depictions of sport, as it reflects his own assimilation narrative within American society.

As influenced by his Brooklyn upbringing, Shaw's short fiction is characterized by his frank portrayals of common individuals and an urban setting, demonstrating Shaw's own existentialist tendencies.[7] His short works depict spaces in which the only cohesion among individuals is achieved in their struggle to remain decent people. In *Irwin Shaw: A Study of the Short Fiction*, James Giles labels the characters within Shaw's fiction as the "gentle people," a reference by which Giles intends to reflect a communal thread of commonality that weaves from story to story:

> The device of placing his ordinary Americans, his "gentle people" in situations that threaten their dignity and sense of decency ... recurs throughout Shaw's fiction ... [h]e is concerned with the necessity and the difficulty of the individual preserving an integrated moral center in an increasingly complex era. Moral struggle, then, is central to Shaw's aesthetic. Clearly, in most of Shaw's stories commitment to a code of decency is the basis of an integrated sense of self and is thus the necessary foundation of individual dignity [3–4].

Shaw's characters express a prevailing code of decency in their collective desire to maintain personal dignity in a world designed to challenge their moral nature. In their struggles to realize a sense of worth and importance, they achieve a greater connection to American society. Morality and value systems within Shaw's short fiction do not derive from characters' religion or class standing, but instead from their distinctly existential self-centeredness. A character's behavior, shown in select instances, becomes the primary determinant by which readers judge that individual's moral foundations and identity. Because short fiction provides only a fragmentary glimpse of a character's reality, this code of morality seems a distinctive thread in Shaw's work.

In this way, Shaw's engagement with the gentle people reveals their key "moments of morality" as a central crux of his short fiction. These moments serve as the existential center of his stories; consequently, expressions of gentility and decency relative to one's community reveal an individual's place within that community. Primarily concerned with American assimilation, Shaw's stories offer portraits of immigrants coming to terms with a nationalistic identity that marginalizes them from American society.[8] Constantly employing "'various uses and manifestations of the flesh ... [that] challeng[e] [his characters] to remain faithful to internal beliefs for which no external verification is possible" (Giles, *Short Fiction* 7), Shaw encourages his readers to acknowledge his gentle people as common individuals defined by their encounters within social spheres. For Shaw, the most revealing social sphere exists within the settings that sport offers.

Not limited to urban settings, Shaw is also prone to place his sport narratives within domestic spaces where characters' moments of moral crisis are frequently similar. These moments reveal the social and communal foundations of his characters. Stephen Riess' *City Games: The Evolution of American Urban Society and the Rise of Sports* provides a context to help explain how Shaw depicts *gentle people* in search of opportunities to assimilate into the American mainstream: "Participation [in sport] was enjoyable and uplifting, provided a means of gaining recognition, and served as a focal point around which urbanites ... could find a community of like-minded fellows in sports clubs that supplied members with friendships, identity, and stability in the alienating and antebellum city" (154). Shaw's gentle people, fragmented and challenged within city spaces, find in gathering at sports stadiums their best chance to assimilate within a larger community.

Within Shaw's short fiction, stadiums function as places of consequence, where an individual's existential experience figures in determining his or her social identity. In a theological sense, these stadiums have a greater impact upon Shaw's characters than any other religious experiences they might have. Replacing religious cathedrals as sites of social gathering, these stadiums infuse Shaw's short fiction, according to Giles, with a humanistic self-reliance that mitigates religious experience:

> Shaw perceives the twentieth century as an age dominated by the obsession with, and the perversion of, the flesh. Modern society, tormented by old beliefs in the preeminence of the soul, is painfully aware of the absence of a moral center to the universe. Random accidents, rather than a benevolent god, control us. For Shaw, belief in humanity is all that is possible in such a fallen world: "believe in man, and take the accidents as they come" [*Short Fiction* 6].[9]

Diminished by the realist elements in Shaw's short fiction, religious experience yields to stadium experiences in determining an individual's social identity.

Within his sports arenas Shaw depicts a type of pseudo-religious experience, where individuals confront not only questions of moral and physical identity, but also those that call their social standing into question. As a natural consequence of these confrontations, the degree of one's belonging within America becomes the focal point of one's existence. Keeping in mind Amy Kaplan's belief in the imperialistic nature of American social institutions, the stadiums within Shaw's fictions depict conflicts of identity within a distinctly American space. They reflect the imperialistic nature of twentieth-century American culture's capacity to absorb individuals and reinvent them in terms of an American identity. Drawn directly from his experiences in visiting the stadiums as a young man in Brooklyn, these spaces provided him with a sphere where he could encounter American life and speech. Tony Williams notes that Shaw's ability and desire to express his own struggle to assimilate originated during trips to watch the Brooklyn Dodgers.[10] As such, a strong connection can be made between Shaw's choice of stadium as symbol and his focus upon the common, "gentle" people within his fiction.

References to baseball and baseball stadiums appear throughout his fiction, providing evidence of Shaw's connecting his own Americanness with his experiences with sport. Specifically, the motif of baseball lent Shaw a sense of this process of absorption into Americanness, a pattern that appears throughout nearly all of Shaw's fiction. In his war novel *The Young Lions*, Shaw references the Dodgers to parallel the routines of war with the routines of American life: "The Dodgers, steadfast — though weary and full of error — had passed through another day of war and thousand edged-death, and despite some nervousness down the middle of the diamond and an attack of wildness in the eighth, had won in Pittsburgh" (221). Because of his Brooklyn origins, Shaw's allegiance to the Dodgers links his usage of baseball as religion with the idea of American exceptionalism and imperialism. Shaw's life-long obsession with baseball is undeniable, extending beyond his seemingly unmitigated passion for football.[11] His own love for the Dodgers expresses Shaw's deep connection to baseball, as, like many other immigrants during the early twentieth-century, he expressed an overriding desire simply to be known as an American. As the son of first generation Jewish immigrants, Shaw did not deny his Jewishness. Rather, as Ben Yagoda mentions in *About Town: The New Yorker and the World It Made*, Shaw was "militantly assimilated, in life and in art ... [as] many ... of his protagonists were identifiably Gentile" (164). Even as stories like "Select Clientele" and "God on a Friday Night" featured distinctly Jewish settings and protagonists, Shaw's stories primarily focus on the common struggle to be American.

These stories rely upon sports imagery to portray this struggle, incorporating stadiums in ways that reveal the moral inclinations of an individual.

"The Eighty-Yard Run," Shaw's most critically respected story, features a football field as the context when a young running back fails in the moment of morality;[12] "The Girls in Their Summer Dresses" presents the stadium as a place where a young married couple considers maintaining the illusion of a happy union, ultimately foreshadowing those acts of marital infidelity that follow because of their refusal to attend a football game; in "I Stand By Dempsey," a discussion between two friends quickly escalates because of a dispute regarding what the men had seen during a recent boxing match; "Return to Kansas City" displays the reluctance of an individual to enter into a boxing arena because it will lead to a possible divorce with his wife; a lesser known story, "Stop Pushing Rocky," details the boxing arena as the place where identity is sold and bought for little more than a meal; "March, March on Down the Field" displays the resilience of football players in the immediate moments before they subject themselves to physical pain within a nearly empty stadium; in "Free of Conscience, Void of Offence," Shaw presents the stadium as a foreign concept for a young college girl, revealing her disregard for accepted social apathy towards warfare and humanity.[13] In using boxing and football motifs, the settings nonetheless influence, and frequently dominate, the unfolding action of those stories. Shaw regularly entwines the message of his stories within the context of a sports arena, exposing how the strength or weakness of an individual — whether that strength be physical or mental — is tied to that arena. For Shaw, decency is found through perseverance and fortitude, which is most vividly revealed within stadium spaces.

However, within Shaw's fiction, the common ground for his gentle people is baseball. They are associated with the group through various symbols and references that reflect Shaw's own desire to belong to America. Like the existentialist themes in his literature, Shaw's consistent return to baseball reflects his desire to belong to American society, and he relies upon baseball as a primary way to Americanize his stories. Often, baseball is associated with violence and uncouth behavior, suggesting the physical struggle that Shaw's *gentle people* must overcome in order to realize a more fully American existence. In particular, the baseball bat itself occupies a specific place as a symbol of foreboding violence in Shaw's fiction. For example, the story "The Greek General" portrays sharp violence of one scene in terms associated with baseball, shown when "Alex ... pitched forward, his head hitting the dashboard with a smart crack, like the sound of a baseball bat on a thrown ball" (362). And in the story "I Stand by Dempsey" Shaw once again invokes baseball to portray violence in suggesting that a character, as protagonist Flanagan states, "punches like he had a baseball bat in his both hands'" (83). In referencing the baseball bat, Flanagan establishes himself as a strong character who views physical strength as the worthiest component an individual can possess. In this same story, Flanagan later imposes his will upon the other characters through sheer force, showing that Shaw depicts baseball motifs in particular to symbolize an individual's power within American society. Finally, in the story "Night, Birth, and Opinion," a bartender uses the threat of "a sawed-off baseball bat he kept under the counter" (167) to quell an argument between two immigrants in his bar. In this story Shaw gives the unnamed, bat-wielding bartender a distinct sense of power and agency, two attributes that reinforce his essential Americanness.

The baseball bat (and thus baseball) is anything but a random weapon in these instances, in fact *replacing* for Shaw the concept of muscular Judaism. The author's writings seldom reference his Judaic heritage, reflecting instead those American influences that point to his desire to be respected as a writer who had distanced himself from his Brooklyn upbringing.[14] As a result, the ethos of muscular Judaism proves inconsequential within Shaw's fiction; his gentle people may be physically strong and accomplished. Yet, without any lasting connection to or associations with baseball, their physical prowess ultimately fails, and this lapse points to their existential and moral failings that rob them of any sense of belonging; portraying these failings is the focus of his fiction.[15] Though Shaw himself was an accomplished and striking physical specimen, his gentle people vary in physical fortitude, further suggesting that something beyond the ethos of muscular Judiaism factors within his stories.[16] Chester Eisinger, one of Shaw's contemporary critics, argues that Shaw refrains from displaying the concept of Muscular Judaism, choosing instead to focus on *how* the Jewish community should blend into the American fabric: "Shaw's concern for the Jew, then, turns out to be, not a hope that the Jew might exist in the United States as a unique person with his own culture who embodies an idea of Jewishness, but a hope that the Jew will assimilate himself to the dominant culture and become like everybody else" (qtd. in Giles, *Short* 208). As a result, Shaw turns to baseball and its stadiums as the predominant motif to show his hope for complete assimilation.

Because many of Shaw's stories occur within or revolve around the various stadiums of American sport, he shows the primary importance that these playing grounds have upon shaping a collective American identity. These spaces parallel Shaw's existentialist worldview, as they equate with everyday negotiations of one's space. Murray Baumgartner mentions that "[b]aseball and city life are experiences in surprise, rewarding alertness to new situations where split-second judgments depend on knowing how to take advantage of the breaks. Like walking in the city, which is a matter of feeling your way through space, so baseball is a game of the individual's constant negotiation with its changing environment" (qtd. in Eisen and Wiggins 77). Indeed, the two short stories that focus on baseball clearly illustrate the concept of American exceptionalism better than any of his other fiction. In his other works involving baseball motifs, however, Shaw invests heavily in baseball as a social institution. Not only is a relation to baseball of primary importance to an individual's narrative of assimilation, but also failing to maintain a proper relationship with the sport reveals a person's alienation from community and society.

Within the story "Main Currents of American Thought," Shaw places Andrew, a serial radio writer, firmly within the assimilationist struggle to belong to America. Perhaps his most autobiographical short story, it reveals that Shaw viewed his early life, and his struggle to assimilate, as experiences in which baseball figured prominently. In an interview with Giles, Shaw states:

> First of all, the character writes for the radio. And I, in fact, have a long paragraph in which he dictated something very much like what I used to dictate ... [a]nd he lives on the street where I lived with my mother and father and my brother. I played football in the field — baseball and football in the field opposite. I was in love with a girl like that one — and I didn't want to marry. Because I knew I'd have to support another family, and then I'd be committed to writing for money all my life [23].

Fearing that he would remain trapped by the limitations of radio writing, Shaw projects this anxiety into the main character, Andrew, of "Main Currents of American Thought." At the story's beginning, we learn that Andrew's primary income comes from the "forty dollars a script" (21) he earns from writing weekly serials. His struggle to maintain financial stability with a sense of personal integrity marks him as one of Shaw's gentle people.[17] Radio work potentially offers Andrew the creative possibility to alter his life; however, as his agent consistently reminds him, "I think you've rather run out of material'" (23). His failure to create quality radio serials parallels his social alienation; and baseball, the same institution that reprieved Shaw, offers Andrew as a means of stability and belonging within America. Longing to escape from the demands of his commercial writing to succeed at baseball, the sport becomes Andrew's reprieve, his means of belonging to America. After being told he "need[s] a vacation" (21) from his work, Andrew's exhausted mind finds respite on a local baseball field. At home seeking slumber, he hears the "neat pleasant crack of the bat and a long time later the smack of the ball in the fielder's glove" emanating from the baseball fields across the street (21).

Just as it offered to Shaw himself, the baseball field offers Andrew a chance at connecting to his society and achieving distance from his personal crisis. The old trees represent the field's timelessness, implying its rootedness in America culture, and the simplicity of the baseball game violently contrasts against the frantic pace of his profession and life. Though the story does not explicitly refer to Andrew as a Jew, Shaw references Jewish culture in a manner that seems to depict his character as a member of this ethnic community on the edges of the American mainstream.[18]

As such, in his struggle to assimilate and grasp at American exceptionalism, baseball is the best part of Andrew's world, and he recognizes its importance by making the physical space of the field his escape from the world around him. One of Shaw's gentle people, Andrew comes to regard baseball as an imperialistic determiner of his identity, one that grants him acceptance into a culture that denies him social worth because of his failure at his profession. As he muses over the amount of work he produces each week, Andrew grows more disconcerted with himself as he realizes how little value his work carries: "Twenty thousand words a week, each week, recurring like Sunday on the calendar. How many words was *Hamlet*? Thirty, thirty-five thousand?" (25), Unsurprisingly, Shaw's existential tendencies reveal themselves in this moment through Andrew's identity crisis; as the young writer's professional identity crumbles, he increasingly turns to baseball as the only meaningful determiner of identity. Baseball is not only an escape for Andrew from his situation, but revelatory of his self-worth. Hearing some boys playing on that nearby field, "Andrew felt like picking up his old glove and going out there and joining them," recalling his college days when he would play "in pickup games until it got too dark to see." Yet, "he was always tired now and ... didn't move his feet right, because he was tired, and hit flat-footed and wild" (24). In contrasting Andrew's former athletic lifestyle against his current professional and personal malaise, the scene depicts Andrew's moments of deepest despair. Within Shaw's existential worldview, this loss of hope and the recognition of one's inferiority marks Andrew's complete inability to belong to society.

Just as his work rejects him, he is also ultimately rejected by baseball, his former claim to American identity. Though a young man in years, Andrew's failures in baseball mark not only his physical insignificance, but also failure at what he believes is his life's calling: "[H]is heart lies not with radio writing, but with the play that sits unfinished on his desk, and with the books he buys but has no time to read" (Shnayerson 54). His life is captured in his diminished baseball skills, his inability to fit the uniform a suggestion that he will never escape from his current mediocrity. Finally deciding to join the game, Andrew "change[s] his clothes and put[s] on a pair of old spikes that [are] lying in the back of the closet," finding as he continues dressing that "his old pants [are] tight on him," bringing forth the realization that "[y]ou grow fat and the lines become permanent under your eyes and you drink too much" (26–7).

His old baseball uniform, much like his fading career, no longer fits him, and in both, Andrew has become a shadow of his former self. First promising

Andrew an escape, baseball ultimately seals his disappointment. In the story's final moments, when Andrew finally escapes to the field, Shaw allows the game to reveal the surprising truth about Andrew to himself — he is world-weary at twenty-five and no longer possesses any aptitude at baseball. The younger players address him as "Mister" (25), affirming his lost youth as much as underscoring the limits of his assimilation, and "he move[s] slowly. His arm hurt[s] at the shoulder when he [throws]" (28).

The second of Shaw's baseball stories, "No Jury Would Convict," takes place almost entirely within a baseball stadium. Though the story is barely over three pages long, it portrays more vividly than any Shaw story the connection between immigrants and their desire to claim an American identity. Written from the perspective of people watching the game, the story details Shaw's existential worldview, while also capturing baseball's imperialistic dimensions among immigrant populations. Published in 1937, the story was Shaw's initial work in the *New Yorker*. It depicts an exhibition game between the Jersey Giants and the Brooklyn Dodgers, centering on the conversation that takes place between unnamed fans of both teams.[19] Their namelessness suggests that these men have the status of gentle people residing within stadium environs that depict Shaw's "brilliant exercise in capturing the talk of rough-hewn New Yorkers" (Shnayerson 78). Their language, supplemented with a few well-placed details, reveals how dependent these characters are upon baseball to supply them with a sense of American identity. For them, baseball becomes a reflection of life and death, compelling these men not only to switch allegiances to root for a winning team, but to desire success at the expense of others. Essentially, the story recreates Shaw's own experiences at Dodgers games, and granting readers a look into how he came to understand assimilationist desires.

Likewise, "No Jury Would Convict" also showcases Shaw writing about American exceptionalism through the eyes of Brooklyn, his depiction of the hometown and people he knew best: "By relying on dialogue, Shaw was playing to his proven strengths ... [b]y setting his characters in Brooklyn, he was wisely writing what he knew ... Shaw's story showed an unabashed empathy for his characters" (Shnayerson 78). Shaw regularly attended baseball games in the 1920s, and used his experiences within baseball stadiums as foundation for the style and language of his works. In both stories, the meticulous description of the game reflects how Shaw came to understand baseball as a civic religion. At the beginning of the story, Shaw suggests that the baseball stadium operates as a sphere of assimilation, as a nameless character who speaks to the desire for collective identity: "'I come from Jersey City,' the man in the green sweater was saying ... 'and I might of just as well stood home. You look at Brooklyn and you look at Jersey City and if you didn't look at the uniforms you'd never tell the difference'" (107). Physically indistinguishable on the field, this nameless grouping mirrors the anonymity in the stands. However, as the fans continue to converse, they supply identities for players even as they themselves remain ambiguous and unnamed.

The focus of the story is a "man in a green sweater" (107), whose only other distinguishing feature is "his dark Greek face" (107). Though the ethnic reference seems out of place, it functions in a much greater role near the end of the story. Subjected to taunts and jeers from his fellow fans because his allegiance is with the wrong team, the man is alien to the community around him. The banter, at least towards the nameless man, is meant to separate him from the civic community of the stadium, marking him as foreign, as Shaw describes the man "put[ting] his hat on again, over his dark Greek face, the eyes deep and sad" (107). To Shnayerson, "[b]eneath the banter lies the poignancy ... of men whose strongest feelings of love and loyalty and despair are stirred by the figures on the field" (78). In articulating his frustrations, the man echoes the frustrations of an ethnic group — in this case, the Greeks — whose social position in America will remain second-rate so long as the Dodgers remain continual losers: "For twenty-three years ... I been rooting for this team. I'm getting tired of rootin for a minor league team in a major league ... [l]ook at them" (108).

As the story unfolds, the man's Greek ethnicity holds increasingly greater significance. As the man "watche[s] the play quietly for a few seconds, his Greek eyes bitter but resigned" (108), the narrative increasingly anchors the man's social alienation within the plight of his beloved Dodgers. When the Dodgers appear close to staging a miraculous comeback, Shaw writes that "the ancient Greek sorrow [was] gone from his eyes for the first time in the entire afternoon" (110). In the word "ancient" (110), Shaw casts the man's sorrow as something far greater than something simply realized in twenty-three years of constant losing. Indeed, the man's suffering recalls the superhuman sufferings in Greek tragedy, rendering him a similarly tragic figure whose hope, expressed through his beloved Dodgers, is to become more American on his own terms. However, this hope is eradicated by one final loss, as after a Dodgers error, "all hope fled from the dark Greek face," and he exclaimed, "'A man on third and one out ... and no score. They ought to shoot Grimes for that. No jury would convict'" (110). His hopes now destroyed, he does what seems best according to Shaw's existentialism: he roots for Jersey City, a winning team.[20] Consequently, "leav[ing] his heart in Brooklyn" (110), the man makes the stadium a burial ground for his ethnic and social identities. Sacrificing his personhood in pursuit of American exceptionalism, the man chooses to embrace belonging to society by switching his allegiance to Jersey City.

Ultimately, Shaw uses baseball within his literature to gain an identity that is distinctly American, as stadiums consistently appear as places where domestic imperialism reveals an individual's desire or inability to belong to American society. Shaw uses historically familiar stadiums like Ebbets Field in Brooklyn to reveal that he too experienced baseball as an imperialistic institution and accepts the level of belonging that the stadium offers. This belonging, as "No Jury Would Convict" illustrates, is the highest concern for any domestic *other*. Because baseball grants and reflects this belonging, the symbol of a stadium and baseball is the most distinguishing factor of identity within Shaw's short fiction. Viewing baseball through the lens of existentialism, Shaw uses its symbols and spaces to illustrate a desire to blend into the cultural milieu of America. Characters that embrace his vision of baseball as American are welcomed into its collective identity, while those who reject it are forever marked as domestic others. Though his stories may revolve around the gentle people, Shaw employs baseball to remind us that one moment, echoing a single at-bat, is all that many characters will experience in their struggle to enmesh themselves more fully within the fabric of America.

Notes

1. In Ethnicity and Sport in American Culture, ed. George Eisen and David Wiggins (Westport, CT: Praeger, 1994), 75. Solomon notes that "[i]n all this concentration of baseball, there is, of course, a "de-Semitization" process, a reflection as in Arthur Miller's plays or Hollywood films about the America of the assimilated Jews' hearts' desire, a place where people have the same non-distinctive names, speak the same unaccented language, and share the same undivided national loyalties" (77).

2. This imperialism points towards Amy Kaplan's definition of American exceptionalism-found in her work The Anarchy of Empire in the Making U.S. Culture-as Shaw's Jewishness, and thus his primary identity, is replaced by baseball. The institution of baseball is, by merit of its distinction as the American pastime, a societal means of transforming Shaw into a member of American society.

3. In Jews and Baseball: Entering the American Mainstream, 1871–1948, authors Burton and Benita Boxerman state, "The decade of the 1920s was a time of somewhat conflicting trends for American Jews–increased anti–Semitism and a growing love of baseball. The anti–Semitism grew out a number of factors . Following World War I ... Jews who came to the United States as part of the mass deportations of radicals from Southern and Eastern Europe were accused of being subversives ... [i]n general, this anti–Semitism meant discrimination and quotas for Jews-in immigration, in their chosen professions, and in the colleges they could attend" (75).

4. Peter Levine's Ellis Island to Ebbets Field: Sport and the American Jew Experience details how baseball worked to integrate the Jewish community despite the cramped confines of urban life: "Whether playing it in neighborhood streets and school yards or following the exploits of major league heroes, baseball, by its very status as America's National Game, symbolically permitted an immediate sense of belonging to a larger American community in ways that few other sportive experiences provided. It is this theme that defines the game's special contribution as middle ground in the process of becoming American ... [a]lthough basketball remained the most popular participatory team sport and the one rooted deeply in the social and community fabric of Jewish neighborhoods, in New York and elsewhere, baseball both informally played in the streets and in more organized settings, always attracted its share of Jewish youth" (88).

5. Eisen notes that "a preponderance of Jewish youth identified their urban roles by their ball clubs: if one grew up in Flatbush, one followed the Dodgers, in 'the shadow of Coogan's bluff,' the Giants, in the Bronx (perhaps) the Yankees" (77).

6. In the introduction to Shaw's collection Short Stories: Five Decades, Shaw presents a view of himself as a man who thrived upon his love for short fiction: "[T]here is the private and exquisite reward of escaping from the laws of consistency. Today you are sad and you tell a sad story. Tomorrow you are happy and your tale is a joyful one. You remember a woman whom you loved wholeheartedly and you celebrate her memory. You suffer from the wound of a woman who treated you badly and you denigrate womanhood. A saint has touched you and you are a priest. God has neglected you and you preach atheism. In a novel or play you must be a whole man. In a collection of stories you can be all the men or fragments of men, worthy and unworthy, who in different seasons abound in you. It is luxury not to be scorned" (i). All future references to Shaw's short fiction will come from this text.

7. A foundational (basic) understanding of Shaw's conception of existentialism is given in David Cooper's Existentialism: A Reconstruction: "First of all, human existence is said to have a concern for itself. As Kierkegaard puts it, the individual not only exists but it 'infinitely' interested in existing.' He is able to reflect on his existence, take a stance towards it, and mould it in accordance with the fruits of his reflection. Or, as Heidegger would say, humans are such that their being is in question for them, an issue for them. Second ... an existing individual is constantly in the process of becoming ... [and] no complete account of an individual can be given of a human being without reference to what he is in the process of becoming" (2).

8. Giles identifies these stories as "an examination of the American character struggling to retain a sense of national decency. The threats to this unique brand of decency are internal as well as external; and fidelity to self is as much a concern as loyalty to groups and causes" (13).

9. By "transcendence," I simply mean this term implies a connection to the divine.

10. Williams notes that "[w]ell before fifteen-year-old Irwin Shamforoff enrolled in the then tuition-free Brooklyn College in 1929, he had already experienced the Brooklyn speech patterns he would employ in his works by regularly attending the Dodgers' games" (34)

11. Shaw's intense love for football is undeniable, yet his stories about football are best interpreted as biographical expressions; the dilemma faced by Christian Darling in "The Eighty-Yard Run," one of Shaw's most frequently published and anthologized short stories, are a direct reflection of Shaw's own feelings of a "peculiarly American brand of arrested development" (Study 23) developed after partaking in World War II. Shaw's loss of innocence, not his inability to belong to America, dominates the story's movements.

12. Christian Darling, the story's protagonist, fulfills his life's ambition to be a successful player only on the practice field, rendering Christian, in the context of Shaw's existentialism, unsuccessful and doomed to isolation.

13. This story revolves around the young girl's inability to connect with her father; central to this disconnect is her failure to relate to the central event of the story, a football game: "This was in the Autumn of 1938, the year Columbia beat Yale 27–14 in the first game of the season" (143).

14. Shnayerson quotes Leslie Fielder as noting that Shaw's seemingly base desire for critical acceptance was critical to constructing his identity as distinctly American: "The two strongest impulses in all of Shaw's fiction, [Fielder] noted, were a 'desire to get the hell out of Brooklyn and stay out,' and a 'great, warm, free-floating cloud of sentimentality' and self-pity that translated into an insatiable need for success" (244).

15. This concept, explained in Todd Presner's Muscular Judaism: The Jewish Body and the Politics of Regeneration, details that "it is no longer sufficient to see the Jewish body as simply 'degenerate,' weak and effeminate and the fascist body as 'regenerate,' strong and masculine; instead, as I argue in this book, the 'muscle Jew is the prototype of the hardened, strong, hygienic, and resolutely masculine warrior" (17).

16. An interview with Shaw in The Paris Review from 1971 humorously describes Shaw's physical prowess: "He has the heavy shoulders and short legs of the backfield star, the muscled forearms of the pelota champion (which, ironically, is one of the few sports he doesn't play), and the large, close-cropped head typical of another of his pleasures-boxing. Ernest Hemingway once told the author Peter Viertel that there is only one way to handle Irwin Shaw in a boxing match: "Rip off your glove and sink your fingers deep into the bulge of his forearm, severing a few of the muscles there and rendering the arm more or less useless" (2).

17. Shaw infused this story with distinctly auto-biographical elements, as Shnayerson notes: "In a few short pages, Shaw captures a sense not only of his own life but of the times in which he lives ... [h]e does this with a storyteller's natural gift, weaving Andrew's brooding thoughts about

how to direct his characters in the next week's radio scripts with the real-life demands put upon him by his family" (54).

18. One of Andrew's radio characters, Martha, seems to embody the same feelings that Andrew feels towards his own situation, as the unclear usage of the pronoun "you" blurs the line between Martha's thoughts and his own: "Martha was Jewish. That meant you'd have to lie your way into some hotels, if you went at all, and you could never escape from one particular meanness of the world around you; and when the bad time came there you'd be, adrift on that dangerous sea" (Short Stories 26).

19. Shaw's amusingly has trouble remembering the title of the story in an interview with Giles, yet clearly remember the story's focus: "'What was the first one in the New Yorker?' 'It was something called "No Jury Would Convict." A baseball story'" (162).

20. The man's final words echo his newfound declaration to only praise the winning team: "'I'm going to root for a winning team from now on. I've been rooting for a losing team long enough. I'm going to root for the Giants. You don't know,' he said to the Brooklyn fan moving along with him, 'you don't know the pleasure you get out of rooting for a winning team'" (110).

Works Cited

Bodner, Allen. *When Boxing Was a Boxing Sport*. New York: Praeger, 2011. Print.

Boxerman, Burton Alan, and Benita W. Boxerman. *Jews and Baseball: Entering the American Mainstream, 1871–1948*. Jefferson, NC: McFarland, 2006. Print.

Cooper, David E. *Existentialism: A Reconstruction*. Malden, MA: Blackwell, 1990. Print.

Eisen, George, and David K. Wiggins, eds. *Ethnicity and Sport in North American History and Culture*. Westport, CT: Greenwood, 1994. Print.

Evans, Christopher H., and William R. Herzog. *The Faith of 50 Million: Baseball, Religion, and American Culture*. Louisville, KY: Westminster John Knox Press, 2002. Print.

Giles, James Richard. *Irwin Shaw*. Boston: Twayne, 1983. Print.

_____. *Irwin Shaw: A Study of the Short Fiction*. Boston: Twayne, 1983. Print.

Kaplan, Amy. *The Anarchy of Empire in the Making of U.S. Culture*. Cambridge: Harvard University Press, 2002. Print.

Levine, Peter. *Ellis Island to Ebbets Field: Sport and the American Jewish Experience*. New York: Oxford University Press, 1992.

Presner, Todd Samuel. *Muscular Judaism: The Jewish Body and the Politics of Regeneration*. New York: Routledge, 2007. Print.

Riess, Steven A. *City Games: The Evolution of American Urban Society and the Rise of Sports*. Chicago: Illinois University Press, 1989. Print.

Shaw, Irwin. Introduction. *Short Stories: Five Decades*. By Irwin Shaw. New York: Delacorte, 1978. i–iii. Print.

_____. *Short Stories: Five Decades*. New York: Delacorte, 1978. Print.

_____. *The Young Lions*. 1948. Chicago: Chicago University Press, 2000. Print.

Shnayerson, Michael. *Irwin Shaw*. New York: Putnam, 1989. Print.

Williams, Tony. "A Fantasy Straight Out of Brooklyn: From *the Gentle People* to *Out of the Fog*." *The Brooklyn Film: Essays in the History of Filmmaking*. Eds. John B. Manbeck and Robert Singer. Jefferson, NC: McFarland, 2003. 33–50. Print.

Yagoda, Ben. *About Town: The New Yorker and the World It Made*. New York: Scribner, 2000. Print.

Setting a Place for Mickey Mantle: Baseball, Class and Local Identity in Philip Roth's Goodbye, Columbus

MATTHEW BRUEN

The notion of local identity, broadly construed, is found in a person's deep-seated attachment to a specific locale, a cluster or habitation such as a town, village, city, borough, or quarter. Local identities often overlap, and residents form parallel identities by sharing experiences and interactions, such as participating in annual parades, reading of the local newspaper, or enduring the devastating effects of a community disaster. Individuals form isolated connections based on personal events that happen in one's hometown (marriages, deaths, meetings with one's closest friends, etc.). Local identity, then, exists in both collective and individual forms. A particular expression of local identity — sports fandom — is revealed in a reading of Philip Roth's *Goodbye, Columbus*. In the novella, Roth uses sports fandom to explore the class-based stratifications inherent in both professional athletics and in the attachments people make with places.

Often, deep-seated attachments to specific locales cause people to support a local sports team. This support usually extends to other fans, as many people feel a special bond with fellow supporters of their favorite team, even if they have never met them. In this sense, baseball fandom is a type of imagined community. As Benedict Anderson has famously argued, communities are "*imagined* because the members of even the smallest ... will never know most of their fellow members, meet them, or even hear of them, yet in the minds of each lives the image of their communion" (6). For Anderson, "communities are to be distinguished, not by their falsity/genuineness, but by the style in which they are imagined" (6). The current cultural phenomenon of "Red Sox Nation" offers an excellent example of how sports fandom is imagined in this manner. Borrowing from the language of nationalism, this "nation" imaginatively unites residents of many New English locales, as well as diasporic fans located across the globe, in collective support of the Boston Red Sox.

Not surprisingly, this type of imaginative construction oxymoronically transcends *and* reinforces class formulations. On the one hand, a Red Sox fan from Boston's gentrified Back Bay neighborhood would possess an imagined affiliation with a working class fan from the city's Dorchester neighborhood. United in their mutual support of and affection for the Red Sox, these fans are defined by their collective participation in the Nation. On the other hand, though, the Back Bay resident will be afforded many more outlets of fandom, such as season-ticketing opportunities, media-related sports packages, and apparel purchases. The Dorchester resident's fandom may be markedly different, although just as powerful, and the two people may find little common ground for non-sports related discourses. Baseball fandom, then, imaginatively marries economically disparate towns, neighborhoods, and peoples, while at the same time ensuring that class-based stratifications remain comfortably entrenched in the ballpark, in the home, and on the streets.

This class-based tension appears in the deluge of writing that occurred after the Red Sox's 2004 World Series Championship. For instance, Stephen King and Stewart O'Nan published *Faithful: Two Diehard Boston Red Sox Fans Chronicle the Historic 2004 Season*, a diary-based chronicle of the 2004 Red Sox. In it, they analyze the obsessive nature of the Nation while remaining particularly sympathetic to the ways by which individuals form connections with the team and the New England region. As King writes, "I heard one fan ... actually saying he hoped the Red Sox would *lose* a couple in St. Louis, so the team could clinch back on its home soil (yes ... he actually said 'home soil')" (392). King goes on to note that this sentiment is unrealistic and potentially damaging to the team: "I had to restrain myself from laying hands on this fellow and asking him if he remembered 1986, when we *also* won the first two, only to lose four of the next five" (392). Despite his incredulity, King understands that Red Sox fans possess an unwavering love of the team — a love that extends to the very soil that lies beneath the cleats of the players. As this anecdote reveals, this specific fan possesses as strong a bond to the soil of New England as he does his beloved Red Sox, the team that represents his hometown, his region, and his imaginative Nation. In fact, he loves the land so much, he would rather the Sox lose so that they may ultimately emerge victorious on home-ground. Indeed, unintentional conflations between place-attachment and baseball fandom, like the one described by King, commonly occur amid significant triumphs.

In the aftermath of the team's monumental win, King focuses on the (imaginative) collectivity that comes with being a participant in Red Sox Nation. According to the Maine-based author,

> Usually when I go to get the papers and my 8 A.M. doughnut, the little store up the road is almost empty. This morning it was jammed, mostly with people waiting for those newspapers to come in. The majority were wearing Red Sox hats, and the latest political news was the last thing on their minds. They wanted to talk about last night's game. They wanted to talk about the Series as a whole. They wanted to talk about the guts of Curt Schilling, pitching on his hurt ankle, and the grit of Mr. Lowe, who was supposed to spend the postseason in the bullpen and ended up securing a magical and historical place for himself in the record books instead [399].

In this idyllic Maine setting, strangers and friends unite, proudly discussing their baseball team over morning coffee and doughnuts. This type of community, though, masks difference, and it will be not be long before the "latest political news" again takes center stage.

While these Mainers enjoyed the successful aftermath of the World Series, they were not, however, afforded equal participation in the actual moment of victory. According to a *Washington Post* article published before the Series began, ticket prices neared "$2000 dollars for some seats" (Finer A3). Meanwhile, the *Post* quotes a posting on Craigslist, in which a person declared "'Trade your World Series tickets for me.... I don't really know what this entails.... Want me to baby sit your kids for 2 months? Want me to paint your house? Serve you coffee? Play the violin at your every whim? Do a dance? Paint a picture? Make a pizza? Pay you money? Tell me what to do'" (A3). Other fans waited in line for days, hoping to score a few standing room-only tickets. As the *Post* reports, "'Look, it hasn't happened since 1918, so this may be my only opportunity to see them win,' [David Millette] said, bundled in the sleeping bag in which he has spent the last five nights. 'I'm not about to miss this'" (A3). In order to attend the 2004 World Series in Fenway Park people needed to part with a considerable amount of money, sell their bodies/labor-powers/sexualities via an on-line advertising website, or spend nearly a week waiting in a line on the streets of Boston.

Stephen King, on the other hand, had the opportunity to walk on the field before the games, speak to the players, and see every play in person. Indeed, Red Sox fans with cash at their disposal did not have to degrade themselves on the Internet or suffer the indignity of living homeless-like in front of the team's ticket offices. In the aforementioned *Post* article, a richer person takes a different approach: "With a larger budget and no desire to sleep under the autumn sky in temperatures quickly approaching the freezing mark, Glenn Baker, 30, of Montreal waited outside the box office and offered to buy tickets from fans picking them up. He bought one Friday morning for less than

$1,000 from a man who was going to the game alone because he had gotten into a fight with his wife. 'Worked out well for me,' Baker said" (A3). While $1,000 was a small amount to Mr. Baker, it would have been unreasonably high to many of the people in King's country store. And yet King, his neighbors, Mr. Baker, and Mr. Millette all remain imaginatively united as Red Sox fans, even if their fan experiences signify their different class statuses. These individuals reside in the same place — New England Red Sox territory — but they do not share equal access, equal social standing, or equal voices. As an expression of place-attachment, baseball fandom almost always glosses over and reinforces social difference.

This phenomenon is not unique to the 21st century, nor is it unique to New England. In his 1959 novella, *Goodbye, Columbus*, Philip Roth explores how baseball fandom quietly but effectively represents the class divisions that mark American society. In the story, the Patimkin family leaves behind its hometown slum in 1950s Newark, New Jersey, for the suburban atmosphere of Short Hills. While the Patimkins seek to disavow their former connection to lower class Newark, they nevertheless maintain their affiliation to the New York Yankees. This vestige of their former local identity signifies baseball fandom's unifying potential while simultaneously highlighting its capacity to foster class stratification.

In order to fully understand the Patimkins' messy relationship with their former hometown and their continued love of the Yankees, one must first examine the history of baseball fandom in mid-century Newark. At this point in its history, Newark began to lose its industrial potency, and increased poverty, improved commuting opportunities, and dwindling middle class housing options drove the city's population sharply downward. In fact, Newark lost over 30,000 residents from 1950 to 1960. Many of those that left fled to the suburbs of Short Hills, Verona, South Orange, and Montclair. And, like the Patimkin family, these emigrants carried with them their affiliation with the Yankees.

Proximity to New York City and the success of the Yankees' primary minor league affiliate, the Newark Bears, made mid-century Newark a hotbed of Yankee support. During this time period, the Bears played ball in the International League, winning a number of championship banners. In 1941, when Newark–born Roth would have been eight years old, the city of Newark staged a celebratory parade for its champions. As the *New York Times* reported:

> Interest in the Bears is running high in Newark and a big civic parade will be held in their honor on Broad Street on Tuesday night. Sixty baseball teams, including semi-pro, amateur, and scholastic squads, will march, as well as more than a dozen bands. A show will follow at the Mosque Theatre, where the Bears will be introduced, with Al Schacht serving as master of ceremonies ["Openers" S4].

Parades, like the one held for the Bears, were often about something more than the titular occasion. In fact, this civic parade celebrated Newark itself, the connections its citizens had with the city, and the city's relationship with baseball. The notion of local identity is on display in this civic parade, which celebrates Newark itself as much as the connections its citizens have with the city and its teams.

Indeed, the Bears' presence in Newark had cemented the city as an important stepping-stone for ambitious young minor leaguers. During the team's run from 1926 to 1949, inaugural Hall of Famer Walter Johnson, and future Hall inductees Yogi Berra and Joe Gordon were affiliated with the team. In addition, Yankee greats Charlie Keller, Spud Chandler, and George Selkirk played for the Bears en route to the major leagues. In 1937, the Bears won 109 games, and overcame a 3–0 deficit in games to win the Little World Series in an epic contest against the Columbus Redbirds. According to the *Times*, the Bears finished '37 with "one of the most astonishing records the International League has seen in its fifty-four years" ("Swept" 12). The *Times* went on to report that "Newark broke all circuit marks by winning the regular season pennant with a 25½–game margin. The Bears ... [are] a collection of youngsters with just enough veteran strength to give the team balance.... The eight-straight record posted by Newark sets a precedent for the playoffs, started back in 1933" (12). This Bears team would later be recognized as one of the best minor league clubs of all time by the National Baseball Association, with many people believing that the '37 Bears were better than many Major League teams.

As baseball historians Bill Weiss and Marshall Wright argue, "Whether or not the Bears could have been competitive in the big leagues is a matter for speculation. The team was located near the New York press machine, which kept feeding the public stories about its prowess. What we do know is that the team completely crushed the competition in one of the three top minor leagues in the land, winning the pennant by a record amount" (431). Playing for the Bears therefore meant two things: a chance to play for the best minor league team in the country, and the opportunity for promotion to the most successful and highest-paying baseball club in American history, the New York Yankees. Being a Newark Bears fan *also* meant two things: firstly, an allegiance to the city of Newark, and almost as important, an affiliation with the Yankees.

As many well-run major league baseball teams continue to do, the mid–20th-century Yankee franchise solidified and enlarged its immense fan-base by maintaining a successful minor league affiliate in a nearby, populated locale. Therefore, to *be from* Newark in the 1930s, 40s, and 50s was to root for the Bears as much as for the Yankees. Not surprisingly, Yankee fandom figures in Roth's *Goodbye, Columbus*, a novella set in the declining industrial locale.

A long-time resident of Newark who spent his childhood rooting for the Bears, Roth has repeatedly noted baseball's impact on his literature. In his essay "My Baseball Years," Roth states that

> I am only saying that my discovery of literature, and fiction particularly, and the "love affair"—to some degree hopeless, but still earnest—that has ensued, derives in part from this childhood infatuation with baseball. Or, more accurately perhaps, baseball—with its lore and legends, its cultural power, its seasonal associations, its native authenticity, its simple rules and transparent strategies, its longueurs and thrills, its spaciousness, its suspensefulness, its heroics, its nuances, its lingo, its "characters," its peculiarly hypnotic tedium, its mythic transformation of the immediate—was the literature of my boyhood [182].

Making great use of anaphora, Roth argues that baseball itself is a type of literature. He is, of course, correct: baseball and narrative are often inseparable, and athletic competition, like fictive writing, operates as a safe psychological substitute for war, violence, and other traumatic events. Sports, however, can also function in a signifying manner. In *Goodbye, Columbus*, Roth employs baseball in this manner, with Yankee fandom marking social stratifications, geographical boundaries, and cultural perimeters.

The story's first-person narrator, Neil Klugman, is a working class librarian who holds a strong bond to his community. Describing "the marquee of a tiny art theatre," which is "jammed between a grimy-windowed bookstore and a cheesy luncheonette," Roth describes Neil's deep knowledge of Newark, an attachment so rooted that it could not help but branch out into affection (22).

Neil weaves his identity around his relationship with his hometown: with his working-class mindset, he maintains an intuitive knowledge of the processes of decay, and still refuses to leave the slowly dying city. Although his Newark local identity is strong, Neil enters into a relationship with Brenda Patimkin, an affluent student whose family has fled from the declining neighborhoods of Newark. By virtue of her family members' disavowal of Newark and their subsequent identification with the suburbs, Brenda's relationship with Neil becomes an intrusion into the Patimkins newly insulated bourgeois life. For Brenda's mother, Neil *is* Newark, and his sexual activity with her daughter serves as a symbolic reentrance of the very local connection she wishes most to disavow.

Much like the Red Sox nation example from 2004, Mrs. Patimkin's repudiation of Neil demonstrates how sports fandom and place attachment are loaded with class considerations. Indeed, peoples' geographical roots often permanently mark them from a specific class. Neil's working class Newark local identity offends the Patimkins, and ultimately serves as the reason that he ends his relationship with Brenda. Indeed, the last line of the novella marks Neil's return to his working class roots. After he returns from Massachusetts, where he has gone to see Brenda one last time, he simply states, "I was back in plenty of time for work" (Roth 97). Neil will continue working in, living in, and loving Newark. Brenda will graduate from college, marry a rich man with a local identity tethered to the suburbs, and produce children that reaffirm her family's connection to this bourgeois locale.

Near the beginning of the novella, we learn that Mr. and Mrs. Patimkin met, married, and started their family in Newark. Once they accumulated a certain amount of wealth, though, they exchanged their Newarkian local identities for suburban ones. But anyone who has ever moved away from their childhood hometown knows that these attachments die a slow, hard death, if they ever die at all. In fact, although Brenda's mother strongly disapproves of her daughter's relationship with a Newarkian, she nevertheless keeps the family's old Newark furniture in storage. By storing this furniture instead of discarding it, Mrs. Patimkin symbolically maintains her former local identity while safely entombing the family's "old furniture" in a vault:

> two wing chairs with hair-oil lines at the back, a sofa with a paunch in its middle, a bridge table, two bridge chairs with their stuffing showing, a mirror whose backing had peeled off, shadeless lamps, lampless shades, a coffee table with a cracked glass top, and a pile of rolled up shades [7–8].

Upon viewing these damaged items, Neil asks Brenda about their origins. She responds by saying they are "from Newark." After she makes this declaration, Neil envisions the two of them living together in a dirty apartment in the old post-industrial city. Despite this fantasy, Neil recognizes that he could never bring her back to Newark, and he realizes that their deteriorating relationship would eventually resemble the family's decaying furniture.

It is not only furniture that continues to tie the Patimkins to Newark. During Neil's first interaction with Brenda's brother, Ron, he is struck by the following interchange:

> "Hey, Bren," Ron said, and pushed a palm flat into the water so that a small hurricane beat up against Brenda and me.
> "What are you so happy about?" she said.
> "The Yankees took two."
> "Are we going to have Mickey Mantle for dinner?" she said. "When the Yankees win," she said so easily she seemed to have turned the chlorine to marble beneath her, "we set an extra place for Mickey Mantle" [13–4].

By symbolically setting a place at the dinner table for Mickey Mantle, the Patimkins unconsciously acknowledge their former connection to the city of Newark. Indeed, they do not really invite The Mick to dinner, but rather a vestige of their Newarkian local identity. The seat at the table, though, remains strikingly empty. In a sense Mantle — and, by extension, Newark — is both absent and present in the Patimkins' bourgeois, upper-class dining room. As a contradictory symbol, then, Mantle's empty dinner space emphasizes the Patimkins' tortured relationship to their former hometown: they can never sever their connection to Newark, but they cannot tolerate its physical presence in their lives.

It is not surprising, however, that the Patimkins choose Mantle as a symbolic stand-in for their connection to Newark, New Jersey. Like the Patimkins, Mantle overcame a humble background to enjoy financial success. Born in Oklahoma in the 1930s, Mantle spent his early years living in relative poverty. As his biographer Tony Castro notes, "The 1930s were hard times in the Oklahoma plains, characterized by the uprooted, impoverished existence of a Steinbeck novel" (4). Like a Steinbeckian character, Mantle's father farmed the Oklahomian land before finding more permanent work as a coal miner. The family survived the Great Depression, and Mickey's athletic talents allowed him to play professional baseball. The rest, of course, is recorded history: 536 home runs, three MVP awards, 16 All-Star games, a Triple Crown, and seven World Series championships.

Mantle's rise from an impoverished background to athletic superstardom spawned a powerful mythology. As Castro eloquently puts it, "In the 1950s, Mickey Mantle came to reflect the appearance and values of the dominant society in the world. He was the hero of America's romance with boldness, its celebration of power, a nation's Arthurian self-confidence in its strength during a time when we last thought that might did make right" (ix). In addition, Mantle embodied the Franklin-esque belief that with hard work, crafty intelligence, and a little luck, any American could overcome hardscrabble origins. For Roth's Patimkins, this is exactly what Mantle represented, and their similar social rise makes Mantle an appropriate — though no less contradictory — symbolic dinner guest.

Near the novella's conclusion, Neil begins to understand that Newark will ultimately separate him from Brenda and her family. As he walks the streets of the city's former Jewish neighborhood, Neil offers the following reflection:

> The neighborhood had changed: the old Jews like my grandfather had struggled and died, and their offspring had struggled and prospered, and moved further and further west, towards the edge of Newark, then out of it, and up the slope of the Orange Mountains, until they had reached the crest and started down the

other side, pouring into Gentile territory as the Scotch-Irish had poured through the Cumberland Gap. Now, in fact the Negroes were making the same migration, following the steps of the Jews, and those who remained in the Third Ward lived the most squalid of lives and dreamed in the fetid mattresses of the piny smell of Georgia nights [64].

Beginning in the 1950s patterns of movement, exodus, and migration decimated the city of Newark. Having lost so many of its citizens (including the fictional Patimkins), the city had fallen into a state of poverty and industrial decay by the mid–20th century. Even so, Neil cannot forsake his hometown. Like the blacks who refuse to let go of their Georgian heritage, Neil spurns the oasis of suburban comfort found in Short Hills, Millburn, Madison, Bernardsville, New Vernon, Mendham, and Chatham. In conclusion, Neil's strong local identity prohibits him from fully assimilating with the Patimkins; conversely, the Patimkins' repudiation of their former Newark local identities causes them to banish Neil from their social circle. And Mickey Mantle, through his empty dinner appearance, functions as a signifier of these tangled threads of class, baseball fandom, and place attachment.

Although baseball skates on the periphery of this novella, its presence reminds readers that team affiliations are often fraught with class considerations. To this extent, baseball in *Goodbye, Columbus* enables readers to grasp the growing class distances that exist between Neil and Brenda, between the Klugmans and the Patimkins, and between Newark and Short Hills. The novel also allows readers to appreciate the roles that local identity and sports fandom figure into their lives.

Works Cited

Anderson, Benedict. *Imagined Communities: Reflections on the Origins and Spread of Nationalism.* New York: Verso, 1983. Print.
Castro, Tony. *Mickey Mantle: America's Prodigal Son.* Dulles, VA: Brassey's, 2002. Print.
"Final Play-Offs Swept By Newark." *New York Times* 25 September 1937: 12. Print.
Finer, Jonathan. "In Baseball-Mad Boston, the Grand Prize; World Series Caps Long Season in the Spotlight." *Washington Post* 23 October 2004, final ed.: A3+. Print.
King, Stephen, and Stewart O'Nan. *Faithful: Two Diehard Boston Red Sox Fans Chronicle the Historic 2004 Season.* New York: Scribner, 2004. Print.
"Openers in Jersey to Draw Throngs." *New York Times* 13 April 1941: S4. Print.
Roth, Philip. *Goodbye, Columbus.* 1959. New York: Bantam, 1970. Print.
_____. "My Baseball Years." *Reading Myself and Others.* New York: Farrar, Straus, and Giroux, 1975. Print.
Weiss, Bill, and Marshall Wright. *The 100 Greatest Minor League Baseball Teams of the 20th Century.* Parker, CO: Outskirts Press, 2006. Print.

Phillip Roth's Comic Corrective
Joshua Daniel-Wariya

Philip Roth's *Great American Novel* (1974) has been called a comic "tour de farce" (Halio). Narrated by Word Smith, an eighty-seven-year-old retired sportswriter who identifies himself as an American institution on the level of Melville and Hemingway, the *GAN* is his account of baseball's forgotten third division, the Patriot League. "P-League" immortals included Gil Gamesh, baseball's only Babylonian-American, and the dashing Luke Gofannon, whose accomplishments rivaled those of Gehrig and even Ruth. In pondering why no one seems to remember the Patriot League, Smith ("Smitty") suggests that it was "not merely wiped out of business, but *willfully erased from the national memory*" (18) after being infiltrated by Soviets during the Cold War. More troubling to Smitty, however, is the American public's complacency with the sham. Mention the Patriot League on the street, he says, and people might call you crazy.

Roth calls *The Great American Novel* an experiment in "comic inventiveness" (*Reading Myself* 76). Gil Gamesh is banned from the Patriot League when he assaults an umpire with a "perfect" fastball; Gamesh later returns as a Soviet spy, having trained in Moscow and graduated from the "International Lenin School for Subversion, Hatred, Infiltration, and Terror, popularly known as SHIT" (357). Luke Gofannon has an affair with Angela Whittling Trust—a former lover of both Babe Ruth and Ty Cobb—but breaks her heart by declaring he will never love her like a good triple. Perhaps most interesting of Roth's comic inventions, however, is his narrator's knack for alliteration. When Smitty's doctor suggests that this tendency toward alliterative word play might be bad for his health, Smitty persists, "Listen to the English language, damn it! Bed and board, sticks and stones, kith and kin, time and tide, weep and wail, rough and ready—" (11).

Just as the *GAN*s opening words—CALL ME SMITTY—recall *Moby Dick*, Smitty's alliteration identifies the book with another American masterpiece, one also heavily invested with alliteration. In Albert Goodwill Spalding's *America's National Game: Historic Facts Concerning the Beginning, Evolution,*

Development, and Popularity of Base Ball (with personal reminiscences of its vicissitudes, its victories and its votaries), his knack for alliteration is especially apparent in the passage where he claims,

> Base Ball owes its prestige as our National Game to the fact that as no other form of sport it is the exponent of American Courage, Confidence, Combativeness; American Dash, Discipline, Determination; American Energy, Eagerness, Enthusiasm; American Pluck, Persistency, Performance; American Spirit, Sagacity, Success; American Vim, Vigor, Virility [27].

Using their common habit of alliteration as a starting point, I read Roth's *GAN* as a parody of Spalding's baseball history, and turn to rhetorical theory to discuss the effects of such a comic account of America's pastime. While many scholars have discussed the variety of sources that inform Roth's novel, including the Biblical story of Abraham and other religious lore (Ardolino, 1985; 1998), oral comedy of the Southwest (Rodgers), an account of a game played at an insane asylum (Wilson Jr.), and patriotic, anti-communist narratives (Crepeau), none have considered Albert Spalding's text as a source for Roth's satiric treatment of the game and the culture surrounding it. Drawing on Kenneth Burke's theory of identification, I suggest that Roth's novel calls attention to class divisions in America by "poking fun" at Spalding's conception of baseball and the American Dream. Spalding writes, "[Americans] are a cosmopolitan people, *knowing no arbitrary class distinctions,* acknowledging none" (7, italics added). By satirizing this point of view, the *GAN* creates a comic spectacle that reveals the sometimes violent class divisions concealed by baseball's mythic ethos, enabling readers to see how both can have problematic, often contradictory meanings within larger conceptions of American identity.

Identifying the American Dream

Kenneth Burke's most important contribution to class-based rhetorical theory involves his reorientation of rhetoric's central concern from persuasion to identification, as he argues that all persuasion is logically preceded by the identification of common motives between people. In other words, people act together to the degree that they see their interests as joined, for good or for bad. As Burke argues, this suggests an inevitable paradox—a "paradox of substance" as he terms it in *A Grammar of Motives*—of the human condition: that people are "both joined and separate, at once a distinct substance and consubstantial with another" (*Rhetoric* 20–21). When one identifies with someone or something, one therefore is inevitably and simultaneously divided. According to Burke, class divisions are particularly emblematic of this paradox. Classes mark boundaries between people from varied backgrounds, yet are manifested in common social goods—money, clothing, education—that mark people as similar. In a society truly devoid of class distinctions, these identifications and divisions would not exist. If the over-arching argument of Spalding's text is that America is that classless society, and that baseball is the proof, a closer reading of it reveals the paradox of class divisions within our nation as revealed by invoking Burke's theory of identification.

Baseball is, of course, commonly identified with American values. Susan Koprince writes, "The game of baseball has long been regarded as a metaphor for the American Dream — an expression of hope, democratic values, and the drive for individual success" (349). In *Making the Team*, Tim Morris writes, "Baseball is American because America is baseball because baseball is American" (13). In *The Great God Baseball*, Allen E. Hye, paraphrasing social critic Jaques Barzun, argues that "[T]o understand America one must know baseball" (13). In *Dead Balls and Double Curves*, Trey Strecker writes that baseball has "fostered the national virtues of integrity, hard work, and self-reliance" (xvi). Bartlett Giamatti famously said, "Baseball is part of the American plot, part of America's mysterious, underlying design — the plot in which we all conspire and collude, the plot of the story of our national life" (qtd. in Evans 13). This small, somewhat random sampling of quotes provides links between baseball and the mythos of the American Dream, and serves to illustrate how commonly the two are identified with one another.

Spalding had a lot to do with this identification, and his Mills Commission, convened in 1905, played a central role in manufacturing baseball's creation story (Evans; Rader). Because the commission enhanced the popularly held myth that baseball was created by Abner Doubleday in 1839 at Cooperstown, Christopher Evans suggests that Spalding almost "single-handedly" created the Doubleday legend. Evans argues that "Even when conclusive proof was presented that Doubleday had nothing to do with baseball's origins," the legend remained because the story served a rhetorical function in establishing baseball's uniquely American ethos (26). In Spalding's presentation of the story, he appears to be torn between competing motives. On one hand, he wants to establish his own importance in the game's history; on the other, he wants the Doubleday legend to carry the status of fact. He reasons that to question the Doubleday story "would be an act of disloyalty to the commission *that was appointed at my suggestion* in 1907" (19, italics added), thereby realizing both motives.

As taken up by Smitty, Spalding's manufacture of baseball's origin story shapes the narrative direction of the *GAN*. The retired sportswriter declares, "First off, as everyone knows, the Baseball Hall of Fame at Cooperstown was founded on a falsehood. No more than little George Washington said to his father, 'Dad, it is I, etc.,' did Major Abner Doubleday invent the game on that sacred spot" (17). Aware of the many myths, lies, and tall tales that permeate baseball's history, Smitty's comic revision of this particular one serves to demythologize baseball's ethos, to cleanse the game of its many falsehoods. This effort seeks to undo the injustice of the Patriot League's erasure from baseball's records. The Doubleday legend serves a rhetorical purpose in positioning baseball as uniquely American, helping to establish the metaphoric bond between baseball and the "American Dream." Spalding presents the American Dream as the realization of a society devoid of class divisions, where all people have a fair and equal opportunity for success. In so doing, he rhetorically positions baseball as a metaphor of this dream through a "rags-to-riches" narrative that constructs the baseball field as an idyllic pastoral where class divisions are dropped and ethics of equality and hard work prevail. Using Burke's terms, we might say that the Doubleday legend encourages Americans to identify baseball with the American Dream, identifying the "classless" image of baseball with their own hopes for upward mobility. Class divisions can be transcended, the image implies, through hard work according to the ethos of the game. Smitty's effort to reintroduce the Patriot League into the ledger of baseball record also serves a rhetorical purpose, prompting readers to rethink, interrogate, and even laugh at that same democratic image that unites America with its national game.

As Spalding sings baseball's praises—and his own—he has to establish the uniqueness of both the game and of America. In doing so, he distinguishes baseball from other games and America from other cultures, and the ideal of class mobility is at the core of his distinctions. Chapter three opens with a sketch of an orphan boy, titled "An Embryo Base Ball Star" (28). The boy is bandaged and appears haggard, wearing only an old catcher's mitt with ragged clothes and no shoes, but he plays a major role in baseball's evolution. Spalding writes, "Placing the Ball in the hands of the first lad who happens along, we may be assured that he will do the rest" (29). Spalding traces the evolution of the game from hypothetical orphan boy until its "perfection" by Doubleday to demonstrate how baseball, like the nation itself, has emerged from a uniquely American, rags-to-riches narrative. Baseball, like America, is not constrained by class, and its upward mobility knows no bounds. This, for Spalding, is what distinguishes baseball and America from other sports and other societies. Comparing America's game to cricket, he—hilariously—writes that while the British cricket player may wear his "negligee shirt" and his "gorgeous hosier," "drink afternoon tea" and have a "jolly, conventional good time," this is simply not true of "the American Ball Player. He may be a veritable Beau Brummel in social life. He may be the Swellest Swell of the Smart Sea in Swelldom; but when he dons his Base Ball suit, he says goodbye to society, doffs his gentility, and becomes—just a ball Player!" (7). Spalding's exhortations proclaim that baseball's, like America's, strongest virtues lie in discarding convention and allowing men the freedom to move up within their respective hierarchies. Baseball is unconventional *because* America is unconventional. Indeed, Spalding maintains that, given the absence of class or convention divisions, baseball spectators can identify with the ballplayers. The baseball field literally serves as the "common ground" upon which identification transpires, and Spalding's powerful investment in this classless, democratic myth of the game's origins underscores his own identification in the American class system.

So what does this all mean for the *Great American Novel*, a text often understood as a misstep in Philip Roth's career (Halio)? Early criticism of the novel was mostly unfavorable, owing partially to comedy's low status in American literature and to the difficulty in categorizing Roth's work (Rodgers; Monaghan; Siegel). According to Derek Parker Royal, "Many critics pointed out the novelist's excessiveness and lack of discipline, his misuses of satire, his problematic narrator, and his overall inability to follow up on the promise of *Portnoy's Complaint*" (153). More recent criticism, however, has revisited the *GAN* and applauds Roth's play with form (Klinkowitz) while noting that the text emerges from 1960s counter-culture (Halio 111). These critics of the novel claim it is best read as an attempt to demythologize cherished American beliefs (Blues), reinventing and illuminating a stylistic antecedent.

Spalding's text helped create the metaphoric link between baseball and the American Dream so that the two conjoin within the larger American consciousness.[1] By satirizing Spalding's history, Roth comedically cracks that link and opens it for critique, even ridicule.[2] Burke refers to this method as the "comic corrective," a method of intentionally disrupting commonly-held associations to comedic ends, suggesting that such an approach "should enable people *to be observers of themselves, while acting,* with an ultimate goal of achieving *maximum consciousness.* One would transcend himself by noting his own foibles" (*Attitudes* 171). Overall, then, Roth's *Great American Novel* serves as an exercise in the comic corrective, interrogating the matter of class mobility in America by making fun of the "national game" that reinforces this very myth. In reading Roth's book about the myth of class as a critical rewriting of Spalding's identification with it in *America's National Game*, the American class structure emerges as something that simultaneously brings together and divides people.

Roth's interrogation of the myths that Spalding identifies with stands out in two specific stories. Spalding provides a history of the umpire and his place in baseball as an unquestioned moral authority. Later, he identifies the baseball field as an armistice setting during the Civil War. In these two examples, Roth's revision of Spalding's "mythic" baseball history participates in the creation of a comedic baseball vocabulary, one comprised of a "baffling mélange of hyperkinetic writing about the mythology of base-ball" (Aldridge, qtd. in Siegel 176). In terms of class divisions and the conflicts they create, this rendering allows one class to proclaim that "we 'win' by subtly changing the rules of the game" (Burke, *Attitudes* 171). So inscribed in Spalding's proclamation of America's classless democracy, and in the ethos of baseball itself, one sees the fullest embodiment of this national ideal. Paradoxically, one also sees the triumph of this self-made industrialist, a sporting goods magnate, who stood at the pinnacle of this "classless" society.

Gil Gamesh, the Immortal: Umpires, War, and Violence on the Pastoral

In retired Major League umpire Ken Kaiser's autobiography, *Planet of the Umps*, he jokes that as an umpire, you must be prepared to "remain calm and collected even when surrounded by a bunch of infantile people yelling and screaming right in your face and kicking dirt on you and threatening you" (Introduction). This lighthearted description of the life of an umpire is not so far from the truth, as shown in episodes such as Roberto Alomar's suspension for spitting in the face of umpire John Hirschbeck in 1996, or Carl Everett's headbutt to Ron Kulpa in 2000. While these two incidents are certainly outside the norm, the notion of conflict between players and umpires is as old as the game itself, and the escalation of that conflict into violence is not without precedent.

According to Spalding's history of the game, however, conflict between players and umpires was simply a product of baseball's early days, forgotten long ago. As American meritocracy developed according to its democratic principles, the baseball field became a playground of fair play; and as a neutral arbiter of this democratic fairness, the umpire has unquestioned moral authority. Ball players should have no reason to dislike or question umpires, who merely enforce values inherent in the game and innate to all Americans. Spalding claims that umpires are so revered because they possess several fundamental qualities: "The umpire must be intelligent ... honest ... quick-witted ... courageous," and, most important, "*wholly without prejudice*" (406–407). While consistently employing a metaphor of "umpire-as-judge," Spalding articulates an interesting paradox: the umpire's authority is absolute, yet he also symbolizes the game's democratic premise of equality, because "as Americans we are committed by nature to stand for 'fair play;' because as men we believe in a 'square deal' for everybody" (415). Even while umpires enforce baseball "law" in order to ensure fair play and equality, fair play also naturally emerges from the baseball field because Americans believe in Roosevelt's "square deal." If baseball is the fullest expression of American values, then umpires both produce and embody those values.

Roth mocks Spalding's umpire narrative in depicting the conflict between a Patriot League umpire, Mike "The Mouth" Masterson, and the most sensational rookie in Patriot League history, a young Babylonian named Gil Gamesh. During his brief career, Gil Gamesh frequently berates, cajoles, and insults umpires. Similar to the god-king from which his name is taken, Gamesh is presented by Smitty as a superhuman on a quest for immorality. Just as Enkidu is called upon by the gods to teach Gilgamesh humility, "The Mouth" is called upon to control Gamesh, and the two have several absurd and violent confrontations. In one game, Gamesh deliberately throws a bad pitch. When the Mouth accurately calls it a ball, Gamesh tells his catcher, "Done it on purpose, Pineapple. Done it deliberate. So's to make sure, so's to make sure the old geezer standing' behind you hadn't fell asleep at the switch! Just to keep the old son of a bitch honest!" (73). The Mouth's hatred for Gamesh grows throughout the season, and he asserts his authority by forcing the pitcher to forfeit two games for insubordination. This comes to a head during Gamesh's final game. Gamesh has recorded 26 perfect outs on 78 perfect strikes. However, on what should be the last pitch of Gamesh's *perfect* perfect game and the conclusion of his ascension to baseball godhood, Masterson's back is turned from home plate (he claims to have spotted the man who kidnapped his daughter over 35 years ago). By rule, the umpire orders the game to resume prior to the previous pitch. Gamesh loses his perfect game on the next throw, but gets revenge by crushing the umpire's voice box with another "perfect" fastball. Smitty claims that the ball, aimed at Masterson's blue bowtie, "was probably traveling between one hundred twenty and one hundred thirty miles per hour" (83). Masterson's voice box is crushed, leaving him mute and jobless, and Gamesh is exiled.

In the figure of Gil Gamesh, Roth invokes the epic of Gilgamesh first to identify, and then to challenge the umpire's position as absolute moral authority. This conflict between pitcher and umpire contradicts Spalding's vision of the peaceful, pastoral ballfield where the ethos of fair play rules. Kenneth Burke writes that "incongruity should be deliberately cultivated for the purpose of experimentally wrenching apart all those molecular combinations of adjective and noun, substantive and verb, which still remain with us. It should subject language to the same 'cracking' process that chemists now use in their refining of oil" (P&C 119). While Spalding's version of the umpire metaphorically fuses one set of terminologies to baseball—honesty, equality, a square deal—Roth engages in Burke's "atom cracking" and creates a new baseball terminology—deceit, inequality, a raw deal—and thus offers an incongruous, comic perspective on Spalding's idealized vision. While Spalding denies the existence of division by presenting the baseball field as a playground of equality, Roth pushes the opposite to its comic extreme: when Masterson deliberately makes his bad call, class warfare ensues. The rags-to-riches version of the American Dream championed by Spalding is, for Roth, little more than the idyllic musings of a fool, and this naïve myth can only be challenged through mockery and laughter.

Spalding's baseball history contains no shortage of contradictions: baseball was invented by Abner Doubleday, but it also sprang naturally from the spirit of the American child. Moreover, Spalding is in no position to argue against the baseball origin story because it was approved by a commission, although he himself created that commission. Additionally, baseball represents a society of fair play with no class distinctions, and yet umpires are moral arbiters that embody a hierarchy of rules and have the power to impose their authority. Finally, as the analogy between baseball and warfare, a common refrain throughout Spalding's book, is pursued, the contradictions concerning baseball and war also emerge: "Cricket is a gentle pastime. Base Ball is War!" (7); "Base Ball, I repeat, is War!" (9). Spalding frequently depicts the baseball field as a battlefield, and it should not go unnoticed that he locates the game's origins in the mind of an Army Officer. "Base Ball had been born in the brain of an American soldier. It received its Baptism in bloody days" (92–93). However, at the same time, Spalding also presents the baseball field as a pastoral space, as an idyllic plane where disputes are put aside and class distinctions are dropped. For Americans, he argues, baseball is "a beacon, lighting their paths to a future of perpetual peace" (93). Through its history, baseball has "healed the wounds of war" (93). And yet it *is* war.

Inattentive to the contradiction that he has introduced, Spalding "proves" the idyllic, peaceful nature of baseball by telling us about a series of games played by Union and Confederate soldiers in Virginia during the Civil War. Apparently, these games were witnessed by over "40,000 soldiers" from both sides with no outbreaks of violence (94–97). While Spalding admits he has never found any witness to corroborate the story, he also uses the games as data to support his claim of baseball as a consequence of American values concerning peace and equality. In Spalding's typical alliterative style, he writes that baseball

> had its best development at the time when Southern soldiers, disheartened by the distressing defeat, were seeking the solace of something safe and sane; at a time when Northern soldiers, flushed with victory, were yet willing to turn from fighting with bombs and bullets to playing with bat and ball. It was a panacea for the pangs of humiliation to the vanquished on one side, and a sedative against the natural exuberance of victors on the other [92–93].

As the embodiment of the American pastoral space, the baseball field is a place where Americans go to set aside difference, avoid hostilities, and forget even the darkest days of their nation's history. To highlight this contradiction, Philip Roth comically critiques this narrative of baseball-as-panacea by igniting the Cold War on the baseball diamond. By identifying baseball with violence and, to a comic degree, with class warfare, he makes fun of Spalding's idealistic identifications of baseball as an expression of democratic equality and peacefulness.

Invoking the novel's pervasive Cold War motifs and the paranoid reactions that result from these, Smitty claims that Patriot League records were expunged from history because the league was infiltrated by a communist regime. The infiltration was such an embarrassment, such an undermining of the values the game was supposed to stand for — Spalding's peaceful, "classless" American Dream — that all those implicated by the scandal had to be removed from the game's history. Roth, however, pushes the Patriot League scandal to a comic extreme with Smitty's wild telling of the tale: Americans are so invested in this American Dream narrative that they are willing to believe the Patriot League never existed, that communism never took hold — even partially — certainly never in baseball, but also never in America. Smitty's quest to reintroduce the league to public memory thus becomes one of the narrative's central threads.

In the later stages of Roth's novel, Gil Gamesh leads a Soviet invasion of America by becoming manager of the Port Rupert Mundys. Gamesh is banned from baseball by Patriot League Commissioner General Oakhart after his "assault" of Mike Masterson. During the years of Gamesh's exile, many Elvis-like rumors emerge about the famed pitcher, but most people assumed he is dead. In the final chapter of the novel, however, Gamesh returns and asks the General to reinstate him to the Patriot League. And just where has he been all these years? After, according to him, having been betrayed by his game and his country, Gamesh claims he trained as a communist soldier in the Soviet Union, graduating as the valedictorian of "SHIT" (357). His SHIT mission? To conquer America from within by infecting its national pastime.

In order to regain entry into the league, however, Gamesh must first persuade the commissioner to believe that he is no longer the brash, loud-mouthed Babylonian with a Southern accent. To achieve this infiltration, he has to prove — as did his mythic namesake before he could transcend death — that he has learned humility. If we achieve persuasion, as Burke says we do, by identifying our ways in terms of the ways of others, by speaking their language, then Gamesh becomes a skilled rhetorician by the end of the *GAN*. In seeking to bring violence to the Patriot League, he modifies his way of speaking to convince General Oakhart that he is no longer the arrogant and prideful man he once was:

> Nor do I feel like that Gil Gamesh any longer. Nonetheless, that is the Gil Gamesh I am doomed to remain forever. I can never hope to unburden myself of his foolishness, his treachery, or his despair. My hair is gone. My arm is gone. My looks are gone. So what. I am what I have been. Can I now become what I would be? It seems once again, General, that my future is in your hands [355].

Gamesh claims to have fully succumbed to violence during the days of his exile. After training as a student of SHIT "14 hours a day, 7 days a week" (358), he plans to return and unleash that violence on America. He claims, however, that on the way to enact his plan, he happened to see a game of the World Series on television and immediately came to realize — and regret — that he had betrayed his country. In making this confession, he follows the example introduced by Spalding, finding the baseball diamond as a place where he can seek relief from his own transgressions and violent impulses.

But despite his contrition, an ideological war is already encoded into P-League battles. According to Gamesh, there are dozens, perhaps more, of Soviet spies already on Patriot League rosters. Since the Soviets still believe the immortal pitcher is working for them, he proposes that he act as a double-agent to expose the growing Red Army in the P-League. Having convinced General Oakhart of the strength of his faith in the idealism of the American Dream, Gamesh is appointed manager of the Port Rupert Mundys—a team he believes is rife with communists—and spends the rest of the novel trying to "discover" traitors by exposing their violent, un–American dispositions. As a double-agent, Gamesh will root out communist infiltrators by pretending to encourage violence on the baseball field according to his "SHIT" training. Players who bring violence to the game — in response to his motivational cues—he identifies clearly as communist spies. In one of the novel's funnier scenes, Gamesh attempts to motivate his players, saying, "You have no friends! You have only enemies! Their smiles oppress you as much as their sneers! You don't want their sympathy! You want their *blood!*" (378). When one player resists, Gamesh says, "Crush his balls, Kid! Defame his wife! Threaten his life! Caluminate his kids! I want blood! I want brawls! I want hate!" (387). Those players who respond to Gamesh's baiting, bringing the violence of war to the baseball field , give the lie to Spalding's rendition of baseball and the American Dream. These enemies of America's game are then exposed as non–American, as Communists. In this way, Roth exposes the problematic status of the peaceful pastoral image of the game that Spalding introduces as much as he challenges its democratic mythos.

Gamesh exposes all but one of the Mundys as Soviets: center fielder

Roland Agni, who does not trust Gamesh. At the conclusion of Smitty's baseball drama, Gamesh stands with Agni in the on deck circle and presents him with a choice: he must succumb to hatred and become great, or remain peace-loving, the very embodiment of Spalding's "embryo base ball star"—and whither in obscurity. Before Agni can decide, a gunshot echoes as Mike Masterson returns and shoots Gamesh from the stands. The magic bullet enters Gamesh's shoulder, turns 180 degrees, and goes through Agni's neck, killing him on the spot. Masterson, so elated to have gotten revenge on Gamesh, flees the scene, gorges himself on a feast of chicken wings, and subsequently dies of heart failure. Those unable to explain his actions label Masterson, too, as a communist. Because of Agni's death, knowledge of Gamesh's McCarthyesque role becomes public. Major League Baseball forms a special committee—as it did at Spalding's request upon the discovery of its origins—and rules that every (living) member of the Patriot League is a Soviet spy. Following Gamesh's execution the league is disbanded, its records erased from history. As much in Roth's novel as in Spalding's *History*, Baseball's history is officially rewritten with little concern for "the truth," but with much attention to those nationalistic myths it is calculated to perpetuate.

Smitty, it seems, is the only one who knows this "real" truth all along, that Gil Gamesh is the uber–Soviet and that he seeks to destroy America by assailing its most prominent institution. Returning to America and managing the Mundys is all part of his grand Soviet scheme to corrupt baseball, his final clutch at godhood. By destroying the Patriot League, the Soviets have succeeded in destroying one-third of America. This, Smitty concludes, is the real reason people have chosen to forget the Patriot League: it represents a defeat in the Cold War era, and so an affront to America's democratic ideals. Just as Spalding had no firm facts to point to in his legitimizing baseball as America's pastoral game, born of warfare but embodying the highest values of democracy, Smitty has no proof to support his account of the events of the *GAN*. Yet he uses those events as evidence of his final claim. While Spalding popularized a metaphor of baseball as the peaceful pastoral, Smitty's tale highlights the inherent contradictions in that metaphor by having the Cold War ignite on the field, thus comically dramatizing the notion that "Base Ball is War!"

Conclusion: The Great American Novel— *Comic Corrective or Comic Inventive?*

Philip Roth has often been asked what he wanted to accomplish in *The Great American Novel*, which retains its status as a "black sheep" in his artistic canon. Roth responds,

> The comedy in *The Great American Novel* exists for the sake of no higher value than comedy itself, the redeeming value is not social or cultural reform, or moral instruction, but *comic inventiveness*. Destructive, or lawless, playfulness—and for the fun of it. Now, there is an art to this sort of thing that distinguishes it from sadism, nonsense, or even nihilism for the fun of it; however, a *feel* for the sadistic, the nonsensical, and nihilistic certainly goes into making such comedy, and into enjoying it [*Reading Myself* 76].

Roth wants us to read *The Great American Novel* as comedy for the sake of comedy. Margaret Daniel asserts that "Philip Roth is a true American historian and the finest stand-up comic ever to lie down on the printed page" (59). Indeed, Roth is a fine baseball historian and a fine comedian in this novel, which serves the rhetorical functions of his comedic strategy by presenting *The Great American Novel* as a comic corrective of Albert Goodwill Spalding's *America's National Game*.

After the manner of Burke, Roth also refuses to see these two "camps" as mutually exclusive, preferring instead to chart their common ground. Writing about the debate between discussing the rhetorical effects of arts, Liz Weiser argues that Burke's career consisted of his intentionally "falling on the bias" between different intellectual camps in order to map their commonalities and differences and thus create new knowledge, which is one reason Burke is often difficult to classify (134). In reinventing Spalding's paean to the American dream in terms that point to its contradictions and points of dislocation, Roth also highlights the value in interrogating mutually exclusive camps. In a discussion of poetics and rhetoric in *Language as Symbolic Action*, Burke claims that "you must write your drama about *something*" before positing that

> since you can't make a drama without the use of some situation marked by *conflict*, even though you hypothetically began through a sheer love of dramatic exercise, in the course of so exercising you tend to use as your subject matter such tensions or problems as exercise yourself, or your potential audience, or mankind in general [29].

Indeed, readers *should* embrace the conflicts of *The Great American Novel* as interrogations of the Great American Dream. Roth's novel is wildly excessive, often just for the sake of its own excess. But in this excess, it also highlights the tensions that arise in dramatizing baseball as the fulfillment of American democratic ideals. Putting it against Spalding's book shows us how baseball truly embodies class in America, speaking comedically to the class distinctions that split us apart. In the end, Smitty is the prototype of the comic fool, the "genius" that shows man how to "transcend himself by noting his own foibles" (Burke, *Attitudes* 171) through the drama of America's great game.

Notes

1. In *Permanence and Change*, Burke refers to this as "piety": He claims, "Piety *is the sense of what properly goes with what*" (74). A commonsense belief, like baseball as a metaphor of the American dream, is an example of piety.

2. Also in *P&C*, Burke more generally refers to this as "perspective by incongruity": "verbal 'atom-cracking.' That is, a word belongs by custom to a certain category—and by rational planning you wrench it loose and metaphorically apply it to another category" (308). The comic corrective is one method of perspective by incongruity. The *GANs* comic pairing of baseball and communism is illustrative of Burke's concept.

Works Cited

Ardolino, Frank. "The Americanization of the Gods: Onomastics, Myth, and History in Philip Roth's *The Great American Novel*." *Arete* 3.1 (1985): 37–60. Print.

_____. "'Hit Sign, Win Suit': Abraham, Isaac, and the Schwabs Living Over the Scoreboard in Roth's *The Great American Novel*." *Studies in American Jewish Literature* 8.2 (1998): 219–223. Print.

Blues, Thomas. "Is There Life After Baseball? Philip Roth's *The Great American Novel*." *American Studies* 22.1 (1981): 71–80. Print.

Burke, Kenneth. *Attitudes Toward History*. Berkeley: University of California Press, 1984. Print.

_____. *A Grammar of Motives*. Berkeley: University of California Press, 1950. Print.

_____. *Language as Symbolic Action: Essays on Life, Literature, and Method*. Berkeley: University of California Press, 1966. Print.

_____. *Permanence and Change: An Anatomy of Purpose*. Berkeley: University of California Press, 1984. Print.

_____. *A Rhetoric of Motives*. Berkeley: University of California Press, 1969. Print.

Crepeau, Richard C. "Not the Cincinnati Reds: Anti-Communism in Recent Baseball Literature." *Arete* 1.1 (1983): 87–97. Print.

Evans, Christopher H. "Baseball as Civil Religion: The Genesis of an American Creation Story." *The Faith of 50 Million: Baseball, Religion, and American Culture*. Eds. Christopher H. Evans and William R. Herzog II. Louisville: Westminster John Knox Press, 2002. 13–34. Print.

Halio, Jay. *Philip Roth Revisited*. New York: Twayne, 1992. Print.

Hye, Allen E. *The Great God Baseball: Religion in Modern Baseball Fiction*. Macon: Mercer University Press, 2004. Print.

Kaiser, Ken, and David Fisher. *Planet of the Umps: A Baseball Life from Behind the Plate*. New York: T. Dunne Books, 2003. Print.

Klinkowitz, Jerry. "Philip Roth's Anti-Baseball Novel." *The Western Humanities Review* 47.1 (1993): 30–40. Print.

Koprince, Susan. "Baseball as History and Myth in August Wilson's *Fences*." *African American Review* 40 (2006): 349–58. Print.

Monaghan, David. "*The Great American Novel* and *My Life as a Man*: An Assessment of Philip Roth's Achievement." *The International Fiction Review* 2.1 (1975): 113–120. Print.

Morris, Timothy. *Making the Team: The Cultural Work of Baseball Fiction*. Urbana: University of Illinois Press, 1997. Print.

Rader, Benjamin G. *Baseball: A History of America's Game*. Champaign: University of Illinois Press, 2008. Print.

Rodgers, Jr., Bernard F. "*The Great American Novel* and 'The Great American Joke.'" *Studies in Modern Fiction* 16.2 (1974): 12–29. Print.

Roth, Philip. *The Great American Novel.* New York: Bantam Books, 1974. Print.
———. "On *The Great American Novel.*" *Reading Myself and Others.* Rev. ed. New York: Penguin, 1985: 99–113. Print.
Royal, Derek Parker. "Fouling Out the American Pastoral: Rereading Philip Roth's *The Great American Novel.*" In *Upon Further Review: Sports in American Literature.* Eds. Michael Cocchiarale and Scott D. Emmert. Westport, CT: Praeger, 2004.
Siegel, Ben. "The Myths of Summer: Philip Roth's *The Great American Novel.*" *Contemporary Literature* 17.2 (1976): 171–190. *JSTOR.* Web. 16 February 2010.
Spalding, A. G. *America's National Game: Historic Facts Concerning the Beginning, Evolution, Development, and Popularity of Base Ball, with Personal Reminiscences of Its Vicissitudes, Its Victories, and Its Votaries.* Lincoln: University of Nebraska Press, 1992. Print.
Strecker, Trey, ed. *Dead Balls and Double Curves: An Anthology of Early Baseball Fiction.* Carbondale: Southern Illinois University Press, 2004. Print.
Weiser, M. Elizabeth. " 'As Usual I Fell on the Bias': Kenneth Burke's Situated Dialectic." *Philosophy & Rhetoric* 42.2 (2009): 134–153. *Communication & Mass Media Complete.* Web. 2 May 2010.
Wilson Jr., Robert F. "An Indisputable Source for the Spirited Account of a Baseball Contest Between the Port Rupert Mundys and the Asylum Lunatics in *The Great America Novel* by Mr. Philip Roth." *Notes on Contemporary Literature* 5.3 (1975): 12–14. Print.

Class (Un)Consciousness: The Unusual Case of Jackie Robinson

ANDREW HAZUCHA

When Jackie Robinson secretly signed a contract to become Vice President of the Chock Full o' Nuts company on December 12, 1956, retiring from baseball the very same day that Dodgers general manager Buzzie Bavasi traded him to the New York Giants, few would have predicted that in his new role as corporate executive he would find time to become one of the most outspoken and determined political activists of the Civil Rights era. And yet, if one traces the arc of Robinson's playing career, one sees that he became an increasingly public spokesperson about racial politics in America even before his retirement, as witnessed by his highly publicized appearance before the House Un-American Activities Committee in July, 1949, and his insistence late in his life that he "once put [his] freedom into mothballs for a [the 1947] season" but soon thereafter "straightened up [his] back so oppressors could no longer ride upon it" (Long 303).

By the late 1950s, the newly retired Robinson had already developed an epistolary relationship with President Dwight Eisenhower and a personal friendship with then-Vice President Richard Nixon, and he closely monitored the administration's record on civil rights initiatives. Alternately encouraged and dismayed by Eisenhower's performance, Robinson increasingly saw Nixon as the one man on the national political scene with the greatest potential to bring about true racial equality in America. Although he admired both Democratic senators Adlai Stevenson and Hubert Humphrey for their bold stances on civil rights, Robinson felt that the 1960 presidential election offered no hope for either man to become a major player on the national political scene that year. In his column for the *New York Post* on December 30, 1959, Robinson declared he "would enthusiastically support Nixon" as opposed to "a weak and indecisive Democratic nominee" (83).

While at first glance it may seem puzzling that the man who broke baseball's color line would not support the eventual Democratic nominee, John F. Kennedy, and would instead campaign for Nixon during the 1960 presidential race, Robinson's allegiance to the Republican Party and Nixon points to his complicated understanding of racial politics at a moment in time when the national Democratic Party was hesitant about supporting legislation that would dismantle Jim Crow. On another level, Robinson simply could not divorce himself from the Cold War ideology that pitted, as Nixon phrased it in a letter to him, "the forces of atheistic Communism" (98) against American leadership of the free world. And yet, many liberal Democrats used anti-communist rhetoric as freely as Nixon was in the 1950s.[1] Even Martin Luther King, Jr.—no friend of Nixon or the Republican Party—would allude to the ostensible evils of a communist regime in his outspoken opposition to the Vietnam War starting in 1967, arguing that the best strategy for confronting the North Vietnamese threat would be for the United States "to remove those conditions of poverty, insecurity and injustice which are the fertile soil in which the seed of communism grows and develops" (King 241). King increasingly saw American military engagement in Vietnam as a problem rooted in social class, a conflict that deployed disproportionate numbers of America's poor black soldiers to fight on the side of wealthy corporate interests and to kill poor people of color on another continent. Unlike King, however, Robinson never publicly articulated the connections between race and class during his career as a civil rights activist. Strangely enough, then, Robinson's unwillingness or inability to attend to issues of socioeconomic class in some measure defines his political activism after his retirement from baseball, helping to explain his uneasy alliance with the party of Richard Nixon. Raised in relative poverty by a single mother and the son of a poor sharecropper father who abandoned the family, Robinson's failure to see race through the lens of class consciousness is the matter that deserves fuller scrutiny.

Race and Class During the Cold War: A Paradigmatic American Story

Some seven and a half months after Robinson announced his retirement from baseball, an African American handyman named Jimmy Wilson was arrested on July 27, 1957, for stealing $1.95 from an elderly white woman for whom he did odd jobs in Marion, Alabama. An all-white jury quickly convicted Wilson of robbery, and the presiding judge sentenced him to the maximum penalty: death by electrocution. Wilson's attorney appealed the decision to the Alabama Supreme Court, which upheld the death sentence; thereafter, the case became a source of international interest and a symbol abroad of

American race discrimination. The man who stole fewer than two dollars in change was to be executed in Alabama not because of the enormity of his crime, but because he was poor, black, and living in the Jim Crow South (Dudziak 3–4).

The international response to Wilson's sentence was swift and essentially uniform. Newspapers from around the world condemned the decision, and disparate groups of citizens began protests across several continents.[2] Eventually U.S. Secretary of State John Foster Dulles intervened, sending a telegram to Alabama Governor James Folsom in which he articulated his deep concern for the negative international attention the Jimmy Wilson case was attracting. Soon after the Alabama Supreme Court upheld Wilson's conviction, Governor Folsom granted Wilson clemency in an effort to put to rest what he characterized as the "international hullabaloo" (6).

Wilson's conviction, sentencing, and eventual release in 1958 dramatized the inherent contradictions in America between a profoundly racist society and the national ideals of egalitarian democracy. To win the Cold War, the United States needed to assure the world that the democratic ideals it espoused abroad were honored and practiced at home. The Jimmy Wilson case, however, laid bare for an international audience the persistence of Jim Crow laws and other, less visible forms of domestic discrimination against African Americans that constituted American apartheid. Thirteen years after the end of World War II and more than a decade after the integration of Major League Baseball, the national moral dilemma in America over how to assure the fundamental equality of all its citizens was no closer to resolution than when Jackie Robinson made his debut as a Brooklyn Dodger at Ebbets Field on April 15, 1947. The fact that Wilson was a poor man — the coins he took from Estelle Barker were not enough money to pay for his cab ride home, and he later noted that he had borrowed small sums of money from her in the past in order to make ends meet (3–4) — meant that he could neither hire a high-profile attorney nor muster the attention of influential advocates until the international press picked up the story. By that time, however, he already faced the electric chair. Even President Eisenhower, a man beleaguered by racial unrest at home, was more apt to focus his attention publicly on communist threats abroad than on the plight of a poor black man's search for justice in Alabama. Eisenhower's central concern, oddly enough, consumed Robinson as well.

Robinson the Anti-Communist

That Robinson was concerned with the global spread of communism and its relation to race discrimination at home is already evident in the fall of 1957, just days after Arkansas governor Orval Faubus employed the

Arkansas National Guard on September 4 to block nine African American students from enrolling in the all-white Central High School in Little Rock (Long 39). Six days later, on September 10, President Eisenhower addressed a group of Rhode Island Republicans and spoke of the need for "patience" regarding the Little Rock crisis (40). Although Robinson had publicly endorsed Eisenhower during the 1956 presidential race, based largely on Eisenhower's declaring his support for civil rights legislation throughout the campaign, the letter that Robinson wrote the president on September 13 indicates both his disapproval of Ike's handling of the Little Rock crisis as well as a shared ideological commitment to the president's numerous anti-communist statements. "A few days ago," Robinson begins his letter, "I read your statement in the papers advising patience. We are wondering to whom you are referring when you say we must be patient." In the next paragraph Robinson directly criticizes the president's inaction, asserting that "a mere statement that you don't like violence is not enough. In my opinion, people the world over would hail you if you made a statement that would clearly put your office behind the efforts for civil rights" (40).

As the news of Little Rock spread across the globe it became "the paradigmatic symbol of race in America," a powerful story of propaganda that laid bare the myth of democracy (Dudziak 16). Robinson's assertion that Eisenhower's inaction would embolden criticism of the United States abroad was certainly well founded. But curiously, in all his letters to the President about race Robinson never focused on the stark economic and social reality that African Americans remained a caste below whites in Arkansas and many other regions of America, even in the late 1950s. For Robinson — as for Nixon in Robinson's subsequent written exchanges with him — concern for potential criticism from the Soviet Union and other communist-bloc states dominated their letters. Their mutual fear was that such criticism would harm America's role as global exporter of democratic freedoms.

Although Eisenhower eventually acted on September 25, 1957, by federalizing the Arkansas National Guard and then deploying the 101st Airborne Division of the U.S. Army to Central High School with orders to escort the Little Rock Nine to their classes, from Robinson's perspective the president's leadership on race relations had suffered irrevocable damage. Robinson wrote a polite note to the president on September 25 thanking him for his decision to send federal troops to Little Rock, but his patience with Eisenhower's policies continued to wane. On December 24, 1957, he wrote a letter to Vice President Nixon in which he voiced dismay at Attorney General William Rogers's statement that the Eisenhower administration would not pursue any new civil rights legislation in 1958. Asserting that he identified himself as "neither a Republican nor a Democrat" (Long 43), Robinson warned Nixon that the

Attorney General's statements were damaging the Republican Party's prospects for the future. Nixon's lengthy reply to Robinson one month later evinced both a defense of Eisenhower's civil rights policies and an invitation for Robinson's continued engagement with the administration's work. Citing the passage of the Civil Rights Act of 1957 and the more recently formed Civil Rights Commission created to enforce the Act, Nixon wrote, "I think you will agree that it would be well to know how effective the present law is going to be before attempting to pass further legislation" (48).

It is difficult to imagine that Robinson did not see Nixon's response as a kind of stonewalling. Indeed, in his reply to Nixon in a letter dated February 5, 1958, Robinson expresses some exasperation with the Vice President when he writes, "those of us who are earnestly concerned about the problems of civil rights and integration must measure progress not in terms of how much progress we have made recently but how far we have yet to go to achieve first class citizenship for the Negro" (49). Nevertheless, when the *New York Post* hired him in April of 1959 to write a regular syndicated column three times a week on any subject he chose, Robinson made it clear that politics would be one of his primary subjects and that he would advocate for Richard Nixon's candidacy in the upcoming 1960 presidential election (64). As the tenor of Robinson's columns for the *Post* seems to indicate, Nixon's hard-line anti-communist pronouncements continued to appeal to him. Concomitantly, Robinson viewed racism and communism as two inextricably related enemies of freedom, and the survival of one ensured the flourishing of the other. Robinson, however, never addressed the conditions that Martin Luther King, Jr. saw as nurturing them both: grinding poverty, a sense of hopelessness, and widespread injustices. Unlike Robinson, King saw in America a society segregated not only by race but by different levels of economic opportunity.

By the spring of 1960 Robinson was firmly in Nixon's camp. In his column for the *Post* on May 23, 1960, Robinson declared that he had met with Nixon over lunch earlier in the month and had formed favorable opinions of the Vice President's stance on civil rights issues. Nixon read Robinson's column, and on June 3 he wrote a letter to him reiterating his commitment to reforming American society so that African Americans would be "entitled to the basic freedoms and opportunities to which you referred in your column" (98). Nixon ends his letter by referring Robinson back to their lunch conversation on May 10, and it is clear from the Vice President's shift to global geopolitics that he wishes to assure Robinson that he remembers their discussion accurately and that they share the same abhorrence of communism. Citing the responsibility of the United States to assert its "leadership of the free world," Nixon declares that the fight against Communism is "an economic as well as an ideological battle. To deny ourselves the full talent and energies of 17 million Negro Americans in this struggle would be stupidity of the greatest magnitude" (98). Nixon's rhetoric suggests that he wants Robinson to believe that for him, a failure to pass meaningful and enforceable civil rights legislation at home would lead ineluctably to the spread of communism abroad. For his part, Robinson never contested this central premise of Nixon's—indeed, he deployed the same argument himself on many occasions, public and private, for the remainder of his life.

Robinson and MLK:
Red Scare vs. Class Consciousness

After Nixon lost the 1960 election, Robinson sent him a letter of condolence, saying, "I hope I am wrong in my appraisal of President-elect Kennedy but cannot help but feel our country is the loser, not you" (123). By 1964, however, Robinson had abandoned any hope that Nixon would be a standard-bearer for civil rights, as Nixon had endorsed for president Barry Goldwater, a man whom Robinson called a "bigot, an advocate of white supremacy and more dangerous than Governor Wallace" (198). After observing President Lyndon B. Johnson's movement on civil rights legislation as well as the nomination of Hubert Humphrey as his vice presidential running mate at the Democratic National Convention on August 1964, Robinson joined the group "Republicans for Johnson" and actively campaigned for the ticket. Three years later, as the Vietnam War escalated under an increasingly disparaged and ineffective LBJ, Robinson wrote the President to voice his support of Johnson's Vietnam policy and to criticize most sharply, of all people, Martin Luther King, Jr. for his anti-war stance. "While I am certain your faith has been shaken by demonstrations against the Viet Nam war," Robinson wrote Johnson on April 18, 1967, "I hope the actions of any one individual does not make you feel as Vice President Humphrey does, that Dr. King's stand will hurt the Civil Rights movement. It would not be fair to the thousands of our Negro fighting men who are giving their lives because they believe, in most instances, that our Viet Nam stand is just" (252).

Coming as it did just two weeks after King's address at Riverside Church in New York City in which King excoriated the Johnson administration and declared that the United States government is the "greatest purveyor of violence in the world today" (King 233), Robinson's letter seems to indicate a failure on his part to see a connection between civil rights at home and militarism abroad. The only connection Robinson saw, as he formulated in a letter to King on May 13, 1967, is one he had never revised over an entire decade of considering the matter: he insisted that America's domestic troubles involving race would lead to a strengthening of communist ideology around the world. "But Martin," Robinson wrote, "aren't you being unfair when you place all the burden of blame upon America and none upon the Communist forces we are fighting. [...] Why is it, Martin, that you seem to ignore the blood which is upon their hands and to speak only of the 'guilt' of the United States?" (Long 256–57). Robinson's letter suggests that King's criticism of the Vietnam War would only embolden communist regimes to imagine African American dissent as, in the words of an official from Hanoi, "A second front ... to weaken US imperialism" (Dudziak 243).

Most telling about Robinson's critique of King's speech — the text of which Robinson seems either to have heard or read, as he alludes to some passages from it in his letter of May 13[3] — is his failure to address King's central argument: that American involvement in Vietnam perfectly dramatizes how race and class come together in a nexus of injustices perpetrated by wealthy whites upon poor people of color. In King's view, the American military-industrial machine exploited both poor Vietnamese peasants and economically disadvantaged inner-city African Americans drafted to fight for corporate executives seeking the "immense profits of overseas investment" (King 240). One of the most memorable passages from King's address alludes to Johnson's War on Poverty and its broken promises in the wake of the Vietnamese conflict's continued escalation:

> A few years ago there was a shining moment in that struggle [the anti-poverty initiatives taken by LBJ]. It seemed as if there was a real promise of hope for the poor — both black and white — through the poverty program. There were experiments, hopes, new beginnings. Then came the buildup in Vietnam and I watched the program broken and eviscerated as if it were some idle political plaything of a society gone mad on war, and I knew that America would never invest the necessary funds or energies in rehabilitation of its poor so long as adventures in Vietnam continued to draw men and skills and money like some demonic destructive suction tube. So I was increasingly compelled to see the war as an enemy of the poor and attack it as such [232–233].

Although it would be another seven months before King launched his Poor People's Campaign, he had planted the seeds for it in this speech, his disappointment with the Johnson administration's waning attention to poverty at the center of his critique. The administration's escalation of the Vietnam War, King thought, would end up bankrupting its War on Poverty, reversing any economic gains that African Americans had made under Johnson's presidency. King dramatized this point further and extended his analysis to class conflict among the Vietnamese people themselves, declaring that American soldiers eventually "must know that their government has sent them into a struggle among Vietnamese, and the more sophisticated surely realize that we are on the side of the wealthy and the secure while we create a hell for the poor"

(238). Significantly, Robinson never took up this moral question with King over the economic disparity between wealthy warmongers and the poor who fight their wars. Although an argument about class difference forms the crux of King's speech, Robinson ignored it entirely.

Military historians have pointed out that African American soldiers suffered a disproportionately high number of casualties during the early years of the Vietnam War. As David Coffey has noted, "Although they made up less than 10 percent of American men in arms and about 13 percent of the U.S. population between 1961 and 1966, they accounted for almost 20 percent of all combat-related deaths in Vietnam during that period" (7). Why, then, would Robinson continue publicly supporting the increasingly unpopular Vietnam War while at the same time ignoring King's linking of American militarism with black poverty? Having served in the Army from 1942 to 1944 and famously court-martialed in Fort Hood, TX, for refusing to ride in the back of a military bus just a few weeks after the Army issued a new rule forbidding segregation on military bases, Robinson was aware of systematic discrimination against blacks in the military (Rampersad 102). But it is also true that in July of 1949 he had testified — at the urging of and with considerable coaching from Branch Rickey — against Paul Robeson in front of the House Un-American Activities Committee, which was conducting hearings on the loyalty of prominent African Americans (210–216).

Robeson had questioned why any African American would go to war for a country that had oppressed black people for generations; Robinson testified that Robeson's statement "sounds very silly to me" (qtd. in Rampersad 214). According to his biographer Lee Lowenfish, Branch Rickey was not only an evangelical Christian but a committed anti-communist, and by 1949 had been "[l]ong antagonistic to Robeson's radicalism" (Lowenfish 472). Having traveled extensively throughout the Soviet Union, Robeson delivered a speech from Paris in April, 1949, in which he praised the Soviet Union for the freedoms it had granted black people. In response, Rickey's animus towards Robeson only increased. He helped with the initial drafts of the statement that Robinson would eventually read before HUAC, a message that balanced the player's feelings about democracy with his opposition to communism (472). Perhaps the real reason Robinson never faltered in his patriotic support of the Cold War generally and the Vietnam War in particular, then, is because he had been mentored and made relatively wealthy by benevolent white father figures, Rickey most notable among them.[4]

By the early 1960s, Robinson's very public political activism on the part of Republican presidential hopefuls Richard Nixon and Nelson Rockefeller had earned him the suspicion of many African American leaders and the enmity of others. His support of the Vietnam War, his anti-communist stances, and his feuds with some members of the civil rights community eventually entangled him in a war of words with Malcolm X, who considered Robinson an Uncle Tom. In a caustic letter to Robinson dated November 30, 1963, Malcolm X called out Robinson on his long-standing association with Rickey and his 1949 congressional testimony against Robeson, suggesting the ballplayer "let [himself] be used by the whites ... to destroy Paul Robeson," who was "condemning America for her injustices against American Negroes" (Long 182–83). The bitter sarcasm of this letter notwithstanding, its importance lies in Malcolm's criticism of Robinson's deference to his "White Bosses."

Like Ernie Banks, who in 1962 ran for Alderman of Chicago's Eighth Ward as a pro–Nixon Republican with significant encouragement from Chicago Cubs' owner Philip K. Wrigley (Wood 103, n.4),[5] Robinson aligned himself ideologically with those who had done the most to help him achieve professional success and material wealth. It is doubly significant, then, that Malcolm X's letter — written just eight days after the assassination of President John F. Kennedy — explicitly links Robinson with an elitist white power structure that will not abide any criticism and will destroy any attempts to dismantle it. Ending his letter not with a reference to the assassination of JFK, but rather to the murder of Medgar Evers, Malcolm warns Robinson that his traitorous activism on behalf of his "White Benefactors" (184) may one day end in violence for him, even should he find the integrity to render a more strident critique of a political system that has systematically excluded poor blacks from a seat at the table. "If you should ever become as militant in [*sic*] behalf of our oppressed people as Medgar Evers was," Malcolm wrote, " the same whites whom you now take to be your friends will be the first to put the bullet or the dagger in your back, just as they put it in the back of Medgar Evers" (186).[6]

Robinson's testy private exchanges with such civil rights luminaries as Martin Luther King, Jr. and Malcolm X make one wonder how the barrier-breaking ballplayer and emblem of racial reconciliation in America ended up feuding with those who both had applauded him as an iconic African American success story and had proudly followed his every move on the ball field. Even Malcolm confessed in his highly critical letter to Robinson that in the early days of Robinson's career he was an "ardent fan," adding, "your speed and shifty base running used to hold me spellbound" (182). Certainly there was much that Robinson, King, and Malcolm X faced in common as they each sought remedies to end racial discrimination in their lives: legal obstacles, white hatred, death threats, violence. On the other hand, it is no condemnation to say that the personal experiences that shaped Robinson's world view differed from those of King, Malcolm X, or for that matter Paul Robeson.

Perhaps Robinson's lack of class consciousness during the Cold War was ultimately the result of his having moved into more affluent white circles where any discussion of class conflict was akin to proclaiming oneself a communist. On the other hand, Robinson's persistent refusal to link race and class in his public pronouncements and private letters leads one to ponder what might have been if Robinson had become more radicalized by his experiences, as Robeson had been. Robeson, who had been an active participant in the campaign to desegregate major league baseball in 1943, forgave Robinson for his statement before the House Un-American Activities Committee during the summer of 1949, insisting that there was "no argument between Jackie and me" (qtd. in Duberman, 362). Others were not so magnanimous. As Malcolm X asked so unforgivingly in his letter to Robinson, "Just who are you playing ball for today, good Friend?" (Long 184).

Notes

1. Senator Adlai Stevenson of Illinois was a case in point. One of the liberal Democratic leaders whom Robinson admired, Stevenson was denouncing communism as early as 1952 while campaigning for the presidency that year. In a campaign speech on September 12, 1952, at the National Guard Armory in Albuquerque, NM, Stevenson declared, "communism is the death of the soul" (Stevenson 126–27).
2. John Collins, Canon of St. Paul's Cathedral in London, was one of many European ecclesiastical and political leaders who urged public protests against the execution of Jimmy Williams. Collins asked every Christian in England to engage in demonstrations against Williams's sentence (Dudziak 5).
3. In his letter to MLK, for example, Robinson paraphrases a line from King's Riverside Church address, saying, "You have called the United States—and unfairly, I feel—the greatest purveyor of violence on earth" (Long 257).
4. The other two most prominent white mentors in Robinson's life were William Black, who hired Robinson as Vice President at Chock Full O' Nuts, and New York Governor Nelson Rockefeller, a moderate Republican who made him deputy director of his 1964 presidential campaign.
5. See Wood for a further discussion of P.K. Wrigley's profound influence on Banks's ideology and post-playing days business ventures.
6. Robinson responded to Malcolm X's letter two weeks later with a letter of his own dated December 14, 1963. Although he doesn't respond to Malcolm's claim that if he were ever to become militant like Evers his "white friends" would kill him, he does reference the recent assassinations of both Evers and JFK. Writes Robinson, "Personally, I reject your racist views. I reject your dream of a separate state. I believe that many Americans, black and white, are committed to fighting for those freedoms for which Medgar Evers, William Moore, the Birmingham children and President John F. Kennedy died" (Long 187).

Works Cited

Coffey, David. "African American Personnel in U.S. Forces in Vietnam." *Encyclopedia of the Vietnam War: A Political, Social, and Military History*. Ed. Spencer C. Tucker. Vol. 1. Santa Barbara: ABC-CLIO, 1998. 6–7. Print.
Duberman, Martin Bauml. *Paul Robeson*. New York: Alfred A. Knopf, 1988. Print.
Dudziak, Mary L. *Cold War Civil Rights: Race and the Image of American Democracy*. Princeton: Princeton University Press, 2000. Print.

King, Jr., Martin Luther. "A Time to Break Silence." *A Testament of Hope: The Essential Writings and Speeches of Martin Luther King, Jr.* New York: HarperCollins, 1986. 231–244. Print.

Long, Michael G., ed. *First Class Citizenship: The Civil Rights Letters of Jackie Robinson.* New York: Henry Holt, 2007. Print.

Lowenfish, Lee. *Branch Rickey: Baseball's Ferocious Gentleman.* Lincoln: University of Nebraska Press, 2007. Print.

Rampersad, Arnold. *Jackie Robinson: A Biography.* New York: Alfred A. Knopf, 1997. Print.

Stevenson, Adlai E. "The Threat of Communism." *Major Campaign Speeches of Adlai E. Stevenson, 1952.* Intro. Adlai E. Stevenson. New York: Random House, 1953. 125–133. Print.

Wood, Gerald C. "Let's Play Two ... in Black and White: Ernie Banks and Race Relations in Chicago." *Northsiders: Essays on the History and Culture of the Chicago Cubs.* Ed. Gerald C. Wood and Andrew Hazucha. Jefferson, NC: McFarland, 2008. 97–104. Print.

Commonwealth: *Hardt, Negri and the Contemporary Class Struggle for the National Pastime*

Carl F. Miller

Debuting on PBS on September 18, 1994, Ken Burns' epic *Baseball* documentary aired at an unprecedented moment of crisis in the history of Major League Baseball (MLB) — a month into a 232-day player strike that would cancel the 1994 postseason, shorten the 1995 season, lead to the use of replacement players, and threaten to alienate the American public permanently. Even so, *Baseball* would go on to become the most watched program in public television history, reinforcing the common belief that baseball is ultimately immune to whatever abuses owners, players, and fans might subject it. Hall of Famer Buck O'Neil, speaking at the conclusion of the documentary, memorably states: "You can't do too much [to professional baseball] because we've done a whole lot of things to hurt it but — I don't care how [much you do] — you can't kill it. You just can't kill baseball."

True to form, MLB would recover astonishingly quickly after the strike, establishing new records for attendance and exponentially increasing its gross revenue. However, the longtime refusal of the Major League Baseball Players Association (MLBPA) to submit to effective steroid testing, the increasing reliance of owners on taxpayers to subsidize their franchises, and an ever-widening economic disparity between big-market and small-market teams have once again called into question the health of the MLB institution. Revealingly, Burns released an addendum to his documentary — titled *Baseball: The Tenth Inning* — in September 2010, in which he addresses the contemporary state of the game. In this latest edition, conservative columnist George Will stresses that "baseball's economic model — individual teams generating their own revenue and keeping as much of it as they could — predates television, radio, flight, [and] the internal combustion engine; it goes back deep into the nineteenth century, and it is utterly unsuited to the modern age." While the current situation lacks the noteworthiness or notoriety of the last player's strike, the question emerges as to whether baseball, in its contemporary form, has quietly reached a moment of class conflict that surpasses that of 1994–95.

One of the most effective means to consider this question lies in an unlikely source: the economic/political/social theory of Michael Hardt and Antonio Negri. Subtle revelations emerge from Hardt and Negri's first collaborative work, *Empire* (2000), which emphasizes the transition from the imperialism of nation-states to the complex Empire of corporations and bureaucratic organizations. Their follow-up book, *Multitude* (2004), focuses on the exploited population beholden to aristocratic and governmental tiers of Empire, and theorizes about the revolutionary potential of this mass to assert their sovereignty and establish an absolute democracy.

The final book in this trilogy, *Commonwealth* (2009), provides perhaps the richest commentary on this inherent conflict between political/private enterprise and the multitude.[3] *Commonwealth* is decisively oriented around the concepts of both globalization and labor, and so is directly applicable to the current class divide within MLB. Hardt and Negri explain that modernity is dialectical in nature and focused on power in the forms of "domination and resistance" (68). Building on Michel Foucault's definition of the "dispositifs" that support the current power structures, Hardt and Negri seek to identify both these contemporary apparatuses and the "common" population over which they hold dominion. *Commonwealth* presents a theoretical "project to win back and expand the common and its powers" (ix), demonstrating in its far-reaching philosophical significance an eminent application to MLB's contemporary class conflict.

Common Wealth and Capitalism

Commonwealth presents an unconventional text for analyzing professional sports, given that it concludes a trilogy that has often been labeled as the *Communist Manifesto* of the twenty-first century. While Hardt and Negri display an innate distrust of capitalist enterprise and hold that neoliberal privatization should be resisted, Major League Baseball is clearly an institution that has been privatized from its very advent. Furthermore, although Hardt and Negri overtly argue that "capital is in crisis" (142), MLB offers a problematic application of this premise, given its hybrid status as both a free-market enterprise and a collection of cooperative franchises that are competitively regulated. For example, while a purely capitalist system would involve free agency in the global sense, a professional baseball player's freedom is still restricted by the draft, seniority requirements, and binding arbitration.

Equally significant, franchises are subject to a payroll threshold that — in the interest of competition — necessitates the payment of a luxury tax on anything spent beyond that limit (set at $178 million for the 2011 season), up to a maximum of rate of 40 percent.[4]

In spite of these limitations, capital is essential to the existence of professional baseball, and MLB offers the oldest sporting example of this in America. Capitalism, Hardt and Negri observe, essentially "order[s] life according to the hierarchies of economic value" (ix). Such a system has inherent and obvious flaws, yet the notion of a non-privatized and non-capitalist system of professional baseball is virtually inconceivable. In explaining this contradiction, *Commonwealth* utilizes John Maynard Keynes' notable assertion that "individualistic capitalism ... is not a success.... In short, we dislike it, and we are beginning to despise it. But when we wonder what to put in its place, we are extremely perplexed" (qtd. in Hardt and Negri 261).

Thus, even if capital is in crisis, such crisis is not inevitably followed by collapse. Hardt and Negri are not predicting or advocating capitalist Armageddon: this premise is important, as MLB — for all its issues — is in no danger of outright collapse. Instead, the emphasis of *Commonwealth* is that the mode of production within capitalism has decisively shifted to the biopolitical, and Hardt and Negri call for the widespread recognition of this reality.

"Biopolitics," in this case, may be defined as the integration of everyday life into methods of dominance and resistance; for example, an MLB franchise relocating to another city is not an exclusively economic matter, but also one that changes the dynamics of everyday life for multiple populations. Hardt and Negri observe that, ever since Marx, "the critique of political economy has focused on the contradiction between the social nature of capitalist production and the private nature of capitalist accumulation; but in the context of biopolitical production the contradiction is dramatically intensified" (149). Contemporary notions of baseball's class conflicts are still largely frozen in time with the 1994 players strike. But the class struggle of MLB has since shifted in accordance with the rise of biopolitics to a more complex, multitiered dynamic.

This trend is difficult to discern, given the general assumption that traditional class conflicts (such as owners vs. players) are perpetually inevitable and contentious. Theodor Adorno and Max Horkheimer contend in *The Dialectic of Enlightenment* that just as "freedom in society is inseparable from enlightenment thinking," even so the "very concept of that thinking ... already contains the germ of the regression which is taking place everywhere" (xvi). In other words, whenever the oppressed emerge as victorious in a class struggle, they will inevitably assume the role of oppressor themselves. Hardt and

Negri take issue with this infinite dialectical loop, lamenting that the model of Adorno and Horkheimer only holds true if one individual sovereign is replaced with another (96).

In addition, *Commonwealth* draws attention to the popular assumption that empires fall from within (235), and — as mentioned prior — the resilience of MLB in the aftermath of the 1994 strike seems to indicate that baseball is immune to even the most severe internal conflicts. In spite of this, Hardt and Negri contend that "the resistance of the multitude" represents the greatest threat to ruling systems (279). Who exactly constitutes this multitude, however, remains the crucial consideration; and this multitude's size and scope is significantly complexified when applied to MLB.

Empire and Globalization

To begin with, *Commonwealth* emphasizes a global multitude, one free of the traditional boundaries and bureaucracies of nation-states, where all countries share "a world that has no 'outside'" (vii). In fact, however, this utopian conception ignores everyday realities, particularly those concerning "geographical divisions of labor and power" (230). Clearly, Major League Baseball is an institution centered on the American people and economy. And yet — even when viewed domestically — professional baseball does not engage with a flat economic system, as each city and each franchise face different fiscal and cultural realities. This difference is evident in the inherent differences between St. Louis and Pittsburgh, two comparatively-sized cities with equally-rich baseball histories and equally-new downtown ballparks. In this case, St. Louis is often considered the best baseball city in America, one whose MLB franchise payroll currently approaches $100 million, while Pittsburgh is a football town, and its Pirates failed to sell out playoff games even when they were winning[5] — and whose MLB franchise has subsequently never carried a payroll of more than $50 million.

These economic disparities within baseball become even more pronounced when applied on an international scale, and here baseball's potential as a non-capitalist institution is best analyzed. A professional league within a developed capitalist nation like Japan wields significant leverage against MLB, as is evident in the lucrative compensation that Japanese franchises receive for posting players to America.[6] Conversely, an undeveloped communist nation like Cuba exemplifies "the bureaucratic and economic straitjacket of the socialist state" (Hardt and Negri 94), as its citizens are legally barred from seeking employment in MLB — effectively making its players the property of the nation, rather than of a specific franchise or league. One of the first moves by Fidel Castro (a former baseball player himself) upon taking power in Cuba was to outlaw professional sports. As a result, Cuba was able to both cultivate and retain its domestic baseball talent, and to maintain a relative advantage in international amateur competition.

In this respect, Cuba presents an effective test case in antimodernity, one which breeds discontent at a greater rate than most any capitalist enterprise. It bears emphasizing that Cuban ballplayers inevitably choose the capitalist straightjacket of MLB to the socialist subjugation of the Cuban state. The end of the Cold War would gave rise to a steady trickle of Cuban refugee talent into MLB, beginning with René Arocha's defection in 1991. Even Castro would come to publicly admit, "If you have to compete against six million dollars versus three thousand Cuban pesos, you cannot win" (Fainaru and Sanchez 639).

Japan would ultimately defeat Cuba to win the initial World Baseball Classic in 2006, and this tournament perhaps best exemplifies the contemporary international dynamic of baseball. For despite America's struggles on the field in this tournament (with a top finish of fourth place in 2009), the World Baseball Classic has paradoxically only served to reinforce America's and MLB's dominance over the game. The first two editions of the tournament (in 2006 and 2009) were held in the United States, presumably the only location that would attain both the desired attendance and revenue and that would ensure the participation of MLB players. Furthermore, while the rules of this tournament — replete with pitch counts and mandatory days off for pitchers — are presumably imposed in the interest of player safety, they are upon closer scrutiny implemented to protect the property of MLB franchises. Instead of holding the tournament in mid-summer — which would likely maximize both viewer interest and player performance — the Classic has been relegated to March, diminishing its stature to that of a higher-stakes spring training league that functions as little more than a prelude to the subsequent MLB season. Accordingly, television ratings have been uninspiring (whether in comparison to FIFA's iconic World Cup or even to FIBA's World Basketball Championships), and the tournament has done little to increase MLB's international presence. Beyond North America, Latin America, and the Far East, baseball has a virtually negligible impact on the rest of the world.

Thus, these facts point to the truth that baseball's international limits are more pronounced than in any of America's other major professional sports, yet even the capitalism of baseball would seem to have its limits. In contrast, the expansionist capitalist practices of the National Football League (NFL), the National Basketball Association (NBA), and the National Hockey League (NHL) have been decidedly more expansive. America still holds unilateral sway over the world's baseball economy. But paradoxically, this transcendent position comes at the price of antiglobalization, as other developed nations remain generally unwilling to submit to U.S. economic dominance.

Class Struggle and the Multitude

While baseball offers comparatively simple external relations to patterns of globalization, its internal system of labor relations and class conflict is exceedingly complex. To begin with, baseball is — in theory — a profession of leisure, rather than labor. As opposed to a factory laborer, an MLB player does not simply approach his job as "fulfilled nothingness" (Hardt and Negri 23); instead, he is highly-visible and handsomely-rewarded, with an average salary of $3.34 million in 2010. Thus, when Hardt and Negri advocate "the establishment of a minimum guaranteed income on a national or global scale paid to everyone regardless of work" (309), they only draw attention to the distorted salary structures of MLB. The sport already has a minimum salary — $414,500 for the 2011 season — which comes across as ridiculously inflated in relation to any potential national scale.

As mentioned before, the class dynamics of MLB are also complicated by the abstract question of who exactly constitutes the multitude. Hardt and Negri speak repeatedly of the "multitude of the poor," who exist within "the mechanisms of social production regardless of social order" (40). In essence, the term distinguishes the haves from the have-nots on a scale that is decidedly comparative. (A chapter in Burns' 2009 *Baseball* documentary characterizing the contemporary labor struggle between players and owners is titled "Millionaires vs. Billionaires").

Hardt and Negri's critical project is thereby predicated on the "republic of property" vs. "the democracy of the multitude" (21), wherein "the republic is defined by property," yet, "the multitude, insofar as it is characterized by property, stands opposed to it" (39). The social objective of *Commonwealth*, accordingly, is to offer a blueprint for transcending this traditional dialectic.

The New York Yankees offer a useful case study to illustrate this conception of "property." They have long been both the highest-grossing and the highest-spending team in baseball, and have accordingly become the default scapegoat for MLB's perceived economic inequalities. However, to characterize the class struggles of baseball as the Yankees vs. the rest of MLB — or, as is more common, large market teams vs. small market teams — also grossly oversimplifies the situation, as the Yankees' influence has helped to drive up the value of franchises and the salaries of players across the whole of MLB. In other words, it is too easy to point to a figure like deceased Yankees' owner George Steinbrenner as a tyrannical despot and assert that the masses must take away owners' rights to establish the rights of the multitude. Rights and freedom are not a zero-sum game, Hardt and Negri emphasize, and the real danger lies not so much in the whims of an individual sovereign as it does within the larger economic structures at hand. Steinbrenner did not change the game of baseball or its inherent class relations; instead, he simply galvanized its play of opposites and became the most visible participant in MLB's contemporary economic system.

Accordingly, this system preys on the multitude, a trend most notably evident in taxpayer subsidies for MLB franchises, similar to how "correct[ing] the excesses of private initiative and guarantee[ing] social welfare" has become a financial, rather than social, approach (Hardt and Negri 145). While the recent corporate bailouts of financial institutions and automakers by the U.S. government have sparked significant controversy, varying forms of social welfare have been in place in MLB for over fifty years. The Boston Braves' move to Milwaukee in 1953 (the first relocation by an MLB franchise in fifty years) set in motion a trend that would see four more teams relocate before the decade was over[7] and MLB franchises emerge with a newfound leverage over taxpayers.

This trend would culminate in 2008 in the nation's capital, with Washington, D.C. financing a new ballpark for its recently acquired Nationals franchise. The already cash-strapped city would ultimately cover a shocking 97 percent of the over $600 million construction cost for Nationals Park, and then grant Ted Lerner — the billionaire owner of the Nationals franchise — a 30-year lease in which he would control all but twelve dates annually, and under which he would be granted total rights to tickets, parking, concessions, and signage (Price 130). Rarely has a case of public financing of private enterprise been more egregious, yet it was widely justified as both normal and necessary within the contemporary corporate climate of MLB.

The Production of Wealth

The conventional caveat to franchise moves and taxpayer-financed stadiums lies in the counterargument that a new stadium and an MLB franchise have a tremendously positive impact on the value of the rest of the municipality/region. Hotels, restaurants, and other ancillary ventures spring up around a new ballpark, which appears to guarantee consistent, MLB-generated traffic through these businesses. Following the prevailing trend of relying upon new ballparks to reinvigorate depressed areas, Nationals Park was placed in D.C.'s troubled Anacostia neighborhood, which carried one of the highest poverty, crime, and homicide rates within the district.

However, the economic revitalization of this neighborhood has been decidedly limited in the subsequent three years. At first glance, this slow pace of rebuilding could be attributed to the economic downturn of 2008; even so it bears mention that virtually all scholarly research conducted by sports economists has downplayed the economic impact of new stadiums and franchises. Roger Noll and Andrew Zimbalist explain that "the standard method of assessing economic impact overstates the extent to which a team generates a net increase in business (its net exports) and then overstates again the multiplier effects arising from this business" (87).

Thus, while the economics of MLB have increased at an exponential rate since the advent of franchise relocation, its generation of wealth—and by whom—poses an ongoing enigma. David Harvey—whose influence bears heavily on *Commonwealth*—has notably argued that "the main substantive achievement of neoliberalism has been to redistribute, rather than generate, wealth and income" (159). With this in mind, one may sensibly question whether MLB generates wealth, or whether it simply reallocates it.

This sort of corporate and political jockeying, it must be emphasized, is played out on a local—rather than a national or a global—scale, and provides for a localized concept of Empire. *Commonwealth* logically articulates that the location of a building represents only part of its value (154). Much like location determines real estate value, so too does location determine franchise value. Hardt and Negri observe that, rather than contributing to the prosperity of the multitude, institutions like MLB franchises are compliant in the corporate seizure of public wealth. Whether a city derives its value from an MLB franchise is debatable, but it is certain that franchises derive their value directly from the common wealth of the metropolis.

In much the same way, one should recognize that cities do not own MLB teams so much as they simply rent them. MLB teams with publicly-financed stadiums invariably sign leases with their respective cities, which generally run in excess of twenty years. Nevertheless, there are a series of extenuating circumstances that can sever these leases—as the Tampa Bay Rays' 2011 threat to file Chapter 11 bankruptcy and end their lease with Tropicana Field has demonstrated. An MLB franchise is not inherently linked to a city but is instead tenuously allied to that city's economic and cultural climate—and both of these climates can shift relatively swiftly.

Exploitation

This temporary alliance between franchise and city illustrates a fundamental component of *Commonwealth*'s claim that "capital is predatory ... insofar as it seeks to capture and expropriate autonomously produced common wealth" (141). As one of the most visible and associative institutions of the metropolis, the potential for exploitation by MLB franchises is exceedingly high. Given the exponential rise in the game's capital, one must question whether the increased salaries and costs are directly associated with material reality, or whether baseball has become an institution whose marketplace is driven by what Hardt and Negri call "immaterial production" (25).

Whether the answer is the former or the latter, MLB remains an institution that offers little direct conflict with the general public. Indeed, this public has little recourse to MLB's economic expansion, mirroring Hardt and Negri's contention that powerful entities eschew force and seek control "by structuring the conditions of possibility of social life" (6). MLB can both pursue and justify the public financing of its private franchises on the basis of the vital role that its teams play in the identity of both a city and an individual person. This sense of possession precisely articulates the cachet for a city's population in having an MLB team, as it creates an illusion of ownership that endows major league status to that city's citizens.

As such, it is both misleading and dangerous to consider an MLB franchise as an indispensable part of a city's identity. The cultivation of this idea represents a Foucauldian apparatus of control, as the wealthy "pretend in the guise of the republic of property to represent the entire society," as opposed to their own "exclusive identity" (Hardt and Negri 45). This illusion of ownership may be categorized as biopolitical exploitation, which Hardt and Negri define as "the expropriation of the common" (141). Teams like the Chicago Cubs, St. Louis Cardinals, and Boston Red Sox may seem to enjoy indissolvable relationships with their respective cities. In truth, however, a twenty-first century MLB team is ultimately a corporate entity with an identity derived more from its owner than from its city — a practice increasingly evident since Walter O'Malley moved his Brooklyn Dodgers to Los Angeles in 1958, shattering the legendary identification that Brooklyn carried with its lone professional sports team.[8]

Furthermore, while the longstanding Reserve Clause remained in place, MLB owners held effective regulation of the economics of the game, as they could independently set the prices for both salaries and tickets, expanding them both in a gradual manner consistent with domestic inflation. The owner's accumulation of capital, however, would reach a tipping point in 1975, when arbitrator Peter Seitz upheld a grievance filed by MLB players Andy Messersmith and Dave McNally, effectively ending the Reserve Clause and beginning the era of free agency. In making his decision, Seitz explained that "the owners were too stubborn and stupid. They were like the French barons of the twelfth century: They had accumulated so much power, they wouldn't share it with anybody" (qtd. in *Baseball*).

In spite of the apparent freedom this new opportunity granted the players, the system of free agency actually replicated baseball's hierarchical economic system. As *Commonwealth* warns, "An even greater danger is that successful revolts end up reproducing the hierarchical power relations of modernity" (117). In this respect, MLB exhibits a distinct *hyper*modernity: While the owner-player conflict continues at a historically-equivalent rate, the dominant exploitation has shifted from that between owner and player to that between MLB and fan. The labor struggles of MLB over the past half-century have allowed *both* the owners and the players to emerge victorious, and have positioned the general public as the oppressed. This trend was already evident at the time of Burns' original *Baseball* documentary in 1994, in former pitcher Bill Lee's commentary on the advent of free agency:

> It was the Emancipation Proclamation of baseball. When the Reserve Clause was overturned, it disallowed the owners from signing perpetual one-year contracts to ballplayers, thereby keeping them in the organization for eternity. So, basically, it allowed us to go from plantation to plantation based on the highest bid of the plantation owner. And the owners got very upset about that because it inflated salaries, and then ticket prices went up, and television revenue went up, and they found out they were making more money, and they found out, "Wow, we had a $1.5 million franchise [before, and] now we have a $150 million franchise." So, they made money; the players made money; the only people that got hurt were the American public, the fans, the integrity of baseball, and—ultimately—the planet Earth.

Exodus

Given the levels of exploitation imposed on the fans and citizens of Major League cities, one can question what options exist within this increasingly hypermodern economic climate. The writings of Max Weber detail how peasant flight to European cities altered existing "forms of servitude," resulting in "objective antagonism of the working class in the face of the capitalist class" (qtd. in Hardt and Negri 77). Far from being an antiquated historical reference, Hardt and Negri stress that "this project of exodus is the primary form class struggle takes today" (164).

However, Hardt and Negri argue with equal clarity that while workers possess "the requirements for resistance ... the requirements for exodus are not so evident" (153). The theoretical threat of exodus lay at the heart of every MLB player strike,[9] but this abstract prospect has largely been a hollow threat on the part of professional baseball players. Clearly, MLB is the most lucrative option players have at their disposal (as opposed to seeking employment abroad or in another field of employment); and—even in the darkest days of the 1994–95 strike—it seemed inevitable that owners and players would ultimately reach a collective settlement.

In fact, the real threat of a player exodus from MLB exists among America's developing amateur talent. While the culture of some nations (namely those in the Caribbean) guarantees that its athletic talent will gravitate toward baseball, the contemporary culture of the United States no longer offers such assurances. Scott Boras—the most successful agent in baseball history—drew attention to this reality with the first client he represented: Tim Belcher, the number one pick in the 1983 draft. Boras demanded the seemingly unreasonable (for that time) signing figure of $120,000 for Belcher. Far from bankrupting MLB, Boras contended that this capitalist maneuver was necessary to preserve the game's quality. "The great athletes aren't going to keep coming to baseball if you keep the bonuses at this [lower] level," he explained, "because some owner *will* pay for that talent. It just happens to be in a different sport. Baseball players play football and basketball, too" (qtd. in McGrath 63).

Other professional leagues also offer sporting alternatives to fans, and make their partial (if not complete) exodus a legitimate possibility. MLB fans have the right to reallocate their dollars to the NFL, NBA, or NHL (not to mention any number of other leisure options), and every MLB team plays in a city with at least one other team from another professional sports league.[10] State-of-the-art facilities and amenities are often seen as the factors that maintain and/or sway fan allegiances, with the lasting nature of these structures presumably guaranteeing interest for the foreseeable future. Even so, Hardt and Negri contend that "today the value of a company depends to an increasing degree on immaterial assets such as 'goodwill' and other intangibles, which can at times be created and destroyed extraordinarily quickly" (312). Winning is—of course—the consummate form of goodwill; but that goodwill rests on the likeability of MLB players and the public's ability/desire to relate to them. The rise and fall of these perceptions has been evident in the vitriol that accompanied the 1994–95 players' strike, the subsequent surge of interest generated on the shoulders of the consummately likable Cal Ripken, Jr./Mark McGwire/Sammy Sosa in the mid-to-late 1990s, and, most recently, the contemporary descent into public distrust in the wake of revelations about player use of performance-enhancing drugs. The significance of immaterial goodwill is essential to any professional sports league, but it is particularly crucial to MLB. Since the abolition of its color barrier in 1947, the sport has carried a decidedly moral imperative that has emphasized purity, simplicity, and equality. However, just as Hardt and Negri contend that the United States' position "as a paradigm for the promotion of rights and law" (214), the same is now true of MLB. Most insightful observers now see MLB as a decidedly human institution that is not immune to the precarious nature of public opinion or the exodus of longstanding supporters.

Solidarity

Exodus is only effective, though, when carried out on a wide-scale basis—a reality that emphasizes the significance of solidarity. While exercises in solidarity will not generally achieve the full extent of their aims or settle class struggles with any sense of finality, wide-scale solidarity is the first crucial step to wide-scale change. Solidarity is generated with the understanding that simply waging battles (regardless of outcome) will inevitably yield tangible results, particularly when events lead to "the restructuring of capital" (144).

In spite of its noble reputation, it is crucial to recognize that solidarity can also be a harmful exercise. The two greatest exercises in solidarity shown by owners of MLB franchises have arguably been in their aforementioned imposition of the color barrier (perhaps the most shameful chapter in the game's history) and in their notorious collusion in opposition to free agents from 1985 to 1987, for which they would eventually have to repay the players $280 million. The latter instance represents an attempt by the owners to revert to their pre–1975 systems of administration and negotiation. This move would presumably have benefited both themselves and MLB fans (by regulating cost inflation) at the expense of the players—a fundamental violation of the progressive universal rights that *Commonwealth* advocates.

Solidarity among MLB players—on the other hand—has proven decidedly productive, as the MLBPA has been recognized as one of the most powerful unions in America since Marvin Miller's appointment as Executive Director in 1966.[11] Over the course of eight work stoppages between 1972 and 1995, the MLBPA has gradually wrested away power from MLB owners and raised the average MLB player salary from under $50,000 a year at the advent of free agency to $3.34 million in 2010. Such change, as Hardt and Negri suggest, is "not simply a matter of refusing the mechanisms of power and wielding violence against them" (16); instead, this transition was rooted in negotiations (however contentious) based on the innate premise that permanent exodus is impossible.

However, solidarity within the MLB player fraternity has also proved damaging to the reputations of individual players and to the group as a whole. The recent decade-long code of silence by MLB players on the issue of performance-enhancing drugs illustrates both the hubris and the dangers of large-scale solidarity, which has eroded public trust and goodwill. And while such consensus agreement is impressive, it is also limited in scale, involving (at most) 1200 well-paid and like-minded individuals at any given time. In contrast to the MLBPA, solidarity among fans is a decidedly localized concept, as MLB franchises can consistently leverage cities against one another to achieve their desired aims. Zimbalist argues that "U.S. team-sports leagues are monopolies. As such, they maximize their profits by reducing the supply of franchises below the demand for franchises from economically viable cities" (57). If Montreal refuses to capitulate to an owner's demands for a new stadium, then Washington, D.C., will gratefully oblige (at the tremendous costs mentioned above). This reality makes the effective mobilization and unification of the multitude so difficult. Even for individual cities to achieve some measure of consensus, Hardt and Negri contend, the production of the common is essential. Yet this production is made all the more problematic by the fact that an MLB team is often the single most effective vehicle for producing the common within a metropolis.

The Production of the Common

The difficulty of both recognizing and making use of the common stands as one of the central messages of *Commonwealth*, and also offers "the key to understanding economic production today" (280). While the common includes the more general categories of knowledge, language, and code, it just as surely involves those institutions that are essential to achieve and maintain social unity within a contemporary cultural climate. MLB franchises stand among the foremost of these institutions, offering both a common rallying point for individual cities/regions and a common frame of reference across the nation.

In classic Marxist terms, Hardt and Negri observe that industry and corporations—while essential to a city's economic viability—are most often alienated from the everyday life of the city. In this way, MLB distinguishes itself from other corporate entities, as ballparks assume prominence in the biopolitical city, bringing together a diverse population into the illusion of a single entity in support of a common cause. Furthermore, Hardt and Negri insist that love is also "an economic power" that "produces the common" (180–81), and nowhere is this more evident than a municipality's collective love for its professional sports franchise and its city. In this respect, the common forges both collectivity and solidarity, ultimately "transform[ing] the multitude into a people" (167). Indeed, MLB teams rank among the primary institutions that "engage and mobilize the common ... and thereby provide important resources for the exodus of the multitude" (Hardt and Negri 164). Paradoxically, these institutions produce that collective solidarity from which the possibility of revolution emerges.

Revolution

However, while *Commonwealth* decrees that "a new humanity must be created" (118), MLB cannot reconfigure humanity by itself. Hardt and Negri ultimately advocate a "Year 0" approach that wipes away "centuries of darkness and blood" (377), but wiping out the history of baseball would destroy perhaps its greatest appeals of nostalgia and historical relevance. In such a way, it can be difficult to discern where exactly a productive multitude can rebel within a climate of exploitation. Historically, outright revolution often entails disturbing images of assault on the icons of power. Therefore, avoiding mob rule as a corrupted form of solidarity, the multitude must adopt a more civil and pragmatic version of these revolutionary impulses to forge an alternative version of modernity that challenges "hierarchical relationships" while also developing "alternative social relations based on the common" (113). In short, baseball must be accessible and relevant to all populations.

In this spirit, *Commonwealth* insists that "capital cannot just write off certain populations as disposable; it needs everyone to be productive in the biopolitical economy" (308). Baseball must follow this mandate, reversing decades-long trends of exodus. For example, the decline of African American players in MLB represents an exceedingly disturbing trend, from a peak of almost 30 percent of MLB players in the mid–1970s to less than 10 percent today. Meanwhile, Little League Baseball has experienced a 25 percent decline in participation over the past fifteen years, with more American children now playing soccer than baseball. MLB's privileging of the corporate classes at the expense of the lower and middle classes not only threatens the growth of the sport, but might fundamentally disqualify baseball's longtime designation as "the national pastime."

In spite of its Marxist leanings, *Commonwealth* stresses the dangers associated with utopian visions of communist reform where the choice "between the private and the public corresponds to an equally pernicious political alternative between capitalism and socialism," both of which are "regimes of property that exclude the common" (ix). In fact, MLB fan bases and municipalities carry legitimate power when they function collectively and focus on a "growing autonomy of the multitude from both private and public control" (Hardt and Negri 311). Such enigmatic attempts at community control have happened in MLB's past. In the late 1980s, San Diego Padres owner Joan Kroc — the wife of late team owner and McDonald's founder Ray Kroc — surprisingly attempted to donate the team to the city of San Diego, along with a $100 million trust to finance the continued operation of the club. Even more surprising, though, was the fact that MLB blocked the donation of the team, stipulating that any transfer would have to be to a private owner. Under the auspices of its private owners, MLB found public/municipal ownership to be incompatible with its existing business model. Dorothy Norris-Tirrell and Susan Schmidt argue that, in theory, "public and nonprofit ownership [of franchises] runs the risk of political interference that is not as great a threat when ownership is private" (111). But while capitalism and socialism are painted as two equally-unsatisfying sides that exploit the multitude, the losers in the case of the Padres were clearly the citizens of San Diego. Kroc would eventually sell the team in 1990 for $75 million to a group of local businessmen led by Tom Werner; at the start of the 2011 season, *Forbes* would value the team at $406 million, with the city still responsible for 70 percent of the costs incurred for the construction of PETCO Park from 2000 to 2004.

Despite the events surrounding the potential sale of the Padres to the city of San Diego, community ownership remains virtually impossible. However, the existing model for such reform may lie in the NFL, instead of in MLB. Among American professional sports franchises, the NFL's Green Bay Packers offer the archetype for a team's symbiosis with the multitude. The team is publicly owned by the city of Green Bay, Wisconsin, and in large measure the city derives both its value and its identity from the team, its coaches, and its players. While the organization is still an economically-motivated institution, with an average ticket cost of $72.36 in 2010, this figure is below the league average and the team maintains a waiting list for season tickets that exceeds eighty thousand (which is more than the current stadium capacity). Playing in a venerated old stadium — Lambeau Field — that has consistently been renovated and expanded instead of demolished, the team's public ownership precludes the threat of relocation. The Packers represent the only major professional sports franchise in America whose financial balance sheet is open to public scrutiny, and the on-field success of the team includes a victory in the 2011 Super Bowl. Admittedly, there are a series of legitimate obstacles to replicating such a model in any other professional league, given the NFL's longstanding revenue sharing policy. Moreover, the team is only eligible for public ownership because it has been grandfathered into the league's current owner policy.[12] However, much as Hardt and Negri emphasize a pragmatic approach to revolution, the Packers franchise provides a working blueprint for an alternative dynamic of ownership, labor relations, and public investiture in which all classes may emerge victorious.

The Future

While the current class struggles within MLB may lack the drama of 1994–95, the commentary of Burns' original *Baseball* documentary is just as relevant in the context of the current crisis. At the end of that documentary, John Thorn — recently named Official Historian for Major League Baseball — says, "Nothing worries me about the future of baseball. I am worried about any number of things, but this is one thing I never, ever worry about. When

I read in the papers that escalating salaries ... are going to be the end of baseball, I love it because [we've] been hearing this ... for 130 years."

Although the future of Major League Baseball seems relatively secure, what that future will specifically look like is a far more pertinent and polarizing consideration. Hardt and Negri's *Commonwealth* is ultimately centered on "a realistic critique of the dominant powers," with the ultimate goal being "free and equal access to the common" (382–83). The collective recognition of MLB franchises as a kind of common wealth distinct from other corporate entities is crucial to this transition. So, too, is the conscientious reevaluation of the exploitation of the general public, whose input is currently excluded from the owner/player power struggles of collective bargaining agreements.

Rather than consider such demands as purely utopian aspirations, Hardt and Negri contend that "the call for happiness is an entirely realistic political project" (377). Marginalizing the demands of the multitude may never kill baseball, but it will, over time, inevitably inspire the kind of cultural exodus that will render MLB a second-tier professional sport. Hardt and Negri end *Commonwealth* with a call for people to eliminate those "attachments to identity" that serve "the institutions that corrupt the common" (383). While the tipping point for such public alienation may be closer than many realize, it is equally certain that Major League Baseball still offers one of the most indispensable sources for the production of the common. And as goes baseball's relationship to the common, so goes its long-term viability as the national pastime.

Notes

1. Quotations from this book are reprinted by permission of the publisher from Commonwealth by Michael Hardt and Antonio Negri (Cambridge: The Belknap Press of Harvard University Press, 2009 by Michael Hardt and Antonio Negri).

2. For comparative purposes within American professional sports, in 2010–11 National Basketball Association teams paid an equivalent luxury tax on any dollar spent above a $70.307 million ceiling, while the National Hockey League enforced a hard cap without a luxury tax that prohibits teams from exceeding $59.4 million in payroll. The National Football League, which for the last two decades has had perhaps the most complex salary-cap system in professional sports, played the 2010 season without an operable cap in the face of labor negotiations.

3. Despite the ability of Pittsburgh's Three Rivers Stadium to hold over 57,000 fans for baseball, the Pirates drew only 46,932 fans for Game 7 of the 1991 NLCS. After being eliminated from the NLCS in another memorable seven-game series the next year (with the last game in Pittsburgh falling over 4,000 fans short of capacity), the Pirates have not returned to the playoffs since. By comparison, the NFL's Pittsburgh Steelers have sold out every home game (regular season or playoff) since 1972-the second longest streak in the league's history.

4. Under the posting system that exists between Japan's Nippon Professional Baseball (NPB) and MLB, once an NPB player is "posted," MLB allows it teams to conduct an immediate silent auction where franchises submit sealed bids for the exclusive rights to negotiate with the posted player. In the most lucrative of these transactions, the Boston Red Sox paid the Seibu Lions over $51 million for the rights to negotiate with Daisuke Matsuzaka in 2006.

5. The St. Louis Browns to Baltimore (Orioles) in 1954, the Philadelphia A's to Kansas City in

1955, the New York Giants to San Francisco in 1958, and the Brooklyn Dodgers to Los Angeles that same year.

6. The Dodgers present a continually fascinating study in such owner/franchise relationships, all the way up to current owner Frank McCourt's dramatic divorce proceedings which involved the firing of his former wife from her position as team CEO, a public court battle between the two for control of the team, MLB's seizing control of the team's day-to-day operations, and the Dodgers ultimately filing for Chapter 11 bankruptcy on June 27, 2011.

7. There have been eight work stoppages in MLB history, beginning with the thirteen-day player strike in April 1972 and culminating in the aforementioned 1994–95 players' strike.

8. This is not the case with the NFL, NBA, and NHL, all of which have multiple teams that play in single-franchise cities.

9. For a detailed account of the MLBPA's rise to prominence, see Marvin Miller's A Whole Different Ballgame: The Inside Story of the Baseball Revolution (Chicago: Ivan R. Dee, 2004).

10. The NFL adopted an ownership policy in 1980 which stipulated a limit of thirty-two owners to a single team, with one of the owners carrying a minimum stake of 30 percent. This has most recently been amended-in the interest of estate planning-in 2009 to require that only 10 percent of a franchise be owned by an individual, although an additional 20 percent must be owned by that individual's family.

Works Cited

Horkheimer, Max, and Theodor Adorno. *The Dialectic of Enlightenment*. Trans. Edmund Jephcott. Palo Alto: Stanford University Press, 2002. Print.
Baseball. Dir. Ken Burns. Prod. Ken Burns and Lynn Novick. 1994. Documentary Film.
Baseball: The Tenth Inning. Dir. Ken Burns. Prod. Ken Burns and Lynn Novick. 2010. Documentary Film.
Fainaru, Steve, and Ray Sanchez. "Emigration in the Special Period." *The Cuba Reader: History, Culture, Politics*. Eds. Avita Chomsky, Barry Carr, and Pamela Maria Smorkaloff. Durham: Duke University Press, 2003. 637–43. Print.
Hardt, Michael, and Antonio Negri. *Commonwealth*. Cambridge: Harvard University Press, 2009. Print.
Harvey, David. *A Brief History of Neoliberalism*. Oxford: Oxford University Press, 2005. Print.
McGrath, Ben. "The Extortionist." *The New Yorker* 29 October 2007. 56–67. Print.
Noll, Roger G., and Andrew Zimbalist. "The Economic Impact of Sports Teams and Facilities." *Sports, Jobs, and Taxes: The Economic Impact of Sports Teams and Stadiums*. Eds. Roger G. Noll and Andrew Zimbalist. Washington, D.C.: Brookings Institution Press, 1997. 55–91. Print.
Norris-Tirrell, Dorothy, and Susan Tomlinson Schmidt. "Community Ownership of Professional Sport Teams and the Role of Social Entrepreneurship." *Sport and Public Policy: Social, Political, and Economic Perspectives*. Eds. Charles A. Santo and Gerard C. S. Mildner. Champaign, IL: Human Kinetics, 2010. 97–112. Print.
Price, S. L. "Going Against the Percentages." *Sports Illustrated* 31 March 2008. 130. Print.
Zimbalist, Andrew. "The Economics of Stadiums, Teams, and Cities." *The Economics And Politics of Sports Facilities*. Ed. Wilbur C. Rich. Westport, CT: Quorum Books, 2000. 57–69. Print.

About the Contributors

Daniel Anderson teaches literature, composition, and American studies at Dominican University, in suburban Chicago. After a brief career as a sportswriter, he obtained an M.A. in English from Boston College and a Ph.D. from the University of Minnesota. His research interests concern sports, literary regionalism and cultural renaissance, particularly as they intersect in New York and Chicago.

Steve Andrews is an associate professor at Grinnell College, where he specializes in 18th and 19th century American literature and culture. His research interests include literary pragmatism, the poetics of landscape and the cultural history of baseball.

Mark Bresnan is a lecturer in the expository writing program at New York University. His research examines representations of popular culture in contemporary literature, with particular emphasis on sport and music. He has published essays and given talks on David Foster Wallace, Jonathan Franzen, Jonathan Lethem, Don DeLillo, and Toni Morrison. This essay is adapted from his doctoral dissertation, "Fantasy Sports: Athletics and Identity in Postmodern American Literature, 1967–2008."

Matthew Bruen is a doctoral candidate in the English department at New York University, studying the intersection of literature, culture and place. His dissertation, "Rooted in Place: Literary Remembrance of Place in Nineteenth-Century America," examines how nineteenth-century Americans used writing to transform real locales into places of cultural memory.

Joshua Daniel-Wariya is pursuing his Ph.D. in rhetoric at Texas Christian University, where he works as a writing instructor and as the assistant director of the New Media Writing Studio. He specializes in digital rhetoric, and his primary research interests involve the intersections of play and writing as well as gaming and new media.

Andrew Friedman is a chancellor's fellow and theatre Ph.D. student at

CUNY's Graduate Center. His interests include experimental theatre, spectatorship and sports, and his research and reviews have been published in *Western European Stages* and *Theatre Journal*. He teaches theatre history and acting at the City College of New York.

Andrew Hazucha is a professor of English and chair of the arts and humanities division at Ottawa University in Ottawa, Kansas. He has published essays on contemporary Irish poetry, William Wordsworth, Nelson Algren, Dan Quisenberry, and the Chicago Cubs. He is co-editor, with Gerald C. Wood, of *Northsiders: Essays on the History and Culture of the Chicago Cubs* (McFarland, 2008).

Ronald E. Kates is a professor of English at Middle Tennessee State University. In addition to co-hosting the annual Conference on Baseball in Literature and Culture, he has co-edited three conference proceedings volumes for McFarland and published other baseball and sports-related essays. While he teaches primarily composition classes at both the upper and lower levels, he also tries to regularly teach the sophomore-level course Sports in Literature and Culture.

Janaka B. Lewis is an assistant professor of early African American literature at the University of North Carolina at Charlotte. Her research focus is black women's narratives of freedom, but her interests extend into nineteenth and early twentieth century African American popular culture, including travel and sports writing.

Carl F. Miller, who received his Ph.D. from the University of Florida, teaches British and American modernism and postmodernism, existential literature, and children's literature at the University of Alabama. His primary research interests are in twentieth-century Anglophone literature, culture, and theory. He has recent publications on the influence of the Cold War in the 1980s graphic novel, the expression of utopia by Michael Jackson in *Captain EO*, and the role of sports in Harper Lee's *To Kill a Mockingbird*.

Scott D. Peterson teaches courses in sport literature, sport journalism, mass communication and technical writing at the University of Maine, where he earned an interdisciplinary Ph.D. in American literature and culture in May 2010. He is the fiction editor for *Aethlon*, the journal of the Sport Literature Association and his baseball research has appeared in the 2007 edition of *Baseball/Literature/Culture*, *NINE*, the edited volume *Baseball and Politics*.

Warren Tormey, a scholar of medieval and early Renaissance literature by training, also does research in Milton studies, the epic tradition, economic history, scientific and technical history, ecocriticism, sports literature, popular culture and technical writing as a member of the Middle Tennessee State University English department. He is co-organizer of the conference on Baseball in Literature and Culture.

Nathaniel Valle spent summers as a batboy for the Delmarva Shorebirds on the Eastern Shore of Maryland. He holds a master's degree from Liberty University and is pursuing additional graduate study.

Index

Adams, Daniel Lucius "Doc" 8, 22
Adorno, Theodor: *The Dialectic of Enlightenment* 175–176
Albee, Edward F. 90–91
Alexander, Grover Cleveland 68
Alger, Horatio 46–47, 49, 54
Algren, Nelson 70, 192
"Along This Way" 113, 121–122
Anderson, Daniel 4, 112–125, 191
Andrews, Steve 2, 7–27, 191
Asinof, Eliot 70, 98–100, 108
Atlanta Journal 108
Augusta Chronicle 39–40

Baker, Frank "Home Run" 101
Bakhtin, Mikhail 44, 49
Banks, Ernie 170–172
Barzun, Jacques 1
Baseball 173, 178, 182, 187
Baseball in Literature and Culture Conference 2, 25, 192
Bavasi, Buzzie 162
Becker, Howard 74, 84
Bender, Chief 110
"Black Manhattan" 112–121, 123, 125
Black Sox scandal 4, 61, 70–71, 82, 98–100, 106–108, 110–111
"The Bone Doctor" 50–52
Boras, Scott 183
Boston, MA 34, 141
Boston Braves 102, 179
Boston Red Sox 96, 104, 107, 109–110, 139–142, 144, 147, 181, 188
Breaking the Record, or the 19th Straight 95
Bresnahan, Roger 68
Bresnan, Mark 3, 60–73, 191
Brooklyn, NY 38, 41, 86, 95, 115, 124, 127, 129, 131, 134–138, 181
Brooklyn Daily Union 38
Brooklyn Dodgers 42, 129, 134–137, 162, 181, 189
Brooklyn Royal Giants 39, 115, 124
Broun, Heywood 47–49
Brown, Mordecai "Three Finger" 109

Bruen, Matthew 5, 139–147, 191
Bucknell University 65
Bulger, Bozeman 3, 44, 47, 49–50, 54–58; "A Major-League Mother-in-Law" 55–56; "A Pinch Hit in Vaudeville" 55–56
Burke, Kenneth 149, 152–154, 156, 159–160
Burns, Ken: *Baseball* 173, 178, 182, 187

Carino, Peter 2, 111
Cartwright, Alexander Joy 2, 7–8, 12–13, 22, 25–26, 29, 65
Castro, Fidel 176–177
The Celebrant 3, 60–73, 74–84
Chadwick, Henry 8, 22, 24
Chase, Hal 49, 69–70, 104, 110
Chicago Cubs 61, 79–80, 94, 100, 172, 181, 192
Chicago Daily News 42
Chicago Defender 4, 124
Chicago Eagle 106
Chicago Tribune 48, 52, 94
Chicago White Sox 52–53, 71, 101–102, 104–107, 109
Cicotte, Eddie 98, 108, 110
Cincinnati Reds 69–70, 82, 97, 160
Cleveland Advocate 39
Cleveland Browns 39
Cobb, Ty 49–50, 66–67, 102, 106, 148
Collins, Eddie 4, 98–111
Columbia University 99, 102, 137
Columbus Buckeyes 39
Comiskey, Charles 53, 98–99, 102–104, 106, 108–110
Commonwealth 174–189
Cooperstown, NY 7, 12–13, 21, 26, 64, 86, 89, 97, 150
Cruse, Harold 113, 125
Cuba 176–177
Cuban Giants 28, 34–35, 39, 115, 118, 120, 124

Daniel-Wariya, Joshua 5, 148–161, 191
The Day Book (Chicago) 110
The Dialectic of Enlightenment 175–176

Index

Donlin, Mike 59, 94
Doubleday, Abner 7–8, 64, 89, 150–151, 155
Douglass, Frederick 28, 30–32, 116
DuBois, W.E.B. 116
Dunbar, Paul Laurence 115

Eisenhower, Dwight D. 162, 164–165
Elysian Fields, Hoboken, NJ 2, 7, 13, 16, 17, 18, 20, 21, 23, 26, 30
Empire 174
Evening Mirror 13
Evers, Medgar 170–171

Federal League 53, 101, 106, 110
Felsch, Oscar "Happy" 99, 103, 105
The Forward 126
Foster, Rube 114, 118, 124–125
Foucault, Michael 174
Frazier, E. Franklin 123
Friedman, Andrew 4, 85–97, 192
Fullerton, Hugh 71, 82, 104

Gandil, Chick 98–99, 104–111
Gehrig, Lou 60–61
Goldstein, Warren 29–30, 32, 35
Goodbye Columbus 139–147
The Great American Novel 148–161
Greenberg, Eric Rolfe: *The Celebrant* 3, 60–73, 74–84

Hardt, Michael 173–189; *Commonwealth* 174–189; *Empire* 174; *Multitude* 174
Harlem, NY 112–115, 117, 119, 123, 125
Harlem Renaissance 4, 112–125
Harlem Stars 119, 124
Hartman, Saidiya 31, 38
Hazucha, Andrew 5, 162–172, 192
Hemingway, Ernest 47–48, 57, 137, 148
Horkheimer, Max: *The Dialectic of Enlightenment* 175–176
The House Un-American Activities Committee 162, 169, 171
Hughes, Langston 112, 117
Humphrey, Hubert 162, 167
Hyde, Lewis 74–80, 82–83

"I Stand by Dempsey" 130–131

Jackson, Joe "Shoeless" 98–99, 104–106, 110
James, Bill 9–10, 13, 24, 67, 72, 86, 125
Japan 176–177
Jersey Giants 134
Jethroe, Sam 109
Johnson, James Weldon 4, 112–125; "Along This Way" 113, 121–122; "Black Manhattan" 112–121, 123, 125

Johnson, Lyndon B. 167
Johnson, Walter 110

Kahn, Roger 62
Kates, Ronald E. 3–4, 25, 66, 73, 74–84, 124–125, 192
Keith, B.F. 90–91
Kennedy, John F. 163, 167, 170–171
Kerr, Dickie 99
King, Martin Luther, Jr. 163, 166–171
King, Stephen 140–141
Kroc, Joan 186–187
Kroc, Ray 186–187

Lajoie, Napoleon 110
Lanctot, Neil 34, 37, 41, 119, 125
Lardner, Ring 3, 44, 47–50, 52–55, 57–59; "You Know Me Al" 52–54
Leibold, Nemo 103
Lewis, Janaka B. 3, 28–43, 192
Little Rock, AR 165
Lorimer, George Horace 45–47, 49–52, 54–57
Los Angeles Dodgers 189

Mack, Connie 68, 101–103, 110–111
"Main Currents of American Thought" 132–134, 137–138
Major League Baseball (MLB) 173–189
"A Major-League Mother-in-Law" 55–56
Malamud, Bernard: *The Natural* 122
Malcom X 170–171
Malloy, Jerry 33–35
Mansch, Larry D. 86, 92–97
Mantle, Mickey 5, 145–147
Marquard, Rube 3–4, 55–56, 75, 78, 85–97
Marxism 71, 112, 175, 185–186
Mathewson, Christy 3–4, 50, 53, 61–62, 65–73, 74–84; *Pitching in a Pinch* 53, 68, 81
Mays, Willie 109
McGraw, John 68–69, 74, 79–81, 83, 94, 102
McKay, Claude 112, 115, 119
Mercer, Sid 92–94
Merkle, Fred 79–81
Merriwell, Frank 52
Middle Tennessee State University 2
Miller, Carl F. 5, 173–189, 192
Mills, A.G. 89, 93, 150
Mills, Dorothy Seymour 23–25
The Mills Commission 89, 93, 150
Morris, Tim 70, 150
Multitude 174
Murphy, Eddie 101, 103

Nathan, Daniel 12, 66–67, 71, 83, 100, 108

Index

National Association for the Advancement of Colored People (NAACP) 113–114, 122
The Natural 122
Negri, Antonio 173–189; *Commonwealth* 174–189; *Empire* 174; *Multitude* 174
Negro League Baseball Players Association 39
New York, NY 8–10, 12–13, 18, 21, 23, 25–27, 29–30, 42, 56 62, 85–86 88–91, 93–95, 99, 112–115, 117, 119, 121, 124, 126–127, 134–136, 142–3, 167, 191–192
New York Age 34, 39, 114, 121
New York Amsterdam News 39
New York Black Yankees 119
New York Giants 55–56, 65–66, 68, 76, 78–81, 85–86, 92, 94–96, 100, 102 124, 136, 138, 162, 189
New York *Globe* 92
New York *Herald* 17–18, 65
New York *Journal of Commerce* 23
New York Knickerbocker Baseball Club 2, 8, 16–17, 29
New York Lincoln Giants 39
New York Post 162, 166
New York *Tribune* 48
New York World 85
New York Yankees 92, 119, 136, 142–143, 145, 178
New Yorker 134, 138
Newark, NJ 5, 15, 142–147
Newark Bears 142–143
Newark Stars 39
Nixon, Richard M. 162–163, 165–167, 169–170
"No Jury Would Convict" 134–136, 138

O'Neil, Buck 173

Pastor, Tony 87, 90
Peterson, Robert 28–29, 32–33, 38
Peterson, Scott D. 3, 44–59, 192
Philadelphia, PA 9, 29, 34, 37–39, 114
Philadelphia Athletics 69, 99–106, 188
Philadelphia Evening Public Ledger 101–102
Philadelphia Phillies 68, 96
"A Pinch Hit in Vaudeville" 55–56
Pitching in a Pinch 53, 68, 81
Pittsburgh, PA 129, 176, 188
Pittsburgh Courier 39, 41, 114
Pittsburgh Pirates 176, 188
Plank, Eddie 102–103, 110
Poe, Edgar Allan 8–9, 12–13, 19–21, 23, 26–27
Polo Grounds 81–82, 86
Pulitzer, Joseph 85

Reserve Clause 58, 101, 181–182
Rice, Albert 119
Rickey, Branch 41, 169–170
Riess, Steven 23, 29, 34, 51, 85 87–89, 92, 94, 128
Risberg, Swede 98–99, 105, 109
Robeson, Paul 123, 169–171
Robinson, Bill "Bojangles" 119, 124–125
Robinson, Jackie 5, 28, 38, 42, 109, 162–172
Rockefeller, Nelson 169, 171
Rogers, Mary 2, 7–13, 17–19, 21, 23, 25–27
Rogosin, Donn 119, 124
Roosevelt, Theodore 50–51
Roth, Philip 5, 62; *Goodbye Columbus* 139–147; *The Great American Novel* 148–161
Rothstein Arnold 70, 98
Ruth, George Herman "Babe" 66, 96, 122, 148

St. Louis, MO 66–67, 140, 176
St. Louis Browns 34, 75, 188
St. Louis Cardinals 75, 176, 181
San Diego Padres 186–187
San Francisco Giants 96, 189
Saturday Evening Post 3, 44–59
Sayles, John 98, 100, 110–111
Schalk, Ray 99
Seymour, Harold 23–25
Shaw, Irwin 4, 62, 126–138; "I Stand by Dempsey" 130–131; "Main Currents of American Thought" 132–134, 137–138; "No Jury Would Convict" 134–136, 138
Solomon, Eric 62, 74, 126
Spalding, Albert 5, 64–65, 89, 149–153, 155, 157–158
Speaker, Tris 102, 106
Sporting Life 120
The Sporting News 24, 96, 120
Sports Illustrated 6, 64, 65, 110
Srebnick, Amy Gilman 9, 12, 18–20, 25–26
Steinbrenner, George 178–179
Stevenson, Adlai 162, 171
The Suffragette Pitcher 86, 95

Tesreau, Jeff 3, 75
Thorn, John 8, 10–12, 15–16, 22 24–25, 27, 187
Tinker, Joe 109
Tormey, Warren T. 4, 25, 98–111, 124–5, 192
Tucker, William H. 8
Turner, Frederick Jackson 23, 50
Tuskegee Institute 35–38
Tygiel, Jules 25, 62

Valle, Nathaniel 4, 126–138, 193
Van Loan, Charles 3, 44, 47, 49–54, 57–59; "The Bone Doctor" 50–52
Variety 86, 95
Vietnam War 163, 167–169

Wadsworth, Louis Fenn 8
Washington, Booker T. 28, 35–39
Washington, DC 34, 119, 179, 185
Weaver, Buck 98, 105–106
Wheaton, William Rufus 8

White, Sol 29, 33–34, 38–41
Williams, Lefty 99, 105
Williams, Ted 109
Wilson, Jimmy 163–164
World Baseball Classic 177
Wrigley Field 42

Yawkey, Tom 109
"You Know Me Al" 52–54

Zimbalist, Andrew 180, 184

www.ingramcontent.com/pod-product-compliance
Ingram Content Group UK Ltd.
Pitfield, Milton Keynes, MK11 3LW, UK
UKHW042007140426
5217IPUK00015B/1040